The Captain's Apprentice

*Ralph Vaughan Williams and the
Story of a Folk Song*

Caroline Davison

Chatto & Windus
LONDON

1 3 5 7 9 10 8 6 4 2

Chatto & Windus, an imprint of Vintage, is part of the Penguin Random House group
of companies whose addresses can be found at global.penguinrandomhouse.com

Penguin
Random House
UK

First published by Chatto & Windus in 2022

penguin.co.uk/vintage

A CIP catalogue record for this book is available from the British Library

HB ISBN 9781784744540

Typeset in 11/16pt Adobe Garamond by Jouve (UK), Milton Keynes

Printed and bound in Great Britain by Clays Ltd, Elcograf S.p.A.

The authorised representative in the EEA is Penguin Random House Ireland,
Morrison Chambers, 32 Nassau Street, Dublin D02 YH68

Penguin Random House is committed to a sustainable future
for our business, our readers and our planet. This book is made from
Forest Stewardship Council® certified paper.

For Pip, Pete and Siân

The Captain's Apprentice

One day this poor boy to me was bound apprentice,
Because of his being fatherless;
I took him out of St. James' workhouse,
His mother being in deep distress.

One day this poor boy unto me offended,
But nothing to him I did say,
Up to the main mast shroud I sent him
And there I kept him all that long day.

All with my garling-spikk I misused him
So shamefully I can't deny,
All with my marling-spike I gagged him,
Because I could not bear his cry.

His face and his hands to me expanded,
His legs and his thighs to me likewise,
And by my barbarous cruel entreatment
This very next day this poor boy died.

You captains all throughout the nation,
Hear a voice and a warning take by me,
Take special care of your apprentice
While you are on the raging sea.

'The Captain's Apprentice'
Journal of the Folk-Song Society
Vol. 2, No. 8 (1906) p. 161

Contents

List of Illustrations

Prologue

The 'B' side

My first copy of *Norfolk Rhapsody* was a gift. A romantic gesture from an Essex boy to a Norfolk girl.

In the early 1980s I left Norfolk to attend Essex University, just outside Colchester. Friends of my brother lived in the countryside nearby and invited me to stay. I stepped off the train at the rural station of Manningtree, walked along a flickering poplar-lined track, past a farm labourer's cottage to a Victorian farmhouse set in the park of a country house. I wore a skirt I'd made from a second-hand 1950s dress, covered in roses, and I held a small tartan suitcase. It was as though I'd drifted into the plot of a Virago Modern Classic. The bohemian world of the early twentieth century – bobbed hair, destitute artists and rural communes – had turned my head.

My soon-to-be boyfriend lodged at the farmhouse and was a thatcher. That visit was in late summer. By the end of the year I'd introduced him to the wild coast of my home county, and for Christmas he bought me Ralph Vaughan Williams's *Norfolk Rhapsody No. 1*. The vinyl record included *Serenade to Music* and *In the Fen Country* on the 'A' side, with *The Lark Ascending* and *Norfolk Rhapsody No. 1* on the other. For years I only listened to the 'B' side and I wasn't conscious of where *The Lark Ascending* stopped, and *Norfolk Rhapsody No. 1* began. The music – plaintive solo viola, rising strings, mournful horns – represented my intense experience of first love. After the relationship ended it became the souvenir of a golden era, a conventional response to the work of Vaughan Williams.

Years later I was given a copy of Roy Palmer's book, *Folk Songs Collected by Ralph Vaughan Williams*, with its chapter of songs from Norfolk. In an idle moment I played through them on my piano. 'The Captain's Apprentice' was the first, and I instantly recognised the tune as the musical theme from the opening of *Norfolk Rhapsody*. Verse one tells of a poor fatherless boy taken out of the workhouse to go to sea – not an unusual subject for a folk song – but then I moved down to a later verse:

> All with my garling-spikk I misused him
> So shamefully I can't deny,
> All with my marling-spike I gagged him,
> Because I could not bear his cry.

The words conjured up an image that made me feel sick.

Palmer noted that the song was based on a real case of torture. I turned the page, wanting to blot out that cruel story with cheerier tales of brave pirates and the merry month of May.

Afterwards, if I happened to hear *Norfolk Rhapsody*, my thoughts no longer turned to romantic love but to the violent death of a defenceless cabin boy.

In 2007 my work took me to that part of King's Lynn known as the North End. I walked slowly along streets of Victorian two-up, two-down terraced houses, taking photographs. Dusty net curtains sagged in the windows, rust-patched cars blocked the pavements, and litter blew down the November street. A man emerged from his house. He was thin and wiry, in his sixties, bespectacled, with straggly hair, and a tea towel clutched in his hand. I braced myself for an aggressive exchange.

'You doing the Council Tax bands?'

I explained that I was a conservation officer, recording historic buildings. His face lit up.

'Oh, are you! Well. In that case, have you been to look at the pub round the corner? They put a plaque up there 'cause that's where Vaughan Williams did his song collecting, off the old fishermen.'

I said I'd definitely visit the pub, and the man went on to tell me about plans for a new building to be named after James 'Duggie' Carter, the fisherman who had sung 'The Captain's Apprentice' for the composer. We shook hands warmly and he stepped back inside to finish drying his crockery while I carried on up the street, mulling over why I was so moved by the encounter.

I walked around the corner, hoping to find a quaint old pub where I could sip at a shandy and imagine Vaughan Williams listening to old salts singing. Instead, I found a modernised building on the edge of a busy road overlooking industrial

The former Tilden Smith pub

wasteland. Clinging to its cement-rendered wall was a plaque marking the centenary of the composer's 1905 visit and his meeting with James Carter.[1] As I waited for a pause in the traffic to take photographs, I felt the irony of the planned commemorative building for Carter that would further obliterate the streets where he and Vaughan Williams had walked. The idea of this potential debasement of memory through the very act of remembering turned my vague musings on 'The Captain's Apprentice' into more precise questions: why was Carter's performance of this song still of such treasured significance, and why had Vaughan Williams been in King's Lynn to hear it?

⌒

That chance meeting with the local 'Northender' was this book's genesis. At the heart of the story are a few moments in time when an old fisherman sang for a young composer. The experience of hearing a song is over quickly but, in the case of 'The

Captain's Apprentice', the sound of it, the particular arrangement of intervals and spaces between notes, embedded itself in the body of the listener. The difference in class and age, the location in a decayed old port, the adventure of being a young man in a strange place – these circumstances all played a part in the strength of the song's impact on Ralph Vaughan Williams. From this musical explosion flew numerous particles in all directions, a combustion which shaped this book, as I tracked the trajectories of those flying sparks during the following years. Some reached into the past, to the half-forgotten story of a child apprentice who died at sea. Some of them travelled into the future, floating through the composer's work to the end. Some even reached into my own musical upbringing, along with all the other British children who came of age during the century following the Edwardian folk revival.

Although the sound of the melody sung to Vaughan Williams in January 1905 began instantly to insinuate itself into his marrow, he was not aware that this pattern of notes, out of many others that he heard through a long life of listening, would stay with him for ever. He made a brief note that it was 'sung by Mr Carter (Fisherman) about 70? Jan 9th 1905 at North End King's Lynn' – but nothing more about the singer, where or how they met, or the quality of the singing. Like the other folk-song collectors of this period Vaughan Williams understood enough about the songs' fragility to realise how important it was to record them. He looked forward to a time when these melodies would be woven once more into the fabric of the nation's music. He recognised some of the significances of the song he heard that day, but he did not delve further into the life of the singer or foresee how this lost context would affect the way we listen to the song now. Not yet established in his career, he could not anticipate our interest in him as a collector and composer, and he was too much a part of his own time to predict the depth of our curiosity about the fisherman. Most of all, his quest was for a 'good tune'. In those few moments in King's Lynn he jotted down everything he needed to know – but I wanted to know more. With no other purpose than to answer my own questions I began to delve into the existing layers of material on Vaughan Williams, folk-song collecting, the singers, and the stories in their songs.

I read about the importance of other collectors who worked alongside Vaughan Williams, such as Lucy Broadwood, Frank Kidson and especially Cecil Sharp, whose campaigning for the cause of English folk-song conservation made him the highest-profile collector of his time. I learnt how Sharp and Vaughan Williams promoted folk song as the means for reviving English national music, and how the publication of collected material in the *Journal of the Folk-Song Society* powerfully influenced twentieth-century composition. I searched through biographies for the significant moments in Vaughan Williams's early life which led him to the folk-song movement and towards King's Lynn, and I became familiar with the oft-repeated stories of his collecting trips. Now and again, something would catch the attention of my peripheral vision – lumps and bumps in the smooth landscape of the narrative – which made me go back and look again. As with an archaeological dig, sometimes I scraped with my metaphorical trowel for days, working through layers of 'natural' soil, before coming across something – an almost indiscernible change in colour or texture – which looked like an embedded ember from one of those original flying sparks. As the years passed, patterns and connections emerged which I felt compelled to piece together through writing. It is those traces, found beneath the more familiar material of the composer's recorded life, that are explored in this book.

Vaughan Williams's road towards folk-music collecting was marked by a sequence of epiphanies, the hearing of three songs which changed the course of his life and his music – 'Dives and Lazarus', 'Bushes and Briars' and 'The Captain's Apprentice'. On closer inspection, documented tales of these encounters are hazy or contradictory; and there is a fourth, 'The Cherry Tree Carol', which offers a glimpse much further back into his awakening consciousness of folk melody as a boy – the moment when he first recognised 'something entirely new yet absolutely familiar'. It is frequently assumed that in his folk-influenced work he intended to evoke a pastoral ideal – several of his early compositions are named after or connected with particular rural areas – but his letters suggest that the impact of landscape on his music was more complicated than that. His response can be deeply personal, sometimes tenuous, never blandly nostalgic. It is often imbued with an emotional attachment to countryside experienced on foot and bike – the allure of the open road underpins his search for folk song in obscure corners of England and his arrival in King's Lynn.

I began to see that the women in his early life were strong influences on his progress, though they usually only pass through the background of his biographies. Without his neighbour, Lucy Broadwood; his first wife, Adeline Fisher; or the aunt who introduced him to 'The Cherry Tree Carol', it is not certain that folk song would have become such a passion. Ingrained in what we know about Vaughan Williams is a fourth woman's voice: that of his second wife, Ursula Wood, a poet who met the composer in 1938. Their relationship began with a kiss in a taxi when he was sixty-six and she was twenty-seven and was ended twenty years later by his death. On that morning, as she wrote in her autobiography, she 'would have been grateful for suttee' but as the weeks went by she embarked on the cataloguing of 'boxes and drawers of manuscripts, letters that had escaped the waste-paper basket, even contracts and copyrights' and began to write the first biography of her husband.[2] The process of exploring his early experiences was 'strange, and sometimes desolating' – it was hard not to have been 'with him while he lived through them'.[3] Wistful longing for the sixty-six years she had missed suffuses the stories of his childhood and folk-song collecting adventures: she lived 'as much in his past as in my own present', and her husband's early life is recalled as if she had been a shadow at his side.[4] So fused are their voices it is often unclear who is speaking: in my attempts to separate them, I found myself living in their past as much as my present, drawn into a beguiling, protected realm where the stories all have a happy ending, a 'paradise remembered' as Ursula framed it:

> . . . its traces here, as I might find
> one golden earring, lost centuries ago,
> gleaming from darkness, still delicate and fine . . .[5]

The words of 'The Captain's Apprentice' always redirected my gaze and brought me back to a harsher world. When

Vaughan Williams published the song in the *Journal of the Folk-Song Society* he suggested that the words were local. Research by Elizabeth James in the 1990s unearthed the potential source for his comment in an old newspaper: the real case of Robert Eastick, a cabin boy from King's Lynn who drowned in 1856 under suspicious circumstances.[6] The testimonies of crew members at the Old Bailey trial of Eastick's captain, Johnson Doyle, reveal the claustrophobic domain of nineteenth-century merchant ships, where despot captains ruled their kingdoms, casual sadism was common, and the word of working-class crew members was often doubted by the authorities. This world of poverty and struggle is found in the shadows of the Edwardian folk-song collectors' sunlit lands: voices that threatened to disturb their constructed idyll were habitually edited out. Because he was a poor boy who lived and died when ordinary people were not much recorded, little evidence survives of Eastick's brief existence. Unless the gaps in the lives of such forgotten people are filled by other means – contextual clues from newspaper snippets, court transactions, surviving buildings, contemporary literature – their stories would remain untold. As with a broken pot, by piecing together scattered facts a more complete picture can be implied by the shape of spaces in between: in the following pages I have used italics for Eastick's story to signal its reconstruction from the fragments that remain.

A thin line threading through the layers between my childhood, Vaughan Williams's folk-song collecting, and the oral tradition, was the most unexpected find: emerging in the nineteenth century from a bog on the western fringes of the Outer

Hebrides it winds its sinuous way back to the eastern counties of 1960s England, and to a Christmas party in my family's Norfolk living room. No one could be more surprised than I was to find that Vaughan Williams had been part of my life from the beginning.

PART I

KING'S LYNN, JANUARY 1905

Approaching King's Lynn

On 15 January 1905 Vaughan Williams wrote from the Temperance Hotel in King's Lynn to his best friend and cousin, Ralph Wedgwood, 'I am collecting most wonderful songs among the fishermen here.'[1] He had arrived in the town a week earlier and, as he scribbled this note, he was looking back on his most fruitful folk-song collecting expedition to date.

The trip had not started in King's Lynn, but in a remote fen village further west –Tilney All Saints – and seems to have been the result of correspondence in the *Morning Post*. Vaughan Williams had responded to a letter which complained about the poverty of folk songs in Essex.[2] Having recently spent several days in that county recording a large number of folk songs, he wrote, 'I believe that we are only now beginning to realize what a store of beautiful melody has existed in our country . . . if they are not soon noted down and preserved they will be lost forever.'

He invited readers to get in touch with the Folk-Song Society if they had information on traditional ballads.

Founded in 1898, the society was part of a wider movement to preserve aspects of rural life in the face of industrialisation which had seen the establishment of the Commons, Open Spaces and Footpaths Preservation Society (1865); the National Trust (1895); the Gypsy Lore Society (1889); and the Royal Society for the Protection of Birds (1889). Its prime object was 'the collection and preservation of Folk Songs, Ballads and Tunes, and the publication of such of these as may be advisable'.[3] Hubert Parry and Charles Stanford, who both taught Vaughan Williams at the Royal College of Music, were appointed vice-presidents. The society had recently taken on a new lease of life when Vaughan Williams and Cecil Sharp – who had 'resolved to fan the dying embers of folk song into a mighty flame which would shine throughout the land' – were elected to the committee in 1904.[4] Working with Lucy Broadwood, who was secretary of the society and editor of its *Journal*, they started a national campaign to collect and publish folk songs. The composer's letter to the newspaper concluded with an offer: 'If anyone knows of traditional songs but does not feel able to note them down correctly, I myself should be happy, wherever possible, to come and note down the songs from the mouths of the singers.'[5]

Three months later, in early January 1905, Vaughan Williams arrived at Tilney All Saints to visit Revd John Henry Newnum, rector of the village. After the train journey from London, the rural station at Clenchwarton could be reached by a single stop along the branch line from King's Lynn, westwards into the Fens. The lane from there south to Tilney is still called Station

Road though the railway line has been buried by the A17. The last leg of the trip was a matter of minutes by pony and trap or bicycle to the vicarage, through a type of landscape familiar to Vaughan Williams from his student days at Cambridge – a straight unmade lane between hedgerows, flat arable fields on either side, the village ahead hidden in a cluster of trees. On a summer's day it might have been a pleasant jaunt, but it was January and strong winds were blowing all along the east coast – an exceptionally heavy gale on the evening of his arrival broke branches from trees, damaged buildings and threatened to sink ships caught offshore in the angry seas.[6]

Tilney All Saints is a tiny hamlet with a large and handsome church in its midst, built from creamy Barnack stone, its tower made elegant by a spire. The vicarage next door survives, a plain brick Georgian box. Vaughan Williams met the sexton, Mr Whitby, but the songs he sang were a disappointment – most had either been collected elsewhere or had already been published. Later that day he travelled to the neighbouring village of Tilney St Lawrence to meet Stephen Poll, an agricultural labourer and fiddler who played for country dancing.[7] On the following day he collected a few more songs from Mr Whitby.

After his disheartening weekend at Tilney, Vaughan Williams booked into the Cozens Temperance Hotel on Blackfriars Road, King's Lynn, two minutes' walk from the railway station.[8] Although it is not known how he met Revd Huddle, the curate who became his guide in the town, it is probable that the Tilney vicar knew about his colleague's contacts with the North End fishermen. Otherwise, the composer surely would have given up and gone home to London.

Vaughan Williams in 1902

In reminiscences about the trip Vaughan Williams turns the next part of the journey into a magical fable. As he continues the quest to save folk songs from the mouths of the people, allegorical figures step into his path: the sailor, the fisherman, the curate. He speaks of how he found a 'good many sailor songs' at King's Lynn 'by pure chance', how he visited 'the country places around', found little of interest, and 'was about to leave the district in despair' when 'a curate at King's Lynn asked him if he would like to see the fishing people in the North Town'. As a result, 'instead of going away he stayed a week'.[9] The curate and the composer both went to hear the fishermen sing, and 'reaped a rich reward . . .'[10]

⌒

Unlike Vaughan Williams, I approached the town from across the river via the West Lynn ferry. The Great Ouse river, which separates West Lynn from King's Lynn, is the port's reason for existing. In the view from the west bank the town retains its medieval shape, its skyscape punctured by steeples, church towers and warehouses, its foreground a long sea wall, interrupted by jetties and slipways. The tide was going out, and the water was low which made it necessary to climb down steep steps to the flat-bottomed ferry, the jetty a tawny-green wall of sea-sculpted timber towering over the passengers. High banks of glistening mud were emerging on both sides of the channel as the water drained out to sea. On the town side, a remarkably flat sandy beach was appearing. I asked if this was almost low tide. 'Not nearly,' replied the ferryman. As we travelled across, I gazed down the broad expanse of the choppy water, out towards the Wash, the view a series of colour blocks: brown river, brown mud, blue sky. Standing on the sea wall later, I watched passengers returning to West Lynn in their Saturday shopping outfits, bags over their arms, tottering down the concrete slipway, along a strategically placed metal plank over a pool, and across an expanse of wet sandbank to where the ferryman waited, almost in the centre of the river bed, with a two-step ladder up into the boat. Once the passengers were aboard, the ferry chugged across the now very narrow channel to the other side, the stepladder left as a surreal sculpture marooned on the line between the sand and water.

The life of the town once revolved around the rise and fall of the tide, this endless revealing and concealing of the river bed. The North End fishermen avoided the strong current in the main river by mooring their fishing 'smacks' in the Fisher Fleet, a tidal creek which formed the northern boundary of their settlement. They could sail out when the channel filled with the incoming sea but had to sail for home before the waters dropped. On the weekend that Vaughan Williams arrived, the strong gale had been followed by an uncommonly high tidal surge, which national papers linked to an earthquake in Gibraltar.[11] At the docks in the North End the tide rose four foot seven inches higher than the normal thirty-eight foot one inch, and parts of the town remained flooded for the week. Several small craft were swept from their moorings, and some were sunk. Although the newspaper report provides no detail, a few fishermen lost their livelihoods that weekend, and others would have been busy patching up their damaged boats.

I happened to be visiting when the King's Lynn festival was on – an annual arts event established in 1951.[12] There was a free Alfred Wallis exhibition at the Fermoy Gallery, close to Ferry Lane, so I wandered in. Wallis, a Cornish fisherman, spent his working life at sea and only began painting in his late sixties. His naive images of ships were taken up by the artists who colonised St Ives in the late 1920s, particularly Ben Nicholson who first brought wider attention to his work. According to Nicholson, Wallis's art was 'something that has grown out of the Cornish earth and sea',[13] echoing the beliefs of the folk-song collectors on the origins of the melodies they recorded. Unlike most of the singers, Wallis was consciously recording his own experiences in the paintings as an act of witness: 'what use To Bee out of my memory what we may never see again . . .'[14] The ships with their square and triangular blocks for sails, cutting through the white surf, would have been familiar to the fishermen and mariners of King's Lynn – barques, brigantines and schooners – each

King's Lynn in 1928 but little changed since 1905: Tuesday Marketplace in the centre; Revd Huddle's former house in the sunlit row at the end; St Nicholas' Chapel with spire, top centre; North End and docks in the top quarter

boat, as Wallis described it, with 'a beautiful soul shaped like a fish'.

A few steps from the gallery I arrived in the grand open space of Tuesday Marketplace, once the commercial centre of the town, lined on four sides with coaching inns, merchant houses and gracious brick terraces. Now filled with cars (except on Tuesdays when there is still a market), it was a spacious tree-lined square when Vaughan Williams arrived. Revd Huddle's house, number 15, is on the north side, part of a range of old buildings unified by an eighteenth-century brick facade of sober beauty. A fine house for a curate, and as close as could be to his congregation, the fishing families of the North End.

When Vaughan Williams came to the North End it was one of King's Lynn's poorest boroughs, habitually described as a 'tight-knit' community whose members did not mix with the rest of the town. After only a week, Vaughan Williams absorbed the sense of 'otherness' in this corner of the port, noting that 'the fishing colony of King's Lynn are a distinct race and still talk of the rest of the town as "foreigners" '.[15] He describes the first two singers introduced to him by Huddle – James 'Duggie' Carter and Joe Anderson – as 'fishermen of King's Lynn, both of them probably with Norse blood in their veins . . .'

To picture the fishermen as descendants of the Viking raiders of the ninth century, with seafaring at their very core, was attractive to Vaughan Williams. It sprang from the idea, widely held across Europe at the time, that isolation from external influences enabled 'peasant' populations to develop and conserve their own characteristic regional cultures. The theory that indigenous oral traditions preserved the artistic soul of each nation brought significance to English folk song as the potential source for developing a new national music.[16] A belief in the power of cultural isolation led Vaughan Williams to conclude that the 'Norse blood' of the fishermen helped to explain the 'wild character' of 'The Captain's Apprentice' melody sung by Carter.[17] It is feasible that some of the inhabitants of the North End were of more recent Scandinavian ancestry – King's Lynn had strong trading links with northern Europe – but it is more likely that, as with all small communities built around a distinctive local industry, in the North End the sense of a separate

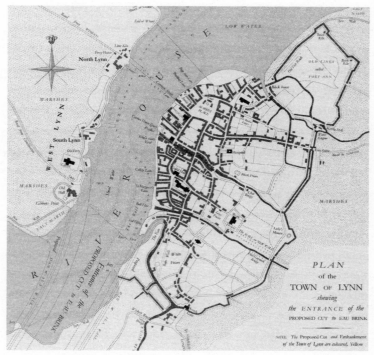

Faden's 1797 map of King's Lynn before major landscape changes.
St Nicholas' Chapel is shown as a black rectangular block towards
the top, with North End clustered around it. The inlet to the north-east
of the chapel is Fisher Fleet. North Lynn is shown on the other side
of the River Ouse.

culture with particular customs and practices grew out of shared
work, shared stories, shared adversity.

Up until the second half of the nineteenth century the North
End consisted of a collection of cottages and tenements grouped
along a handful of streets and alleyways bounded by the Great
Ouse and Fisher Fleet. These waterways gave access to fishing
grounds in the shallow bay of the Wash, and the North Sea. The

north bank of the fleet was a place where families could go for a stroll, and was a favourite subject of local artist Henry Baines (1823–94). One view, taken from the mouth of the creek in the 1860s,[18] looks back towards the North End on a summer's evening, the sky tinged with red. A group of women in pink and green dresses sit on the bank of the fleet, holding babies on their laps, while the men stand chatting behind them, hands in pockets. Youths lie on their stomachs on the soft grass, trousers rolled up after a paddle in the creek, and along the embankment other groups can be seen wending their way back to the town. The tide is out and a man stands up to his ankles in the channel, checking the underside of his boat. The fleet is full of 'smacks', small fishing boats designed for shallow waters, their masts leaning at all angles, their red sails draped and loose, as if they too are relaxing.

Fisher Fleet Looking East. Kings Lynn Norfolk *by Henry Baines (1823–94)*

Sunset, North End *by Henry Baines*

In another painting Baines has turned round to look the other way, west into the sunset, and towards the isolated hamlet of North Lynn (not to be confused with the North End) on the opposite bank of the River Ouse.

In the mid-nineteenth century major embankment and drainage works in this area began an irrevocable transformation of these views. The Norfolk Estuary Company diverted the Great Ouse river down a new channel – the Lynn Cut – which was excavated across the land west of North Lynn. Where the river had once flowed, the land was drained and reclaimed for agriculture. North Lynn Farm, which had gazed over water, now gazed over an expanse of flat pasture, while the big ships sailed along the new deep channel behind its back. In this remodelled landscape North Lynn was joined to the east side of the river, a new neighbour to the North End.

Soon after, the reclaimed marshes which now lay between the North End and North Lynn were earmarked for the construction of state-of-the-art docks. Two were to be built, one on either side of the Fisher Fleet – first Alexandra dock (completed 1869), and then Bentinck (1883). During construction of the second dock it was planned to fill in a section of the Fisher Fleet, leaving only a short stretch at its mouth where fishing boats could continue to moor – change that the Northenders vehemently opposed. A complaint from the fisherfolk submitted to the town council in 1880 was dismissed by the mayor who pointed out that the work had been approved under an Act of Parliament and that 'full accommodation' would be given to the fishermen: a landing stage was promised near the mouth of the fleet to compensate for loss of their traditional moorings.[19] Although the mayor intended to silence opposition with the crushing authority of Parliament, the following year saw a series of protests against the changes. In February 1881 a group of fishermen visited the homes of the contractor and foreman in charge, and threatened them with violence, and destruction of the dam that was to be built across the fleet. A month later, when there was a ceremony at the start of works, the polite applause of spectators was disrupted by the 'hootings and other expressions of disapprobation' of the fisherfolk. At the end of May 1881 an order was sent out for all fishing smacks and boats to be removed from the area that was to be blocked up. A chain was slung across the fleet, but the fishermen were defiant and attempted to sail up the channel on the designated day, while their wives and children – possibly some of the people depicted in Henry Baines's idyllic paintings from the 1860s – lined the banks shouting and swearing at the fifty dock labourers and the police who were there to enforce order.

In the 1950s, an elderly fisherman, Charlie Fysh, remembered the events from his boyhood. 'A gret [sic] big fellow', fisherman

Tom Bunn, shouted, 'Come on – don't let the hounds have it!' as he knocked off the helmets of several policemen and threw mud in the face of the white-gloved superintendent.[20] The newspapers reported that Northenders armed with boat hooks and hatchets threatened to 'chop down the officers, and to throw them in the river'. The disturbances went on for three hours before reinforcements were brought in and the police managed to clear away the angry crowds. There was more trouble on the following three days but in the end the community could not stop the works and half the Fisher Fleet was buried for ever. The dock company failed to consult the fishermen about the design for the replacement moorings – and so they were built too high, on the wrong side of the fleet and without the necessary tramline to transport their catch off the quay. Although the town council agreed that the fishermen had a legitimate grievance, nothing was done. Aged nearly ninety, Charlie Fysh was still bitter: 'King John, he left the fleet and that chapel with the steeple there . . . wholly and solely for the fishermen, and they took it to make the new dock. They stole it from us, they stole it from us.'[21]

By October 1883 the docks were officially opened. The *Boston Guardian* relates how the lock which joined the old and the new dock had been built across the bed of the Fisher Fleet, 'the harbour for many years of the fishing craft of Lynn; and the locality altogether has undergone such an entire transformation that very few of its original features remain'.[22] With my twenty-first-century eye, I expect the next line to acknowledge the negative impact of such obliteration – but this is the Victorian era and there is no looking back. The reporter singles out the economic benefits of using hydraulic power to scour the Fisher Fleet which will be 'a matter of interest to the shareholders'. After the opening ceremony on the dock '250 ladies and gentlemen accepted the invitation of the dock directors to partake of an excellent luncheon'. We can be sure no fishermen were at the party.

Meeting 'Duggie' Carter

The first version I heard of the meeting between Vaughan Williams and Duggie Carter was based on a local narrative of delicious chance and coincidence: it was said that due to the unusually bad weather of that January weekend in 1905, the North End fishermen had retreated to the Tilden Smith pub, to wait for the storm to blow over.[1] If the weather had been good, the pub would have been empty, Vaughan Williams might never have heard Carter's version of 'The Captain's Apprentice', and the composer's whole oeuvre would have developed differently. This was the story behind the commemorative plaque I saw on the old pub wall, and was the series of events that the man I met in the street believed to be true. It is a good story, one based on the common knowledge that Vaughan Williams regarded pubs as fruitful venues for finding tunes. In the months prior to the King's Lynn visit he had noted down songs in several pubs around the country, and when he published his collection in the Folk-Song Society's *Journal* of 1906 he wrote, 'I could imagine a much less profitable way of spending a long winter evening than in the parlour of a country inn taking one's turn at the mug of "four-ale" . . . and with the ever present chance of picking up some rare old ballad or an exquisitely beautiful melody, worthy, within its smaller compass, of a place beside the finest compositions of the greatest composers'.[2]

In my mind's eye, I see the snug room of the Tilden Smith, with a good fire and high-backed wooden benches to keep out the draughts, where the fishermen sit smoking their clay pipes and drinking small-beer. Vaughan Williams steps out of the cold wind and rain into the warmth of the pub, accompanied by the Revd Alfred Huddle. The composer is tall, large-framed and well fed, and by all accounts often dishevelled and clumsy. The cut of his clothes and his accent set him apart from the regular drinkers. He is not the kind of figure who can slip into the Tilden Smith unnoticed, however affable he is. The pair bring a chill into the comfortable atmosphere of the bar, as everyone turns their gaze on the stranger. Chatter ceases, singing is silenced.

Settling down at a table, Vaughan Williams takes out his notebook and pencil, and politely asks those present whether they might entertain him with a song or two. The air is thick with woodsmoke and tobacco, the sour tang of old beer, the aroma of fish and oil emanating from woollen 'ganseys' and weathered boots.

Someone says, 'Come on, Duggie, bor, give us a song.' Out of the awkward silence, the raw voice of a man 'advanced in years' rises up, singing a melody of such ethereal beauty it would influence Vaughan Williams's composition for the rest of his life.

⌒

Despite the long-held belief that Vaughan Williams visited the Tilden Smith, it turns out there is no evidence he was ever there.[3] Although it was a popular singing pub during the 1950s and '60s (in 1955, travel writer John Seymour found the fishermen's songs so good he went back later to record an evening's session for BBC radio[4]), no pubs are mentioned in Vaughan Williams's notes for this particular trip – perhaps due to the influence of his guide, the Revd Huddle. In practice, Edwardian collectors found that pubs were not always suitable locations for the painstaking task of setting down a melody, words and any variants for each verse, as this required the song to be performed more than once. Pubs were the places where 'promises of meetings to sing in quieter surroundings could be exacted and which were always honoured'.[5] Younger singers living in the North End, who might have been kept at home by the gales or the tides, could perhaps have been found in one of the singing pubs – including the Tilden Smith – but it seems that Vaughan Williams never met them.[6] His days in the town were divided between an older group of twelve men and women living in the North End and six men who were resident in the workhouse, the order of visits dictated by when the fisherfolk were available.[7] In later years Vaughan Williams recalled the experience in a talk he gave on folk music for the BBC. He spoke about 'On Board a Ninety-Eight', one of the airs he used in *Norfolk Rhapsody No. 1*: 'This was sung to me in King's Lynn by an old sailor. I spent many happy mornings with him and his friends listening to their almost inexhaustible stock of splendid tunes.'[8] The song was sung by Robert Leatherday in the workhouse. The singers were generally over seventy and 'though their memories were good the thin voices of old age sometimes made it difficult to note the tune'.[9] In his plea for the preservation of songs passed down through the oral tradition, Vaughan Williams argued that 'it is the elder people to whom we must go': it was in their company that he hoped to be taken back in time, to the early 1800s and beyond.[10]

⌒

Revd Huddle, dressed in black suit and dog collar, steps out of the front door of his town house for a two-minute stroll that takes him from the pomp of Tuesday Marketplace to the church at the centre of North End. I follow in his imagined footsteps. The church-like building of St Nicholas is a medieval chapel-of-ease, dedicated to the patron saint of fishermen. When Vaughan Williams was here in January 1905 the Northenders continued to rely on fishing to make a living, though the building of the docks had made it more awkward. Revd Huddle, a recent arrival in the parish, had gained the trust of local people and had managed to persuade well-respected figures, such as James 'Duggie' Carter, to be confirmed in the church.

A black-and-white image shows Carter, Huddle and another singer, Joe Anderson, in a formal pose. Carter, clean-shaven, wears a neckerchief and an elaborately patterned 'gansey' jumper of a type that all Norfolk fishermen wore, tight-knitted and oily to keep out the wind and rain. On his head is a peaked cap and, clamped between his teeth, a clay pipe. His adopted daughter 'never knew him with anything but a blue jersey and a peaked cap'.[11] He has a determined, almost bullish look. Aged sixty-one when he met Vaughan Williams, he had been in his late thirties when the Fisher Fleet riot took place.[12] He looks like the kind of man who would have stood his ground against the docks, even though after retiring from fishing he worked there as a labourer. The other two men are seated in front of him. Mr Anderson looks careworn and more elderly with an old-fashioned beard, his head slightly tilted to one side. The balding curate is fresh-faced, plump-cheeked and enthusiastic.

The photograph might have been taken especially for Vaughan Williams.[13] During his visit he noted down songs from eighteen

From left to right: Joe Anderson, James 'Duggie' Carter, Revd Huddle

of the town's inhabitants, but in the preface to the *Journal of the Folk-Song Society* in 1906, he specifically thanks Carter and Anderson as well as Huddle who 'so kindly helped me by finding out singers . . .'[14] Rather than meeting these singers at the pub, it appears that the curate escorted – or directed – Vaughan Williams from house to house. Carter was the first singer Huddle introduced to the composer, around the corner from the chapel, in Watson's Yard.[15]

Addressing an audience five years later about the trip to the North End, Vaughan Williams commented that the slums were the worst he had ever been to and that he was 'very forcibly reminded of the fact that the appeal of the folk song was to the ear and not to the nose' – a comment met with laughter, but which might be considered ungracious coming from a stranger welcomed into the homes of these 'very hard-working and very poor fishermen' as he described them.[16]

The North End was a jigsaw of 'yards' – clusters of buildings that had grown up around numerous narrow passageways and courtyards. There was no running water, electricity or drainage, and large families lived in tiny spaces. True's Yard, the sole survivor of slum clearances, is now a museum. At around the time Carter was growing up nearby, a two-room cottage here (one-up, one-down) housed a family with nine children. The ground-floor kitchen and living space, entered straight off the yard, had an open fire, or a modest coal-fired range, for heating and cooking. There was little room for knick-knacks, but the hearth was brightened by a traditional rag rug, made from multicoloured scraps of material. A winding wooden stair next to the fireplace led to the bedroom. Six of the children slept in the only bed, while the baby was placed in a chest, and their mother lay on the floor next to them, a few embers from the downstairs fire placed in the grate for warmth. The older children, who lost their place in the bed as younger children came along, stayed over-night with relatives. In the winter their father slept downstairs, and in the summer on one of the fishing smacks. The contents of chamber pots and, later, outside loos, were sometimes dis-posed of in the street. Hauls from fishing trips were brought back to the house, sorted and prepared, and the waste washed out into the yards. The air was pungent with the odour of fish guts, coal smoke, raw sewage and thick mud.[17]

Neighbouring Watson's Yard, where Carter lived, was no dif-ferent. An inquiry into sanitary conditions in 1853 found it a 'vile place – fish refuse; no proper pavement; excrement . . . The whole place covered with shrimp and mussel refuse, and only two water-taps for about 10 houses, and 50 or more people.'[18] Fifty years later there had been improvements in water supply and sewage control but living conditions remained poor until the 1930s when Watson's Yard was swept away in a slum-demolition programme. The composer and the curate stepped into a cramped and sparse house on that cold January day when they visited Carter. The fisherman's wife had died in the previ-ous year, his five children were grown up and his adopted daughter, Lottie, aged twelve, was at school, so it was probably just the three men gathered in the kitchen. The curate's knock on the door with a stranger at his side must have been quite a surprise. There is no record of how Carter felt about this unex-pected visit from a well-to-do Londoner who wanted to hear him sing. When interviewed in the 1970s Lottie did not report that it had been a momentous day in the life of her father, or something he often spoke of.

The fisherman performed five songs that day and made time to sing further songs later in the week. Above the first, 'Deeds of Napoleon', Vaughan Williams wrote those brief notes: 'Sung by Mr Carter (Fisherman) about 70? Jan 9th 1905 at the North End King's Lynn'.[19] From the manuscript it looks as though he found it easy to jot down the melodies as Carter sang them – there are no corrections – suggesting that the fisherman had a confident and tuneful voice, which made it clear which notes he intended. In contrast, later in the week when the retired sailor Mr Woods sang 'Napoleon's Farewell', Vaughan Williams wrote next to his notation, 'doubtful because he was very hoarse'.[20]

'The Prentice Boy' as Carter named it – or 'The Captain's Apprentice' as it is more widely known – was the second song he chose to perform. This air is more complicated than 'Napoleon's Farewell'. The line of the melody at the beginning of the first verse differs from the following verses and Carter changed the final phrase at least three times. Vaughan Williams would have asked him to sing the song more than once, while he carefully noted down these variants, and then the words.[21] Additional pencil notes show that he returned to the manuscript later to think about how he would present these variants in the published version. There are no other marks, signs or comments in the notebook to suggest that he was particularly struck by the melody, though Ursula claimed it was 'always one of his favourites'.[22]

When the song was published in the *Journal* Vaughan Williams wrote, 'The words are evidently local. "St James' Workhouse" is

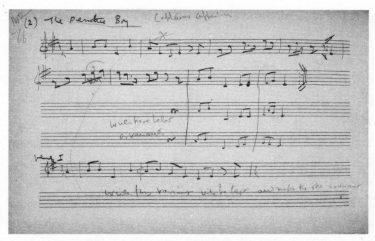

Vaughan Williams's manuscript of 'The Captain's Apprentice'

the King's Lynn Union.' A further note states that the ballad 'was probably called forth by a particularly brutal case of ill-treatment, similar to that narrated in it, which occurred some twenty or thirty years ago'.[23] These cryptic comments invite the curious to look for a local story: in the 1990s a possible candidate for the 'brutal case' was discovered by museum curator Elizabeth James, in a copy of the *King's Lynn Advertiser* of 12 September 1857 under the headline 'Cruelty at Sea'.[24] The report describes how Captain Johnson Doyle had been charged with a series of aggravated assaults on an apprentice, a King's Lynn boy called Robert Eastick, carried out during a trip to Ceylon (modern-day Sri Lanka) on a ship known as the *John Sugars*.

James Carter was twelve when the news of Eastick's death reached the town. Being so similar in age – Eastick had been fifteen – this tragic news may well have made the words of 'The Captain's Apprentice' particularly significant for him, enough to keep the song in his repertoire until old age. Lottie recalled her father singing it at home when she was a child: 'I remember they were cruel to this boy, and in the finish they lashed him to the rigging . . .'[25] But was that boy Robert Eastick?

⌒

The 'wild' melody of 'The Captain's Apprentice', as sung by Carter, became the main theme in Vaughan Williams's *Norfolk Rhapsody No. 1* and deeply influenced his later work. In old age the composer claimed that the cadences of the tune 'finally opened the door to an entirely new world of melody, harmony and feeling'.[26]

At St Nicholas' Chapel, visitors can listen through headphones to sung verses of each of the three tunes Vaughan Williams used in *Norfolk Rhapsody No. 1* – 'The Captain's Apprentice', 'The Bold Young Sailor' and 'On Board a Ninety-Eight' – with an invitation to compare these to a recording of the composer's piece. His brief visit to North End more than one hundred years ago is still an event to be proud of, perhaps to cling to. The music captures the imprint of a community that was swept away shortly afterwards: the faint pattern of musical notes marks the line of their high tide.

Turning right out of the chapel, it is a few yards to the end of North Street. True's Yard Museum stands on the corner – a shopfront, with the pair of tiny furnished cottages and work-shops at the back. Beyond its door a great wave of modern development has crashed along the course of the old Fisher Fleet taking most of the North End with it. Out of the wreckage has grown an industrial area, buddleia and brambles caught behind high-security fencing. Watson's Yard is occupied by red-brick flats arranged in a kind of ziggurat style overlooking the car wash. Scything across the east end of the street is the John Kennedy trunk road, built in the late 1960s, named to commemorate the assassinated president. The Tilden Smith is stranded on the other side, its plaque still in place. A nineteenth-century photograph shows the former setting of the old pub, a plain brick building perched on foundations at one end of a bridge, its two sash windows looking down the channel of the Fisher Fleet. On the north bank, boats are drawn up from the water to lie on the mud slopes below a crowded line of cottages. On the south bank the tramline and warehouses of the first dock are visible. The image might have been taken to record the view before the second dock was built, and the river buried.

Fisher Fleet at low tide, looking back towards the town, c.1880. The Tilden Smith pub is the detached building in the centre

The Tilden Smith has not moved, but its original appearance is now masked by render and plastic windows, and the landscape around it has been transformed. The process of this building's desecration feels symbolic of a wider loss. There has been a stripping away of patina, setting and context. Even its name was changed in the late twentieth century, to the Retreat – a name that aptly sums up the sense of the North End community's enforced withdrawal.

Behind this building, along Hextable Road, is the small housing development called Duggie Carter Court. It is not the office block I had envisaged when first told that the singer was to be commemorated by a building, but a modest row of terraced housing. The naming of the terrace after a real-life person is in the tradition of the King's Lynn yards, but True's Yard records the name of the landlord – the person with money and status. Duggie Carter Court commemorates a man who had no expectation, outside the circle of his family and friends, of being remembered. As a result of the chance encounter with Vaughan Williams his name is set next to the famous American president in perpetuity.

Not all of the old North End is lost. Hidden down a footpath behind the ziggurats there is a stub of Pilot Street, a row of buildings all different shapes, sizes and dates, squeezed along a narrow brick lane. Remove the yellow lines, and you can think yourself into 1905, a shimmer of Vaughan Williams walking ahead along those bricks.

Under increasingly grey skies I made my way along busy roads, past the Victorian railway station and the former Temperance Hotel, before cutting through St James' Park to reach the King's

Lynn Union workhouse on Exton Road. A large part of it survives, now used as health authority offices. Completed in 1856, two years after the collapse of the old St James' workhouse, its red brick is enlivened by decorative white diamonds, crosses and banding, though it was not designed to be an attractive place for inmates. When it opened, the local press reminded the workhouse guardians that they were required to provide only the 'necessaries of life' and to 'withhold everything which would render the lot of the pauper better than that of the independent man who supports himself at his own exertions . . .' Half a century later, attitudes had softened. In the week prior to Christmas every workhouse child was given sixpence, and on New Year's Day young and old inmates were treated to a special tea with music and presents. The King regularly sent a festive hamper from nearby Sandringham: prior to Christmas 1904 the workhouse received ten pheasants and sixty rabbits from the royal estate. After their feast the inmates stood to sing the national anthem. Three weeks later they sang for Vaughan Williams. This is where he spent 'many happy mornings', collecting more than twenty songs in the workhouse despite the thin voices of the elderly men. By the time he left King's Lynn he had written down over sixty songs in his manuscript books.[27]

The health authority offices were closed, and it began to rain. Walking back towards the town, instead of turning right into St James' Park, I turned into Goodwin's Road. On the right-hand side, set back from the pavement, I spotted a row of cottages, the long, low exterior punctuated by timber bay windows, the gables decorated with semicircular patterns of blue engineering bricks. Mounted over the central porch, a commemorative stone plaque announces: 'SUGARS ALMSHOUSES. ERECTED 1887'. These quaint old buildings were funded through a bequest in the will of John Sugars – town councillor, builder, architect and shipowner. Standing in the drizzle on the side of the road on that grey afternoon, this was my first tangible connection with the story of Robert Eastick.

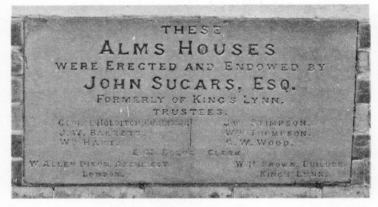

Plaque for Sugars's Almshouses

St James' Workhouse

(King's Lynn, 13 August 1854)

At a quarter to eleven on the morning of Sunday 13 August 1854 the clock on the central tower of St James' workhouse stops. This is unexpected as Mr Andrews, clockmaker of the town, visits twice weekly to check the mechanism and had wound it up only the day before. Inmates and staff of the workhouse and local residents rely on the hourly chimes of the cupola bell to regulate their day. At night the face of the clock is illuminated. Mr Nelson, master of the work-house, sends for Mr Andrews to check what is amiss.

A group of old men are standing in the yard below the clock. These workhouse inmates, whose sleeping quarters are in the tower, have often been woken in the night by ominous cracking noises. Fissures between the great stone buttresses and the ancient walls had appeared more than two years previously and were declared unsafe by a visit-ing surveyor. On this Sunday morning, the men were disturbed by lumps of mortar falling into their room. Alarmed, they gathered outside from where they observed that the doorway leading into the tower had separated from the main wall.

Revd Bransby calls in on his way to deliver a service at the West Lynn hospital. After discussing the problem with Nelson, he sends a brief note to the Governor of the Court of Guardians requesting an urgent assessment of the building's condition. Everyone is ordered out of the men's day room on the ground floor of the tower. Despite these circumstances – the men milling about in the yard, the creaking walls, and the visibly distorted doorway – Andrews and Nelson enter the building to inspect the clock.

Together they climb the steep stone steps inside the eighty-foot-high tower, knowing full well that it is a dangerous undertaking. As they reach the clock turret, Nelson sees that the cracks are wider than on the previous day. Half an hour later, the old men in the yard below watch amazed as the tower roof begins to sink in front of their eyes. In a split second the whole edifice comes tumbling down. The tremendous crash is heard across town and brings crowds running to the scene. Immense clouds of dust surge in all directions, coating everything with a ghostly white film.

News of the catastrophe spreads quickly. Church sermons are interrupted as pleas for help go out to doctors, builders and able-bodied men who might lend their strength to clear the rubble and save those trapped beneath. John Sugars rushes to the scene after hearing the boom of the building's collapse. Even as he helps clear away the rubble he is thinking about a location for the new workhouse, and how the pauper lads might be helped. Teams of navvies from the Norfolk Estuary Company claw away at the stone with their bare hands, while the air fills with choking powder and the shrieks of womenfolk. The residential wings on either side of the

tower, usually occupied by boys and young men, were partly demol-
ished by the fall. In amongst the chaos, it is not immediately realised
that they had been at church and are safe. Policemen are brought in
to preserve order.

Within the first few minutes of the rescue mission, three old men
are pulled from the rubble, smothered in lime but without life-
threatening injuries. The cheering townsfolk are entreated to be
quiet while the navvies listen for the sound of further survivors.
They hold their breath. A whisper of dust cascades down the ruined
walls. A broken timber creaks. Then, from beneath the huge pile of
stones, comes a weak 'halloo'. It is Nelson, his life saved by two masses
of masonry wedged above his head which protected him from falling
debris. He is freed with only a dislocated shoulder and severe bruis-
ing. Poor Andrews is not so lucky. The clock which he had been sent
to inspect has killed him. He is found crushed beneath its weight, the
key of the turret door still in his hand.[1]

During the following days, there is hardly a soul in King's Lynn
who does not visit the site of the accident to view the ruined build-
ing, marvel at Nelson's lucky escape, and shake their heads over the
death of the clockmaker. Ten-year-old Duggie Carter runs over with
his friends from the North End to gawp. Thirteen-year-old Robert
Eastick joins the crowd. He lives with his mother in a yard behind
the workhouse where they felt the rumble of the collapse under their
feet. He is destined to become an apprentice on John Sugars's ship.
Two years and one week after that August Sunday, the teenager
would be dead and John Sugars's name in all the papers.[2]

PART II

LOST VOICES

The Hebrides Connection

South Uist

I don't remember hearing 'Kishmul's Galley' before my mother taught it to me when I was sixteen. Sitting at the kitchen table, waiting for something to cook, she sang each line to me separately, and I sang them back, imitating the same phrasing, the same solemn tone, the same depth of emotion. The song is sung on 'the day of days' by someone standing high on a mountain called the Ben a Hayich as they watch a ship battle against the sea to reach the safety of Kishmul (now known as Kisimul) Castle. Against the odds, the galley arrives and there is great celebration with red wine, meat and harping. Throughout, there is a repeated chorus, a kind of keening: o-*hee* a *ho*, *fal*-oo-*o*. It felt like an old song to me, full of Scotland's 'ancient glory'.

At that time, I was very conscious of my Scottish roots – my great-grandmother was Glaswegian, and I believed it was from her that I inherited my red hair. From my mother I had imbibed the importance of the 'national bard', Rabbie Burns, and the heroic romance of Scotland's past. I loved the wistful Scottish air I learnt in the kitchen. Afterwards, I often sang 'Kishmul's Galley' at family parties, then I sang it to Mum when she was ill, and then I sang it at her funeral.

In the 1990s I arranged 'Kishmul's Galley' for a small choir. I tried researching the song's origins but the World Wide Web was still young. I discovered only that Kisimul Castle exists, built on a rocky outcrop off the shore of Barra, a tiny island at the end of the Outer Hebrides archipelago. It occurred to me then, that I had inherited the mysterious 'Kishmul's Galley' from my distant Scottish ancestors through the oral tradition. I was happy to cradle this idea, and not pursue it, but in 2008 I came across a website which mapped surnames across the world using Victorian census data. In the nineteenth century almost everyone with my great-grandmother's name – MacIsaac – lived in the west of Scotland, and especially on the Outer Hebridean island of South Uist, near Barra.

I mentioned to a friend this new-found MacIsaac link to South Uist. The following Christmas he bought me a book: *Carmina Gadelica*, an extraordinary collection of Gaelic poems, charms and songs, collected by Alexander Carmichael in the late nineteenth century. I opened the book and there in the introduction was Carmichael's account of visiting a Hector MacIsaac and his wife in 1871 at their house in a 'peat-moss' at Ceannlangavat, South Uist. Hector was an 'unlettered cottar': an uneducated farm labourer or tenant occupying a cottage in return for labour. The walls of the couple's 'hut' were made from turf, the roof of reed. It was fifteen feet long by ten feet wide, and five feet high. Carmichael writes, 'There was nothing in it that the vilest thief in the lowest slum would condescend to steal.'[1] There was, in fact, great treasure within the four walls, which Carmichael took away with him: Mrs MacIsaac gave him many secular runes, sacred hymns and fairy songs, while from Hector he recorded numerous heroic tales, poems and ballads.

I felt the name 'MacIsaac' jumping out of the text as a physical jolt, as if Mrs MacIsaac had reached her hand through time and grasped mine in affirmation of my own impulse to sing and tell stories.

Hector MacIsaac and his wife (her name is not given) were undoubtedly related to me, though how closely, I don't know. My great-grandmother Jessie Bell MacIsaac was born at around 1853 in Glasgow so her branch of the family had already left South Uist behind when Carmichael met Hector. But this tale of my distant ancestors offering up their material to the grand visitor marked a subtle shift in my relationship to the research – it placed me firmly in the camp of people from whom songs were collected, rather than the collectors.

In 1871 Hector was the poorest of the poor, living in a decrepit hut in the remote bogs of a far-flung island. According to Carmichael he had never in his whole life left the island of his birth, and he spoke only Gaelic, a language that was actively suppressed. Yet here is his name in black and white, set down in a book that has been republished several times since the original edition of 1900. Like James 'Duggie' Carter, someone who was destined to be forgotten has been immortalised.

⌒

In the spring after my mother's death my partner and I spent a week on South Uist. Since learning about the MacIsaac connection, I had often considered visiting but was put off by the distance, a long journey by road from Norfolk in the east to the far Western Isles. But singing the old Scottish songs to my mum during her last illness had rekindled the idea. I thought I might find Ceannlangavat, where Hector MacIsaac had lived, and visit the real-life Kisimul Castle.

On the first day, we visited the settlement of Tobha Mor set behind the *machair* – the low-lying grassy dunes found along much of the west coast of South Uist. Two or three croft dwellings survive in the hamlet. The thatched roofs of these single-storey cottages are protected against Atlantic gales by netting weighted with heavy stones, like antique sugar-bowl covers, beads dangling. One has been converted into a compact hostel. Close to the austere twentieth-century Catholic church are the ruins of a medieval monastic settlement, with a series of cell-like buildings made from stone. It's a spot where you can imagine the island before bungalows. When we arrived, three or four men in overalls were standing around a cow, tied by rope to some metal fencing, and a bedraggled calf. While we watched, one of the men lifted the calf, pulling it nearer to its mother. She was bowing her head down and straining at the rope, furious at being constrained, and uninterested in the wet creature she had just birthed. We crept past, trying not to disturb them.

After exploring the ruins we walked back past the cow. Now there was only one man waiting by her. He was perhaps in his early sixties, with white hair, blue eyes and a weathered face, his woollen jumper smeared with mud. I asked him about the ruined chapel, and we talked about the newborn calf and its angry mother.

'We have trouble with this cow every year. She's a bitch of a cow.' The harsh word sounded almost affectionate in his gentle lilt. She was tangling herself in the rope, rolling her eyes and kicking. 'I'll have to let her go.'

He asked where we were staying. I mentioned that I was hoping to explore my MacIsaac connections, and I wondered if he knew where Ceannlangavat was.

He said, 'My mother was a MacIsaac – this land we're standing on belonged to her.'

'Then we must be related!' I laughed, quite thrilled to think that the first person I had spoken to on the island was connected to me, even though in the most tenuous of ways. I shook his hand while he looked bemused at my excitement. He recommended that we visit the museum at Kildonan. As we left he let loose the cow and she stumbled off, kicking her back legs.

On the following morning we drove south to the museum along the 'main' road, a narrow ribbon of tarmac floating across the surface of a treeless, waterlogged landscape. The western side of the island seems to be ninety per cent loch, sea inlet, and tawny wet bog, a land saved from submersion by the ballast of mountains along its eastern edge. Kildonan Museum holds some beautiful, bleak black-and-white photos of the old life there, women in aprons and boots living in tiny 'blackhouses' with earth floors, cooking fires in the centre, the smoke finding its way out through the thatch. There was no information available about my branch of the MacIsaacs and no reference to 'Kishmul's Galley', but a member of staff thought the museum at

Barra would know more, so she took my contact details. I bought a slim book in the shop about the collector Alistair Carmichael. In it there was a reference to Hector MacIsaac living on the island at Cárnan, Íochdar.[2]

On the map, we could see that Cárnan was just a mile or two from our holiday cottage, on the northern tip of the island, so we went to have a look. It is a straggle of two or three modern houses along a narrow lane, bog on one side, the sea inlet between South Uist and Benbecula on the other. In the saturated fields are the remains of cottages – mostly a few jumbled stones marking out the rectangles of the old places. Any one of them could have been the site of Hector MacIsaac's home. As I took photographs, a lapwing hovered over one of the ruins close by, making that strange swanny-whistle call, and for a fanciful moment I imagined it was crying, 'This one, this one!' One of the crofts was still standing, though derelict. A window was open and inside was a kitchen table and chairs and a mug on the

Abandoned croft, South Uist

rust-eaten cooker, as if the occupant had been spirited away after breakfast.

My idea of the relationship between Alexander Carmichael and Hector MacIsaac, evoked by the introduction in *Carmina Gadelica*, was in tatters after reading the book bought in the museum. I had assumed that Carmichael used the same collecting techniques in 1871 as Vaughan Williams and the other Edwardian collectors did, thirty-five years later – they made special journeys to rural places, used local contacts and tip-offs about the best singers, and then visited to record material. In fact, Carmichael lived in various houses on South Uist and the adjacent isles for around sixteen years, and he visited Hector several times. His notes from one of these meetings give a picture of the cottar as a man with strong opinions:

> Hector MacIosag [MacIsaac] despises mythological tales and says they are great rubbish . . . He says that he heard tales read as repeated by persons whom he knows and that the tales were so garbled and mangled that he hung down his head and closed his ears for very shame . . . He dec[lares] that there is no man from the Butt of Lewis to Barra Head – 200 m[iles]. – who has the history of the Fing[alians] so well as he . . .[3]

I had previously imagined Carmichael sitting in the turf hut at the feet of the venerable old couple, noble in their utter poverty and want, while he noted down their unique knowledge in a rescue mission before they died. In these field notes Hector is out and about, planting potatoes, he has a young daughter in the house who has no interest in his legacy of poetry and prose, and he talks freely of travelling twenty-one miles over difficult terrain to Benbecula to share his material with the collector.

The initial two volumes of *Carmina Gadelica* were not published until 1900, when Carmichael was nearly seventy and had lived away from the islands for many years. During the thirty years between the field notes and the publication of his massive work, his tone changed from amused observer to respectful acolyte. His 1866 declaration that reciters are 'the most egotistical set I have ever met' is not repeated in the 1900 publication. Instead, Hector is portrayed as the picture of modesty, 'polite and well-mannered and courteous . . .'[4] I am attracted, though, to the other Hector, the one with numerous ancient stories crowding his head, out in the wind and the rain, his hands thrusting seed potatoes into the peaty soil, boasting of his own eloquence to the mainland scholar, calling over his shoulder a chiding remark to his disaffected daughter who is only interested in new things.

In Search of a Good Tune

I am gazing into the eyes of Mrs Lucy White of Hambridge, Somerset, as she stands outside her cottage over one hundred years ago. She looks straight into the camera, amused, one corner of her pursed lips upturned. Her left arm is held awkwardly by her side, her elbow stiff. Behind her, the door is open, as though she expects this pause on the front step to be brief before returning to her chores. There is no attempt at the picturesque, no formal backdrop – just Mrs White in her shawl and apron, grey hair tied back from her face. The photographer is Cecil Sharp, collector of folk songs.

White has sung several times for Sharp and Charles Marson, the local vicar, sometimes at the parsonage, sometimes at home. Sharp takes down the tunes while Marson scribbles the words.[1] The two men have become familiar to her, and she feels certain that they are genuinely interested in her repertoire. At some

Lucy White photographed by Cecil Sharp

point she gives them 'Blow Away the Morning Dew'. The vicar's hand falters momentarily as he writes out the lyrics. In the published edition it is noted that he found it necessary to 'soften' the words.

The ballad was published in the early seventeenth century as 'The Baffled Knight' but was probably in circulation before that.[2] There are several alternative titles but in all versions a man comes across a 'pretty maid' on her own in the countryside. Sometimes the man is a knight, sometimes he is a farmer's son or a shepherd – perhaps a reflection of changing times and the regions where it was sung. Whatever his rank, the man is filled with lust – in the 1609 lyrics he declares:

> If I have not my will of you,
> Full soon fair lady I shall be dead.

Despite this, the woman persuades him that it would be more comfortable to go back to her house. When they arrive, she escapes inside from where she taunts him for his naivety. Lucy White sang:

> We have a cock in our barton [farm building]
> That never trode [*sic*] no hen
> And I think to my very own self
> That you are much the same.
>
> When she came to her own father's gates
> So nimble she popped in
> Saying you're a fool without
> and I am a maid within.[3]

In the published collection Sharp observes that 'the air is not an ancient one but it is eminently suited to the breezy character of the words'.[4]

In the 1960s my father watched *Farming Diary* on television at Sunday lunchtimes, while the joint finished roasting. Although I didn't know it at the time, this was my earliest introduction to the music of Vaughan Williams: the theme tune was 'Blow Away the Morning Dew', taken from the third movement of his *English Folk Songs Suite*. In this orchestral arrangement of White's air, a jovial clarinet bobs along with the melody, like the cooing of a collared dove, answered by other bird-like wind instruments, until they are gathered up by the brass and strings – as though the wind has blustered into a gale and thrown them into the sky. The music used to evoke for me queasy feelings of Sunday *ennui*, the flavour of gravy, and the stable order of things – the countryside looked after by men in Harris tweed hats, tractors ploughing the soil, white showers of seagulls rising and falling behind the big wheels. Now I am unsettled by the thought that while listening to the opening credits of *Farming Diary*, I was tapping my toe to the remnants of a Tudor song which encouraged men to take sexual advantage of women when given the chance, or risk mockery:

> Now if I ever meet that girl again
> A little below the town
> I won't mind [take any notice of] her squalling out
> Nor the rumpling of her gown.[5]

Vaughan Williams was conscious of the awkward relationship between earthy lyrics and the beautiful airs that accompanied them – he never made public the titles of folk songs he used for hymn tunes because 'a lot of narrow minded people refuse to use the tune if they think it has Sexular (i.e. secular!!) associations'.[6] He turned to folk music for melodies not words. Out of this comes a disconnect between the sex, trickery, violence and death in the texts and the distilled renditions in orchestral pieces such as *English Folk Songs Suite*. In the same way that he transformed a ballad about predatory sex into a piece redolent of a heart-lifting breezy day in the English countryside, he captured the intensely tragic melody of 'The Captain's Apprentice' and used it to conjure the melting dawn mist on a Norfolk marsh, haunted by the repetitive calling of lonely birds.

⌒

As I sift through Sharp's photograph collection of singers there is a sense of familiarity, the same faces still seen today in every street, but framed in archaic ways: the men often with beards shaved back to a white ruff under their chin and dressed in waistcoats and jackets, the women with their hair hidden under bonnets and elaborate broad hats, or scraped back from their faces, clothed in voluminous skirts and long white aprons. Men and women wear practical boots – the streets and country lanes were still barely more than muddy tracks. The most touching images capture moments of intimacy when the photograph ceases to be a two-dimensional document and starts into life. In one photo Phillander Fitzgerald and her husband sit side by side with stern faces. A well-nigh identical photo follows, except that now their hands are entwined and, by the subtlest of movements in her face muscles, she shows her quiet contentment. The expressive, melancholy eyes of an unidentified 'Cotswold Fiddler' linger in the memory. Lucy Carter stands in the street, still and serious, but the young girl at her side is puzzled, as if she's just asked how the camera works, and the woman standing on the doorstep behind has her hand to her mouth, possibly in astonishment. Shadrach Hayden, in his eighties, sits on a chair in his vegetable garden, looking at the lens, his gaze faintly quizzical: on one knee he holds a great-granddaughter, on the other a black-and-white kitten. The little girl is probably Ivy, three years old, with shiny, ruffled hair, in a puffed-sleeved dress and a white apron.[7] Perhaps the kitten was there to encourage her to sit still, but it wriggles in her great-grandfather's hand and extends its paw onto her lap, and Ivy is not sure she likes it – she looks, with the beginning of a frown on her face, towards someone outside the image, presumably her mother. Seconds later, the cat is away under the rhubarb leaves, the child set on her feet to toddle off, while the old man shakes his head with a chuckle.

I'm in danger of romanticising the image. Shadrach lived a hard life as a labourer and shepherd, and he and his wife supported their daughter and her children when her husband died. Grandson Harry, a labourer and scaffolder, stayed with the old couple even after he was married, and had a growing young family of his own (five children by 1911 including Ivy) – all squeezed into just three rooms.[8] The vegetable patch on a summer's day cannot tell us much about a whole life.

The photos of Lucy White and Louie Hooper, two of Sharp's most prolific singers, show them dressed in standard, sombre, plain clothes, hair tied back and aprons on. There are no clues to

Shadrach Hayden (and Ivy) photographed by Cecil Sharp

the turbulent times they had lived through. White had a baby boy when she was twenty and before she had a husband. This first child died, but she went on to have two more babies before she married – then she had seven more. Hooper worked from the age of ten making gloves and shirts. She married when she was twenty-four but her husband died five weeks after the wedding. She did not remarry but went on to have four children, the father unrecorded. She also lost a son.[9] The lives they looked back on were reflected in the lyrics they sang – they were not coy about stories of sexual infidelity and betrayal:

> With child pretty maid & so you may be
> The child is none of mine
> Unless you can tell me where and when
> The very first minute & time
> Fol the dol fol the dol dee.

> O yes I can tell both where and when
> The very first minute of time
> 'Twas up in my father's garden behind the rose bush
> When the clock was striking nine
> Fol the dol fol the dol dee.[10]

In the face of such explicit verses, Sharp argued that folk songs were '. . . sung freely and openly by peasant singers in entire innocence of heart . . .' although he admitted that these 'noble and beautiful sentiments' would not be understood in the 'primitive, direct and healthy sense' by modern-day listeners.[11] The stories of betrayal, tragedy and murder told in the songs should have been enough to bring down to earth those high-minded ideals of his.

In King's Lynn Mrs 'Lolly' Benefer[12] sang to Vaughan Williams 'The Banks of Sweet Dundee' (or 'The Farmer's Daughter') which sounds like a pretty pastoral ballad but actually tells the story of a woman whose lover is beaten up and press-ganged while she kills the squire and her uncle to escape a forced marriage. Lol Benefer was born Harriet Bailey. In 1882 at the age of eighteen she and other members of her family got mixed up in a fight with a neighbour in Whitening Yard (in the 1852 survey described as having 'abominable accumulations of dung and filth'), just over the road from James Carter's place in Watson's Yard. The argument was about whether the younger children from each family should play together. Nineteen-year-old James Stannard, who was beaten about the head, died of his injuries. Benefer, her mother and her sister were convicted of manslaughter and served eight months in prison, while her father got twelve months' hard labour.[13] Unmarried Lol was pregnant at the time and gave birth in prison – the father left town while she was incarcerated. This miserable story brings home the claustrophobia of living conditions in the yards: small houses, large families, cramped outdoor spaces, privies and taps shared by many, each knowing the other's business, and the everyday tensions that poverty, sickness and insecurity bring. Twenty-three years later, when Benefer sang for the composer, she was a married woman with nine children, her conviction far behind her, and Vaughan Williams was unaware of her troubled past. James Carter knew about it, though – not just because it was a big news story in the town: his adopted daughter, Lottie, was Benefer's niece.

Louie Hooper photographed by Cecil Sharp

With only the briefest of enquiries into the lives of singers, Sharp's vision of pastoral 'peasants' singing with 'innocence of heart' like children is exposed as an absurd delusion.[14] White and Hooper probably had a giggle together when they closed the door behind him.

⌒

Folk songs are made from two elements – the words and the tune. The name of a folk song – such as 'The Captain's Apprentice' – refers to a particular set of lyrics. In contemporary Western music we are accustomed to lyrics being sung to a tune exclusively associated with them. We wouldn't expect to hear 'Bohemian Rhapsody' or 'Imagine' sung to a different melody: the two elements are inextricably linked to make a whole. In the folk tradition this was not the case. As collectors travelled around the country they often found a song's words sung to different airs; or well-known airs used with different words. A contemporary illustration of the former would be the words of Christina Rossetti's poem 'In the Bleak Midwinter' sung to two well-known settings, one composed by Gustav Holst and the other by Harold Darke. For a tune adapted to different words, try singing the first three lines of 'Twinkle Twinkle Little Star' and 'Baa Baa Black Sheep'.

Some airs developed separate identities. One of Vaughan Williams's most popular pieces is based around five variants of the melody known as 'Dives and Lazarus' which is used for other sets of lyrics including 'The Star of the County Down' and 'The Unquiet Grave'. 'The Captain's Apprentice' was no different from other folk songs in the variation of the air to accompany its words.

In January 1905 'The Captain's Apprentice' was sung by James 'Duggie' Carter to the melody Vaughan Williams later used in his orchestral piece, *Norfolk Rhapsody No.1*. Two days later a Mr Bayley performed the song with the same melody; and a couple of days after that, still in King's Lynn, Mr Harper sang a variant of the melody, but his lyrics were from the song called 'Oxford City'.[15]

Vaughan Williams collected another version of 'The Captain's Apprentice' in the Broads village of Filby during a trip to Norfolk in 1910. The tune was different to Carter's, but most of the lyrics were the same, so he only noted down the last verse which was an addition:

To Newgate gaol then I was brought
To Newgate gaol I was condemned;
For if I had by my men been rul'd
I might have saved a poor boy's life and my own.

When material was published in the *Journal of the Folk-Song Society* it was usual for fellow collectors, such as Cecil Sharp and Lucy Broadwood, to add notes and comments. When the 1910 version of 'The Captain's Apprentice' appeared, Sharp reported that he knew a Somerset variant sung by a Bridgwater sailor.[16] Under this note Broadwood pointed out that the tune sung at Filby was very similar to one Vaughan Williams had collected in Essex from Ann Humphreys – but her lyrics were about a woman keen to marry a sailor, a song known as 'Tarry Trowsers'. This song was published in the journal in 1906, with notes from Sharp and renowned collector Frank Kidson. They had found further versions of 'Tarry Trowsers' in Yorkshire and Somerset.

Vaughan Williams – the great-nephew of Charles Darwin – applied evolutionary theory to the development of folk music. He believed that as songs were handed down from generation to generation they would change and develop into different melodies; inept variations would fall by the wayside, good variants would be adopted widely. A folk song, he said, is 'like a tree, whose stem dates back from immemorial times, but which continually puts out new shoots'.[17]

In 1915 'The Captain's Apprentice' was collected on the Norfolk coast again, this time by the composer Ernest Moeran at Winterton, just six miles from Filby.[18] This was a third melody, and the words are subtly different – here the boy is still fatherless but he is bound apprentice for ten long years and is taken from St Giles' workhouse rather than St James', as in the King's Lynn version. An extra verse reads:

> Now my crew they do object to me,
> Seeing how as I done wrong,
> Down in my cabin close confined me,
> And brought me to London in irons strong.

⁓

According to Vaughan Williams, 'scoffers' would often suggest that some of the old chaps had *invented* the tunes they sang to him, with the implication that they were therefore inauthentic. He would reply that if this was the case it would only make the tunes more valuable to him: 'In one aspect the folk-song is as old as time itself; in another aspect it is no older than the singer who sang it.'[19] After Mr Potiphar of Ingrave sang to him, Vaughan Williams asked the old man if he could tell him anything about the origin of the melodies. His answer was, 'If you can get the words the Almighty sends you a tune.'[20]

⁓

In 1921 Moeran collected yet another version of 'The Captain's Apprentice', at Potter Heigham – a village about six miles from Winterton, and a similar distance from Filby, where Vaughan

Williams had found the song eleven years earlier. This makes a total of four different melodies for the same lyrics in one county, three of them within six miles of each other.

The Potter Heigham air, sung by Harry Cox, was in a major key – something you might expect to accompany a happy love story – but the three previously collected airs were performed in various 'modal' scales. It was the unfamiliar sound of these scales that proved so alluring to many collectors.

Listeners to music instinctively identify the different soundscapes created by modal scales in genres such as Folk, Jazz, Blues, Raga, Klezmer. Each uses a different pattern of intervals between the notes, each creates a unique mood. Eight consecutive notes played on the white keys of a piano, starting on 'C', will create the sound of a major scale – the 'Ionian' mode. The same exercise, starting on 'D', sounds different – more like a folk song – and is called the 'Dorian mode'. Starting on 'E' will produce the 'Phrygian' mode, present in much Middle Eastern music. The bright sound of the 'Lydian' mode is created by starting on 'F'; the scale from 'G' is 'Mixolydian' – another folk mode. Beginning on 'A' produces a third common folk scale, the natural minor – or 'Aeolian' – mode; the rarer 'Locrian' starts on 'B'. A further feature of modal scales is the common use of only five notes – the 'Pentatonic' or 'gapped' scale. The song of the lark ascending at the end of Vaughan Williams's most popular work is pentatonic.

For centuries, European composed music had been based largely on just two scale systems – major or minor. Folk melody allowed musicians to break free from the chains of Old World classicism – as Vaughan Williams signalled at the start of his 1912 article, 'Who wants the English Composer?', with an extract from the American poet Walt Whitman:

> Come Muse migrate from Greece and Ionia,
> Cross out please those immensely over-paid accounts,
> That matter of Troy and Achilles' wrath, and Æneas',
>   Odysseus' wanderings,
> Placard 'Removed' and 'To Let' on the rocks of your
>   snowy Parnassus,
> Repeat at Jerusalem, place the notice high on Jaffa's gate
>   and on Mount Moriah,
> The same on the walls of your German, French and
>   Spanish castles, and Italian collections,
> For know a better, fresher, busier sphere, a wide untried
>   domain awaits, demands you.[21]

The wider use of modal scales in music during this period was such a radical change, that when Sir Charles Villiers Stanford, editor of *The National Song Book* for schools (1905), included traditional airs from Scotland, Wales and Ireland he was concerned that 'English children may at first experience some difficulty in grasping the peculiar scales and intervals of Keltic tunes . . .'[22]

It was a long-held belief that the choice of mode for a melody created particular moods and effects, 'for songs make men sleepy, and wakeful, carefull [*sic*] & merrie, angry and merciful'. The writer of this sixteenth-century treatise, translated by John

Dowland in the early seventeenth century, goes on to claim that the Dorian mode 'is the bestower of wisedome [*sic*] and causer of chastity', that the Phrygian 'causeth wars' and the Aeolian 'doth appease the tempests of the minde [*sic*]'.[23] In the medieval period the Ionian (or major scale) was called the lascivious mode (*modus lascivus*), and was banned from use in church because of its associations with smutty popular songs.

Despite this background, Vaughan Williams questioned whether the modes were essential to folk song when commenting on a draft of Cecil Sharp's book, *English Folk Song: Some Conclusions*. In what proved to be his magnum opus, Sharp set out theories on the communal origin and evolution of folk song, based on his experience of collecting (at that point) fifteen hundred in the field. Vaughan Williams advised him to omit the chapter on modes, but it remained in the published version (1907), though Sharp commented that the subject is 'only indirectly related to that of folk song'. It is true that most folk songs collected were in the conventional major key, but modal melodies were deeply attractive to collectors and musicians as a source of inspiration 'throbbing with the pulse of life . . .'[24] Only forty per cent of the songs Vaughan Williams noted were modal, but they made up sixty-seven per cent of the material he chose to publish.[25] The three folk tunes which influenced him most – 'Bushes and Briars', 'Dives and Lazarus' and 'The Captain's Apprentice' – are all Aeolian; and he frequently worked with the Dorian, Phrygian and Mixolydian – all scales with the characteristic 'flattened' seventh note. This sonic landscape creates the 'pastoral' atmosphere in his best-known music.

Cecil Sharp

Later commentators have criticised the Edwardian partiality for modal melody over tunes in the more common major scale as a misrepresentation of the true scope of traditional song.[26] Song collectors were certainly not systematic in the organisation of their task – they began with preconceptions about what folk music should sound like; they favoured rural areas over towns and missed a whole subgenre of workers' songs from industries such as coal mining. Much of the material they heard was dismissed by them as 'popular' or 'music-hall' and never made it into their notebooks. The ability of each self-appointed collector was variable and, apart from the few phonographic recordings that have survived, there is little objective evidence on whether their work was accurate. No training, university qualification, appointment process, or project plan was required to participate – they were essentially amateurs, each with their own agenda. Collectors like Vaughan Williams, Sharp and the composer George Butterworth, were looking for tunes to break 'fresh ground', and which could offer 'a wider horizon, and new possibilities to the modern composer'.[27] It is no wonder they were drawn towards the more 'exotic' melodies of the modes.

A Kind of Folk-Song Symphony

Between noting down his first folk song – 'Bushes and Briars' – in December 1903, and a spree of collecting in the vicinity of his family home at Leith Hill, Surrey, during Christmas 1904, Vaughan Williams had already collected over two hundred and fifty songs and tunes in ten counties before he arrived in Norfolk in January 1905.[1] The modal intervals and cadences he had heard were seeping into his creative bones, reflected most clearly in his 'symphonic impression' *In the Fen Country*. This orchestral work, finished initially in April 1904, but revised in 1905, 1907 and 1935, sounds 'folk-like' but contains no identified folk melodies. It was only after the week in Norfolk that he attempted to set a series of collected folk tunes for orchestra.[2] Excited by the material he had discovered during the King's Lynn trip his immediate response was to compose the *Norfolk Rhapsodies Nos 1, 2* and *3*.

In a series of articles on Vaughan Williams written by Edwin Evans for the *Musical Times* of 1920, the composer's voice can be heard in the description of his characteristically pragmatic approach: 'When he came upon some tunes that appealed to him so strongly that he thought people ought to hear them, he provided the opportunity by weaving them into a rhapsody.'[3] Evans noted that the three *Rhapsodies* were originally planned to form 'a kind of folk-song symphony' in which *No. 1* would correspond to the introduction and first movement; *No. 2* to the slow movement and scherzo; and *No. 3*, the finale, in the form of a quick march and trio.[4] *No. 1* was performed in August 1906, the second and third in September 1907.

The *Concise Oxford Dictionary of Music* defines a musical rhapsody as 'a composition in one continuous movement, often based on popular, national or folk melodies'. The form was in vogue in early twentieth-century England, with other county- or country-based rhapsodies written by composers in Vaughan Williams's circle, such as Gustav Holst (*Somerset Rhapsody*, 1906), Frederick Delius (*Brigg Fair: An English Rhapsody*, 1907) and George Butterworth (*Rhapsody, A Shropshire Lad*, 1911). The ancient Greek origin of the word described the recitation of parts of an epic poem at a single performance: *rhaptein* 'to stitch' + *ōidē* 'song'. In the three *Norfolk Rhapsodies* eleven songs were 'stitched' together in three separate pieces. The poetry of their names conjures up maritime and pastoral 'old England', populated with sailors and pirates, farmers and poachers:

'Basket of Eggs'
'The Captain's Apprentice'

'A Bold Young Sailor, He Courted Me'
'Ward the Pirate'
'On Board a Ninety-Eight'
'Young Henry the Poacher'
'All on Spurn Point'
'The Saucy Bold Robber'
'The Lincolnshire Farmer'
'John Raeburn'
'The Red Barn'

The story of the three *Rhapsodies* puts me in mind of the folk-tale trope of 'trebling', where three sons or daughters – or little pigs – are sent out into the world, one after the other, to make their fortune. Each encounters a challenge along the way. Two will fall by the wayside and fail the task; only one succeeds.

Norfolk Rhapsody No. 1

The first performance of *Norfolk Rhapsody No. 1* took place at Queen's Hall, London, on 23 August 1906 and attracted generally positive reviews, the correspondent of the *Globe* remarking that the piece was 'as rich in beauty and intellect' as anything Vaughan Williams had previously produced. It was so well received that the composer was 'compelled to emerge from that retirement in which his modesty, apparently, prompted him to remain', to take a bow on the stage.[5] The *Norfolk Chronicle* pointed out the special interest for its readers of the new work, noting that the melodies collected in the county 'present admirable contrast, and possess an individuality which has been cleverly accentuated by the composer'.[6] The air of 'The Captain's Apprentice' was highlighted as 'remarkable for the freedom of its rhythm'.

The *Rhapsody* discussed in these reviews is not the one we would recognise today. Programme notes from the premier describe how the melody of 'Basket of Eggs' and 'Ward the Pirate' were woven into the piece, the last section combining phrases from 'The Captain's Apprentice', 'On Board a Ninety-Eight' and 'Ward the Pirate' before ending 'brilliantly' – that is, with climactic gusto.[7] In this form, *No. 1* was performed several times around the country in the following years, to general acclaim – 'a genial, bright, spontaneous-sounding composition',[8] 'redolent of the countryside and the morris dance and the spirit of a merrier England'[9] – but Vaughan Williams was not happy with it. By May 1914, when it was performed at the Bournemouth Pavilion, he had made significant changes. In the notes for the relaunch, he wrote it had 'lately been entirely revised and much curtailed. The concluding section is entirely new.'[10] He further highlighted that the construction of the piece was now 'very simple' and has been 'much modified', implying that he had come to feel that the original five themes were excessive.

In the revised scheme, references to the melodies of 'Ward the Pirate' and 'Basket of Eggs' are almost entirely removed. As a result, the sombre mood of 'The Captain's Apprentice' becomes the ribbon running through the piece. It opens with the vestigial Morse-code rhythm from the beginning of 'Basket of Eggs' – da-da-daa-daa-daaaa. Muted violins respond with a short phrase snipped from the end of the second line of 'The Captain's

Apprentice'. In current parlance, Vaughan Williams has 'sampled' these two tunes and spliced them together to create the underlying open texture of a lonely landscape on a quiet morning. The repeated phrase on strings is taken up by the clarinet '*a piacere*' ('to your liking').[11] This instruction – to introduce flexibility and emotion – is the composer's attempt to recreate the free-form of folk singing, re-emphasised six bars later with his direction to play 'freely as if improvising' as the viola enters unaccompanied. Its lone voice starts up in the emptiness and sings the full melody of 'The Captain's Apprentice', gently encouraged between lines by the rising bubbles of the clarinet – perhaps the closest we will ever get to Duggie Carter's performance in the kitchen with his enthralled audience of two.

The melody's uneven rhythm is taken up by the strings, emerging in oceanic surges between the wistful 'Bold Young Sailor' played in 'singing style' (*cantabile*) by the woodwind section, and the frenzied 'On Board a Ninety-Eight' at the centre of the piece, before ending, not 'brilliantly', but in a mournful dwindling, as the solo clarinet returns over sparse *pizzicato* cello and bass. The long, virtually imperceptible high notes of violins replicate the tinnitus-like ring in the ears heard when standing alone in a silent space. 'Genial' and 'merry' no longer suit the pervasive melancholy.

This revised arrangement, published in 1925, remains popular but no manuscript of the original survives.[12]

Norfolk Rhapsody No. 2

Norfolk Rhapsody No. 2 endured a more perilous journey. Along with *No. 3* it was first performed at the Cardiff Festival in

September 1907 but was not heard in London until 1912 after which it vanished from the scene.[13] An unpublished manuscript of the score survived in Vaughan Williams's collection, with two pages missing – around nine bars in total – making the piece unplayable. It fell into a deep slumber for ninety years, only to be revived when, in 2002, Stephen Hogger was invited to fill the gap. He was able to include three bars discovered on a fragment of manuscript paper written in Vaughan Williams's hand and tucked into the back of the original manuscript – a ghostly message of encouragement from beyond the grave.[14]

Norfolk Rhapsody No. 3

The third *Norfolk Rhapsody* was lost. This quick march and trio was performed at least once after 1912, a review in the *Westminster Gazette* of 21 November 1913 describing it as 'a very vigorous and jolly work'. After this it appears to have been destroyed by the composer. Commenting on its disappearance, Ursula confirmed that her husband was 'all his life, a great waste-paper-basket man'.[15] Evans acknowledged the composer's leaning towards 'ruthless extermination' and confirmed the fate of *No. 3* in his 1920 article, remarking that 'the composer has decided to discard the third, and is doubtful about the second, which may be overtaken by the same fate unless its friends intervene'.

The suggestion that the *Norfolk Rhapsodies* were, in effect, Vaughan Williams's first attempt at a symphony, has been a provocation for completists. Once *No. 2* was revived, the resurrection of *No. 3* was inevitable. The 1907 programme from the

Cardiff performance is helpfully detailed, with a description of its form, the order of the songs used, instrumentation, and even the number of bars in one section. David Matthews was commissioned to reconstruct the piece by the Ralph Vaughan Williams Society, and it received its premier in May 2016, under the title of *Norfolk March*. Rather than a 'vigorous and jolly' work Matthews felt that, in the centenary of the worst year of the First World War, the march should reflect a more 'dark and sinister' mood. His arrangement ends with a funeral march and an allusion to 'the last post'.[16]

The creator of the three *Norfolk Rhapsodies* sent them out into the world and found them wanting. They returned from their journey transfigured – leaner, wounds barely healed, darker in mood. Never performed together at one concert in their original form (although interest in such an event was expressed in newspaper reviews at the time) the 'kind of folk-song symphony' Vaughan Williams first imagined can never be experienced. We can catch an echo of it if we listen in sequence to the curtailed *No.1* , the repaired *No. 2* and the obliquely referenced *Norfolk March* but, as Evans remarked in 1920, '. . . since it no longer has the composer's approval, the symphony must remain truncated'.[17]

⌢

Despite Vaughan Williams's matter-of-fact claim that he wrote the *Norfolk Rhapsodies* to provide opportunities for people to hear the tunes, the combination in the title of a well-known part of the country, alongside a word frequently used to describe ecstatic enthusiasm, brings an expectation from the listener of a tone-poem, of 'lonely birdcalls keening across a coastal land-scape'.[18] But when he wrote the pieces the composer's knowledge of the Norfolk coast was limited to a brief trip out into the agricultural flat lands of Tilney, several days in the industrial port of King's Lynn, and a day at the seaside resort of Sheringham. He had no time for emotional immersion in the bleak landscapes of the county's wintry salt marshes – for most of the trip he was in towns and indoors. Unlike most of his fellow collectors, Vaughan Williams did not accept the antithesis of town and country and did not insist that folk songs could only be authentic in a rural setting.[19] He was happy to gather material from the ancient port and it was no surprise that most of it was about sailing and the mariner's life rather than country life – as he reported to Cecil Sharp, he 'got hardly anything but sea songs from the sailors at Lynn'.[20]

It was understood by 1905 that just because melodies were collected in a particular county such as Norfolk, it did not mean that they possessed intrinsic 'Norfolk-ness'. When the King's Lynn songs were included with collections from other counties in the 1906 *Journal of the Folk-Song Society* Vaughan Williams emphasised this point: 'Indeed the more wonderful fact elicited from the search for folk-songs is that the same tune may be heard, with hardly any variation, in Norfolk, Sussex or Yorkshire' – that is, they reflected a national tradition.[21] The 'Norfolk' label he gave to the *Rhapsodies* is not there to conjure up the county's essence through its locally distinct Norfolk airs, but to indicate where the material was collected.

On the other hand, his comment on the origin of 'The Captain's Apprentice' – the possible Norse ancestry of the fishermen of the North End – takes us in the opposite direction, further from a wider landscape to a very small and culturally specific urban location, quite separate from the surrounding country-side.[22] The singularity of the melody was the source of its fascination for the composer, an exception that proved the rule and, perhaps, a reason why he allowed *Norfolk Rhapsody No. 1* to survive. After spending several intense days in the North End it is improbable that, when he sat down to compose this rhapsody, his mind turned to lonely coastal marshland. The Morse code-like rhythm of the opening clarinet theme is undeniably reminiscent of the redshanks' call, and he may have heard their cry as they waded in the shallow waters of the tidal Great Ouse below the sea wall. The sound is an opening glance at the quiet morning river before the hard work of sailing begins. He had seen the shining mud banks of the Fisher Fleet, squeezed along dark passageways in the yards, inhaled the stink of fish and open sewers. He had greeted weather-beaten fishermen and old sailors in their tenements and workhouse wards and listened to their cracked voices singing him tales of life under sail. I think, as his hand hovered over the blank manuscript paper, his mind was filled, not with images of pastoral Norfolk, but with the cry of seabirds following the ships, and the unpredictable rhythms of the raging sea.

⌒

'The Captain's Apprentice' sank deep into Vaughan Williams's imagination. All the characteristics he was searching for, he found in the tune – unbound melody, fluid rhythms and exotic rarity. To come across this after the disappointment of the thin pickings from Tilney, for it to be only the second song sung to him in the North End, performed by an archetypal fisherman with Viking blood in his veins, was an experience never to be forgotten. Thenceforth, the tune was embedded in the 'crude life-force' of his musical thought.[23]

This is how Elsie Payne described it in her seminal 1954 article on his oeuvre. She made the case for folk song as 'the most powerful source of inspiration' in the music of Vaughan Williams, highlighting 'The Captain's Apprentice' and 'Bushes and Briars' as the most influential. He used 'The Captain's Apprentice' overtly just once – in *Norfolk Rhapsody No. 1* – but Payne argued that it held a persistent power over his writing at a subconscious level, emerging as melodic and rhythmic embellishments. She discerned fragments embedded throughout his work, ranging from the 1908 *Quartet in G minor* to *Dona Nobis Pacem* in 1935, including *A London Symphony* along the way.

Although her emphasis on the influence of folk song may be overstated – early Tudor music is just one other obvious source of inspiration – it is easy to trace the colour of folk music permeating Vaughan Williams's composition. In his remarkable survey of folk-song quotations, Adam Harvey identifies phrases from over a hundred and twenty songs in around thirty separate works by the composer, adding *A Pastoral Symphony* to the list of those which quote 'The Captain's Apprentice'.[24] Ursula agreed that folk music brought a new vocabulary to her husband's work. It was a process in which phrases from the melodies he had collected became 'part of the texture of his own invention'.[25]

⌒

The importance of saving the old songs was agreed by all collectors involved – but what did a saved song look like?

Words used to describe the process by which a cultural artefact, at risk of being lost for ever, can be saved – to renovate, preserve, conserve or restore – carry subtle differences of intent. The objective – to save a building, a landscape, a painting, a folk song, a rhapsody – is simple; the route to this outcome is complicated.

Because I'm an ex-conservation officer, familiar with investigating old buildings and discussing their repair, I picture a jumbled house which has grown over centuries, wood, mud, brick and concrete, thatch and tile all cheek by jowl. It looks atmospheric, full of stories, but tired – the chimneys are crumbling, the roof leaks, there is only one loo. The new owner, the builder, the antiquarian and the conservation officer each wish to save it. The owner wants to *restore* it to its former glory – they love the old parts but are not so keen on the 1960s concrete extension and would like to knock that bit down. The *renovation* builder points out that the cheapest route is to gut the building, take out the decrepit ceilings, floors and windows, strip off the thatch, start again – this is easier than trying to repair the existing fabric. The antiquarian's instinct is to *preserve*. They argue that to change any part will be akin to partially erasing a person's memory. The *conservation* officer looks for compromise – a house must be lived in to survive, but a balance must be struck between keeping the historic fabric and introducing modern living standards. I offer these stereotypes as a way of entering the world of Edwardian folk-song collectors and their approach to the songs in their care.

The material collected by Vaughan Williams in King's Lynn was extensively sifted, reworked and moulded. The composer made choices along the way, in the belief that the work of the collector called for both 'scientific discovery and artistic presentation'.[26] He agreed that every traditional tune ought to be carefully stored for posterity, but only those which had 'beauty and vitality' should be made more widely available: 'For the student a folk tune may be worth preserving for its historical or archaeological interest – for the singer and dancer there is only one test – is it beautiful?'[27] This subjective search for beauty was at the centre of his own motivation – to demonstrate how folk music was a 'living force' with 'something to say' to future generations, and which could nurture a revival of English music.[28]

He collected over sixty songs during the King's Lynn trip but published just nineteen of them in the 1906 *Journal* – these were the airs he felt were the rarest and best examples of 'exquisitely beautiful melody'.[29] They were presented unadorned and unaccompanied, set down as accurately as hand-notation by ear could manage. Two years later he published an even more select collection (seven, of which 'The Captain's Apprentice' was one) which Cecil Sharp, the editor of *Folk Songs from the Eastern Counties* (1908), was keen to emphasise had not been 'improved' in any way: '. . . no melody will find a place in this series except in the precise form in which it was noted down by a competent musician from the lips of some folk-singer'.[30] But in this format Vaughan Williams made the airs more generally palatable by providing piano accompaniments suitable for a parlour setting. These introduce harmony that no old folk singer would have imagined, but which a middle-class audience expected.

The words were also modified. Sharp makes a general case in the preface for editing lyrics. Reasons included the need to correct the 'corrupt' cheap printed versions (known as 'broadsides'), or rectify mistakes due to lapses of memory, the awkwardness of varied lengths of lines, and the 'somewhat free and unconventional treatment' of themes, which made it necessary to fill gaps, reconcile rhymes, correct bad grammar and 'soften' or omit verses.[31] This last measure led to the deletion of the most graphic verse of 'The Captain's Apprentice', the detail of torture and the mention of thighs clearly too shocking to be heard coming from the lips of young ladies.

In the *Norfolk Rhapsodies* Vaughan Williams undertakes a more radical reworking, the tunes spliced, sampled and mixed, and wrapped in a contemporary orchestrated setting of layered harmonies. In these works he takes 'artistic presentation' to a new level. With it, the words and meaning of 'The Captain's Apprentice' vanish. The melody takes on a new character, evoking an atmosphere that seems 'to express the very spirit of the English countryside'.[32]

It is unlikely that the fishermen of King's Lynn ever attended a concert to hear the *Norfolk Rhapsodies*. If they had, they might have found it difficult to listen to the composer's setting of melodies with orchestral arrangement and multiple harmonies – as did a Dorset countryman quoted by Vaughan Williams. On hearing a professional singer perform a folk song with piano accompaniment, the old man complained about the unnecessary distraction from the melody and words: 'Of course, it's nice for him to have the piano when he's singing, but it does make it very awkward for the listener.'[33]

The Unromantic Truth

Origins of 'The Captain's Apprentice'

'The words are evidently local.' In the editorial notes under 'The Captain's Apprentice', published in the *Journal of the Folk-Song Society* in 1906, I can hear Vaughan Williams's voice, emphatic and enthusiastic. '"St James' Workhouse" is the King's Lynn Union.'

The composer had never seen the lyrics of 'The Captain's Apprentice' before, with their strange words – 'garling-spikk' and 'marling-spike' – and their detailed description of torture. To him it was self-evident that the words were rooted in King's Lynn. Besides, he knew the old workhouse in the town was called 'St James" just as in the song – he had walked past its ruins.

He also had an opinion on the singer – here are his words again: 'Mr Carter belongs to the colony of fishermen who inhabit the "North End" at King's Lynn. They possibly have a Norse ancestry . . .' The origin of the unique melody seemed obvious. Vaughan Williams had been on an expedition into an unknown world and stumbled upon a tribe who in their isolated colony had preserved ancient Nordic ways, including their musical culture. It was an amazing story.

Beneath Vaughan Williams's comments, another voice interjects. 'The ballad was probably called forth by a particularly brutal case of ill-treatment, similar to that narrated in it, which occurred some twenty or thirty years ago.' Frank Kidson, aka 'F.K.', was too polite to directly contradict Vaughan Williams, but he gently unpicks the composer's excited remarks. 'The ballad "Oxford City" to which this air evidently belongs, is found on broadsides of the Catnach period.'[1]

Kidson believed that the words of 'The Captain's Apprentice' did not originate in King's Lynn but were taken from a preexisting ballad that had been revived in response to a more recent case. As for the melody, it appeared to have been adapted from one sung more usually to accompany an entirely different ballad, 'Oxford City'. He considered that the words of this song, sung to Vaughan Williams by Mr Harper, fitted the tune better and could be traced back to printed verses produced by renowned London-based publisher James Catnach.[2] His cheap popular news-sheets – 'broadsides' – produced from the early nineteenth century, carried political gossip, crime stories and song lyrics (not melodies) to the masses: 'Oxford City', which tells the tale of a jealous man poisoning his lover, was typical fare. Kidson was sure that the melody was originally made for these lurid lyrics. Vaughan Williams's belief in the local source of the song is appealing but Kidson's matter-of-fact approach cannot be ignored.

Frank Kidson

Frank Kidson, a founding committee member of the Folk-Song Society, was a collector with a longer pedigree than either Vaughan Williams or Sharp. During the last decades of the nineteenth century he had gathered together a large personal library of old books, manuscripts and broadsides, and had published collections in the 1890s. Unlike the other two men, who believed that folk songs were generated in an oral tradition from within mainly rural labouring communities, he argued that the majority were remnants of composed popular songs most of which he could trace back to printed sources. His mission was to help collectors avoid 'that wild domain of vague conjecture, random assertion, and romantic untruth which is apt to entrap the enthusiast'.[3] The initials 'F.K.' appear on many of the *Journal*'s pages – akin to a quick shock of cold water – next to his carefully documented sources for songs in earlier printed form.

Vaughan Williams did not agree with the supremacy of the printed source: 'Other thinkers', he wrote in Kidson's obituary some years later, 'consider it doubtful whether one can always refer to a printed copy as an "original" version; they think rather that a printed version of a ballad or tune is often itself a distorted version and that folk-songs can be more readily found in their pure and idiomatic form in the minds of traditional singers.'[4] Cecil Sharp's opinion on the matter was less circumspect: 'To search for the original of folk songs amongst the printed music of olden days is mere waste of time.'[5]

Nevertheless, I am compelled by curiosity to look for the truth – romantic or otherwise: was Kidson right to pour cold water on Vaughan Williams's idea, or is it still possible to believe that the words and tune of 'The Captain's Apprentice' emanated from the old port of King's Lynn?

⌒

The only evidence Vaughan Williams offers for the local aspect of 'The Captain's Apprentice' is the coincidence of St James' workhouse being referenced in the song, and the building's previous existence in King's Lynn. It is not known whether Carter, Huddle or another Northender gave him more details. In a different approach, Kidson suggests that the text is about a case from twenty or thirty years previously, which could not have been Eastick's, as that story was nearly fifty years old by 1905. He goes on to suggest that when this unspecified tragedy was on everyone's lips, the pre-existing song was 'brought forth'

by someone – a retired sailor who had heard it on his travels perhaps, or a local printer with entrepreneurial spirit who reissued
a broadside of the text – before it was taken up by local singers
and became part of Carter's repertoire. If Kidson's scenario was
correct and the ballad was not written specifically about Robert
Eastick, where did it come from?

In England during the early years of the twentieth century,
versions of 'The Captain's Apprentice' (with different tunes)
were collected in other parts of Norfolk, and in south-west
counties: Dorset, Devon and Somerset (Corscombe, Beamin-
ster, Bridgwater). They may have been circulating in other places
too, but where no collector ventured. Although the known texts
are very alike, there are small but significant differences and
omissions.

Returning to the pages of Roy Palmer's book of songs collected
by Vaughan Williams – where I first read the words of 'The
Captain's Apprentice' – I noticed that he included two extra
verses, absent in Carter's version, but which were found stuck in
the composer's scrapbook.[6] These lines refer to the 'Bristol
shore', which locates events in the south-west, where the song
was clearly popular; and it aligns the text with an obscure ballad
sheet entitled 'A New Copy of Verses Made on Captain Mills,
now under Confinement in Newgate, at Bristol, for the murder
of Thomas Brown, his Apprentice Boy'.[7] A single surviving copy
appears to date from no later than 1800, and could be much
earlier (an historic record of the Thomas Brown case has yet to
be uncovered).[8] The verses are very similar to the song sung by
Carter, and their pre-1800 date rules out the possibility that
they were written in direct response to the Eastick case. Kidson's

belief that there was an older origin for the ballad was correct –
and yet this does not entirely sever the potential connection
between the song, the boy and King's Lynn.

  'Captain Mills' has forty-eight lines compared to the twenty in
Carter's 'The Captain's Apprentice' – but these twenty are almost
identical to verses in the broadside, suggesting that Carter had
either forgotten some of it, or learnt a shorter version, or omitted material that was not relevant to the story he wanted to tell.
In both ballads the boy is fatherless, apprenticed out of St James'
workhouse, because of his mother's distress.

'Captain Mills'	*'The Captain's Apprentice'*
This boy to me was put apprentice,	One day this poor boy to me was bound apprentice,
Because that he was fatherless,	Because of his being fatherless;
I'd him out of St. James's workhouse,	I took him out of St James' workhouse,
His mother being in distress	His mother being in deep distress

Carter omits a verse which identifies the West Indies as the
destination (Eastick died on a ship bound for Ceylon/Sri Lanka),
and in which the captain admits he killed the boy, but the next
verse is, again, well-nigh identical:

Poor boy one day he me offended,	One day this poor boy unto me offended,
Tho' nothing unto him did say,	But nothing to him I did say,
Strait to the mizen shroud I seiz'd him,	Up to the main mast shroud I sent him
There I kept him the whole day.	And there I kept him all that long day.

Carter then misses out a verse in which the crew 'earnestly request' Captain Mills to free the boy which only makes him more 'exasperated'. The verses which describe the torture contain similar sentences but they are in a different order. Carter's later rendition gives the impression of a list that has been slightly muddled over time:

With his legs and arms extended,

His face to windward too likewise,
And with a hand-pit I him gagged,

Because I would not hear his cries.

For with the crogic-brace I beat him,

Most inhuman I can't deny,
So he, poor soul, with my ill-treating

In agonies did the next day die.

All with my garling-spikk I misused him
so shamefully I can't deny,
All with my marling-spike I gagged him,
Because I could not bear his cry.

His face and his hands to me expanded,
His legs and his thighs to me likewise,
And by my barbarous cruel entreatment
This very next day this poor boy died.

Captain Mills attempts to buy the crew's silence, but they confine him to his cabin and, once Bristol is reached, he is taken to Newgate prison, where he confesses his crime and heartily repents. Carter omits this part of the story, but finishes with a warning which in the Captain Mills version is at the start:

'Captain Mills' Verse 1

You Captains all throughout the nation
Advice and warning take by me,

'The Captain's Apprentice' Verse 5

You captains all throughout this nation,
Hear a voice and a warning take by me,

| And not like me ill use your servants, | Take special care of your apprentice |
| When they are on the raging sea. | While you are on the raging sea. |

By the time Carter performed the song in 1905 the words had been shared orally – and perhaps via other broadsides now lost – over at least a century through multiple mouths and ears, with the inevitable small changes of words and word order this method of learning brings. It remains plausible that he (or the person he learnt it from) moulded the words to fit Eastick's case: having grown up in King's Lynn in the 1850s, perhaps with his own dreams of travelling the world under sail, knowledge of the local boy's death would have been inescapable. Although Eastick was not from St James' workhouse, he had lived adjacent to it; he *was* fatherless and poor; and the coincidence of the work-house name anchored the song to King's Lynn. By leaving out references to Bristol and the West Indies the lyrics could be experienced as local and directly relevant.

In the late 1930s Herbert Halpert, a song collector in the New Jersey and Delaware River areas of New York, noticed a tendency for singers to believe in the factual basis of their songs, and the intensified emotional connection they felt with the stories as a result.[9] Cecil Sharp also recognised this: if he praised a singer for the rendition of a long ballad, the singer would often say, 'Yes, Sir, and it is true,' with the implication that this made the song more significant. Sharp went on to say that 'to heighten the sense of reality' a singer 'will often lay the scene of his story in his own locality'.[10] For Tony Green, writing in the 1970s, singers who talked of the 'truth' of a song were not necessarily referring to documented historical facts but to 'a moral statement' with application to their experience and to the people they shared it with. In 1904 there was a popular song doing the rounds of Southwold pubs called 'It's the Poor that Help the Poor':

> Up came a beggar with his clothes threadbare
> 'Turn him away,' said the master there.

The fishermen would yell, 'That's right enough, too! . . . You can't get a rich man t' help you.'[11] Green argued that variation of details in a song's content should be seen as 'an attempt by particular ethnic, religious, social or occupational groups to accommodate a song to their own special view of life . . .'[12] A belief in the truth of a story, and its continuing relevance to the singers and their audience, were powerful influences on the material they chose to perform. As one Suffolk septuagenarian put it in 1975, 'Those old songs have a meaning in them, really.'[13]

There is no direct evidence that Carter claimed 'The Captain's Apprentice' as true – it was Vaughan Williams who asserted it was 'local', and Kidson who suggested it referred to a real historical case. Even so, it is certainly possible that Robert Eastick's death and its emotional impact on the King's Lynn community stimulated the choice of the song for performance in the 1850s, followed by its wider spread into other parts of Norfolk, and its survival in Carter's repertoire into the twentieth century.

⌒

The origins of the melody which Vaughan Williams so admired are equally obscure. Airs which accompanied versions of the words collected in the south-west, and other parts of Norfolk, were not the same as Carter's. That tune, sung to Vaughan Williams three times during his stay in the North End – by Mr Carter, Mr Bayley and Mr Harper – was not found anywhere else in England.[14] Kidson thought it was adapted from a tune for 'Oxford City' but it could equally have been the other way round: Mr Harper may have decided to use the air for 'The Captain's Apprentice' to accompany the 'Oxford City' words. Several different melodies for this song about a poisoned lover were recorded during the period. Kidson might have rolled his eyes at Vaughan Williams's idea about Norse ancestry but it is possible that Carter's melody came from even further north, out of the icy waters around Greenland's coast.

From at least the early seventeenth century ships sailed out from King's Lynn to the seas east of Greenland to hunt whales for the precious oil used in lamps. From the 1770s a government payment of thirty shillings per ton, coupled with import duties on whale oil, made the trade lucrative, and a small fleet of five or six whaling vessels sailed each spring to the 'Greenland fisheries', near Svalbard, returning in late summer with their catch which, in a good year, could amount to ten or eleven whales per ship.[15] St Margaret's church bells rang out to welcome home the returning sailors after their perilous journeys. The fleet was small compared to those from other east-coast ports such as Hull which sent out as many as sixty-five vessels, jostling for space with large fleets from the Netherlands.[16] By the turn of the century whale stocks were so reduced, their hunters were forced to explore more distant and treacherous waters on the west coast of Greenland, in the Davis Strait and Baffin Bay, competing with North American ships from Nantucket, New Bedford, Mystic and Martha's Vineyard.

In the late 1820s the availability of gas lighting produced a drop in demand for whale oil in England, causing the trade from King's Lynn to end, but whaling continued in other oceans throughout the nineteenth century and beyond.[17] The crews were drawn from all continents, and singing was part of every-day life on board. This mixing of world cultures is recreated in Herman Melville's *Moby-Dick* in which his imaginary crew from across the nations dance and sing together on board the ill-fated *Pequod*.[18] There were further opportunities for song exchange along trading and fishing routes between England,

Eighteenth-century mug depicting a King's Lynn whaling ship, the Beleana, in 1799

North America and Canada. For example, Joseph Elliot of Todber, Dorset, left Dartmouth with about sixty other men to crew fishing boats in the waters around Newfoundland in the mid-nineteenth century. In 1905 he provided the collector, Henry Hammond, with twenty songs he had learnt during his fishing career, one of which was 'Nancy from London', also collected in Newfoundland in the early 1920s.[19]

Some crew members of whaling ships kept journals on these long voyages, which could last up to four years, and occasionally they noted down lyrics. It was in one such journal that in 1768 a sailor aboard the *Two Brothers* wrote down words for a song called 'Captain James'.[20] The tale has much in common with the 'Captain Mills' / 'Captain's Apprentice' texts. The story is told in the form of the captain's confession, opening with the cautionary verse – *Come all you noble brave commanders / Come and warning take by me*. It moves on to name Richard Spry (later copies give different names), whose parents 'bid me prentice bind him'. After a 'trifling act' by the apprentice which puts the captain's 'bloody heart' in a rage, he ties the boy to the mainmast and keeps him there for several days. The crew protest but are threatened by the captain who thinks he will be able to silence the murdered boy's poor parents with money – but the 'tender mother' is not bought off and James is hanged.

The mid-twentieth-century song collector Gale Huntington found the *Two Brothers* text, and two further versions in journals from the ships *Walter Scott* (1840) and the *Cortes* (1847). In his book *Songs the Whalemen Sang* he provides a melody for 'Captain James' that closely resembles Carter's tune – with the implication that it may have travelled between the remote waters of the Davis Strait and Norfolk's Great Ouse. The *Walter Scott* made her first three voyages (in the 1830s and 1840s) out of Nantucket, and her final three from Martha's Vineyard, under Vineyard captains. The *Cortes* was based in New Bedford, but her first two voyages after 1847 (that is, after the song was written down aboard the ship) were also commanded by a Vineyard captain.[21] The Martha's Vineyard connection is significant because Huntington's wife, Mildred Tilton, came from a long line of Vineyard seafarers. According to Bow Van Riper from the local museum, Tilton's uncles were whaling captains, coastal schooner captains and fishermen, and one of these, William 'Bill' Tilton, was a chanteyman on both British and American vessels in the mid- to late nineteenth century. In this role he would lead the crew in singing rhythmic songs – chanteys or shanties – that helped them work together as a team. The entire Tilton family were known for their singing. Huntington got to know the family when he was courting Mildred in the early 1930s, and they provided material for his earliest research into sea songs. Bow pointed out that the Tilton brothers were only a generation younger than the Vineyard men who shipped on the *Walter Scott* or the *Cortes*, and it was plausible that one of these sang 'Captain James' to Huntington and that this was the source of the tune printed in the book.[22]

The possibility that this remarkable melody was shared and adapted by multicultural whaling crews on the high seas, before travelling back to Martha's Vineyard and to King's Lynn, is tantalising – but it is straying into the 'wild domain of vague conjecture' which Kidson would have had something to say about. Huntington does not cite his source for the tune in his published collection, but he does mention the version of 'The Captain's Apprentice' published in the *Journal of the Folk-Song Society*; and Vaughan Williams's *Folk Songs from the Eastern Counties* is listed in the bibliography. The more likely explanation is that he adapted Carter's melody from these published sources for use in his book.

It remains true that this mysterious melody, heard three times by Vaughan Williams in King's Lynn, was collected nowhere else during the period. Kidson and Vaughan Williams might each have won part of the argument: though the words were not written locally, the tune's origin in King's Lynn cannot be ruled out.

⌒

Though it is established that the 'Captain Mills' ballad is a precursor of 'The Captain's Apprentice' it is not necessarily the 'original' or earliest version of the song. The broadside locates the action around the port of Bristol but, though the city had a Newgate prison in the eighteenth century, there never was a St James' workhouse. London had both – St James's workhouse in Westminster, and the notorious Newgate prison in the City. It is possible that an earlier London-based broadside was edited by a printer in response to a crime near Bristol, in the same way that King's Lynn singers might have omitted geographical references to make the song more relevant to Eastick's case. The lack of a name for the boy or the captain in 'The Captain's Apprentice' version made it easy to adapt the ballad to any new situation and reflects the generic experience of defenceless boys in this lowly position aboard ships.

Across the Atlantic, the inspiration for the 'Captain James' verses written down in the whaling-ship journals appears to have been a broadside printed in Newburyport, near Boston, USA, entitled 'Captain James, who was hung & gibbeted in England for starving to death his cabin-boy'. A British broadside survives with an almost exact replica of the text but a different title: 'A Copy of Verses, Made on Capt. Eldeb's Cruelty to his Boy'.[23] Both seem to date from before 1800, but it is difficult to say which came first.[24] These macabre broadsides provide more detail on the torture of the apprentice which includes flogging, forcing him to drink 'purple gore' from his own wounds, and to eat the captain's 'dung'. The 'Captain James' lyrics were printed again, in early nineteenth-century Boston, and were included in a number of 'songsters' (books of lyrics) printed in the New York area in the 1840s.[25]

The 'Captain Eldeb' / 'Captain James' cluster of texts and the 'Captain Mills' / 'The Captain's Apprentice' group tell similar stories with similar language and in a similar sequence and they share phrases and details: the *Walter Scott* text reports that the boy was apprenticed by his *mother*, and in versions from both groups, the boy commits some small unspecified offence but is punished by being tied to the mainmast '*With his legs and arms extended*' as expressed in 'Captain Mills', in a distant echo of the King's Lynn line '*his face and his hands to me expanded . . .*' Like Captain Mills, Captains Eldeb and James explicitly murder the boy by leaving him tied to the mast with no food or water for several days.

Despite these similarities the lyrics are rarely exactly the same. For example, here are versions of the cautionary verse:

'Captain Eldeb' (before 1800)

Come all you noble Commanders,

that the raging ocean use,
Let my ruin be a warning,

your poor sailors don't abuse;

'Captain Mills' (before 1800)

You Captains all throughout the
       nation
Advice and warning take by me,
And not like me ill use your
       servants,
When they are on the raging sea.

'Captain James' (Two Brothers version, no later than 1768)

Come all you noble brave commanders
Come and a warning take by me
See that you don't abuse your seamen
When you are on the raging sea

This lack of exact replication continues throughout, to the
extent that the editors of *The Ballad Index* held at California
State University consider 'Captain James' and 'Captain Mills' /
'The Captain's Apprentice' to be separate entities, although they
agree that one 'probably set the pattern for the other'.[26] The
British-based Roud Folk Song Index lists 'Captain James' under
the same number as 'The Captain's Apprentice', recognising
that the two are closely related.[27] It appears that the two groups of
texts – 'Captain Mills' / 'The Captain's Apprentice' and 'Captain
Eldeb' / 'Captain James' – developed along separate branches,
the differences in detail consolidated and embellished by the
intermittent editing and printing of broadsides on both sides of
the Atlantic. Decades later the two songs emerge as cousins
rather than identical twins.

Identification of the original source for the story would be more likely if it was known which of these 'cousin' songs set the pattern for the other. In the 1768 text from the *Two Brothers*, Captain James threatens his crew with hanging for piracy 'if ever to England we got o'er' which suggests a British origin, as does the reference to him being 'hung & gibbeted in England' in the early nineteenth-century Boston broadsides. But it is still not certain which of the English sources – the 'Captain Eldeb' and 'Captain Mills' ballad sheets – was the first. The vital piece of evidence would be documents relating to a real-life case involving one of these named captains and their apprentice.

Palmer published the 'Captain James' lyrics in another of his books, *The Oxford Book of Sea Songs*, with a passing reference to a historical case mentioned in the *Gentleman's Magazine* from 17 April 1766.[28] The magazine text sounds strangely familiar:

A marine belonging to one of the men of war at P[ortsmou]th being found in liquor upon duty, after being severely beaten, was ordered by the commanding officer to be fastened to the mizzen shrouds with his arms extended, and in this situation being left all night, in the morning he was found dead. It was then ordered that he should be privately buried, but his brother marines insisting that a jury should sit upon his body, the commanding officer thought proper to abscond.[29]

This report was replicated in newspapers across the nation. A slightly different version appeared in the *Public Advertiser* which stated that being tied in the 'shrouds' was a usual 'slight' punishment for drunkenness, but that the marine had mistakenly been left there overnight.[30] It is feasible that by 1768 a song developed from this event could have reached the *Two Brothers* – ships frequently sailed from Portsmouth to the eastern seaboard of North America, to South Carolina, and to Newfoundland, which was then a British colony.[31] But with no names given in the newspaper report, this case is difficult to trace. A printed 'ur-text'– the crumpled sheet of a conveniently named and dated broadside languishing in a Portsmouth attic – is unlikely to survive.

Whether or not an original real-life case is ever identified, it is clear that there was a demand throughout the eighteenth and nineteenth centuries for ballads which brought attention to the cruelty of captains towards their subordinates at sea, and which attempted to hammer home a warning to violent masters of the punishment that would await them once they returned to shore. These words were shared through singing on board sailing vessels and in ports, and transported back and forth across the world, adapted along the way to suit the detail of local experience. As Sharp would have said as a way of ending the argument, 'The method of oral transmission is not merely one by which the folk song lives; it is a process by which it grows and by which it is created.'[32]

Cruelty at Sea

The appetite for ballads that set out the plight of cabin boys across the world was fuelled by a continual supply of true-life cases. I still feel the shock of that first reading of 'The Captain's Apprentice'; but to understand the context of the song, it is necessary to travel further into the horrors of life at sea for young apprentices. As well as the 1766 case of the marine in Portsmouth, Palmer refers to a Liverpool case in 1764 in which Captain Wilson of the *Free Briton* was acquitted of murdering his cabin boy;[1] and to the killing of a nameless boy in 1798 noted down in the diary of Serjeant Benjamin Miller. Miller was aboard the *Loyal Briton* which was transporting soldiers of the British army from Gibraltar to 'take the island of Minorca'. At the time of the murder the ship had been becalmed for two weeks. Miller notes in a single dispassionate sentence that the captain 'killed his Cabin-boy by striking him on the head with a handspike' and 'was ordered back to England for trial'.[2] Though he does not elaborate on the circumstances, it is easy to imagine the claustrophobic conditions on the vessel with its cargo of soldiers and crew, bobbing around in a flat and windless sea, nothing much to do, nothing much to eat, and no means of escape, the captain finally venting his frustration upon the person on board least able to defend himself.

Boy apprentices were at the very bottom of the strict hierarchy of the crew, from a long list including Captain (or Master), First Mate, Second Mate, Quartermaster, Boatswain, Rigger, Master at Arms, Purser, Helmsman, Carpenter, Cook and Able Seaman. A high proportion of the boys were recruited from workhouses, reformatories or orphanages and had little control over the form of servitude they were signed up for. If they tried to escape, the master, mate, shipowner or the police had the power to take them back on board without a warrant, or they could be imprisoned for twelve weeks for desertion.[3] During one year in Grimsby, 200 deserting boys were sent back to their ships and 258 were kept in prison, 51 of them for the second or third time. Some were only thirteen years old.[4] A skipper who was apprenticed in the 1860s remembered that he got 'more hidings than good dinners'.[5]

The apprentice was at the beck and call of the whole crew, and was required to help in the kitchen, keep the gear tidy, scrub the deck, make sure the lights always had enough oil and were in good working order, fetch and carry and run messages to the crew on watch – often his sleep was interrupted with an errand or task.[6] The time endured in this lowly position was an open-ended torment compounded by a helpless reliance on the wind and sea currents, or the violence of storms. Sometimes landfall was not made for months. Worst of all was the physical confinement of the vessel – the sole escape from a blow to the head was a leap into the ocean, described on the fishing smacks in the North Sea as 'the fisherman's walk'.

The ship in the 'Captain Mills' ballad was sailing from the West Indies, not to Minorca, so it does not fit with the documented murder on the *Loyal Briton*. Despite the lack of evidence for the cases involving Captain Mills, Eldeb or James there is no reason to think they were fictional, the supply of true stories being so numerous. One such is supplied by *The Ballad Index* which tells of W. Parker Snow, born in England in 1817 and apprenticed at the age of sixteen to a merchant vessel, who recorded how he was flogged, tied to the mast, sleep-deprived, starved and his body tarred. Although he survived, he sustained a brain injury which affected him throughout his life.[7]

A verifiable story in this horrible catalogue of torture at sea which *was* recorded in a ballad, was the murder of Andrew Rose:

> Andrew Rose, the British sailor
> Now to you his woes I'll name
> 'Twas on the passage from Barbados
> Whilst on board of the Martha Jane.

Henry Rogers, captain of the *Martha and Jane*, tortured crew member Andrew Rose for several weeks during a voyage from Calcutta in 1856. Aided by the first and second mates,

Captain Rogers beat Rose nearly every day with a rope-end or riding whip, and the ship's dog was trained to bite him. On one occasion he was gagged with an iron bolt, on another he was forced into a small barrel fixed to the side of the vessel for twelve hours during which he was given no water; on another he was forced to eat his own faeces. He was regularly kept in irons and denied rations. Finally, the three men hanged him by the neck from the mainmast until he was nearly dead. He did not recover from this cruelty, and his broken body was thrown overboard a few days later. Once back in England the crew reported the captain and mates to the police. The text of the trial was published in the following year with the hope that the conviction and execution of Rogers for murder would serve as a warning to vicious captains and 'prove to our hardy Mariners, that the law watched over them, however distant they may be from their native shores'.[8] It was reported that at least fifty thousand people attended the execution of Captain Rogers at Kirkdale prison in Liverpool in September 1857.

The stories told in songs and the documented cases of murder at sea emphasise the common occurrence of such violence. As the opening paragraph of Captain Rogers's trial states, the government undertook his prosecution because 'The recurrence of oppressive tyranny, and disgusting cruelties on the part of Captains of Merchant Ships . . . has unfortunately, of late, become so frequent.' What is striking about the Rogers case is the identical nature of the cruelties meted out to the victims in real life and in ballads – Andrew Rose was forced by the captain to eat his own excrement and he begged to be put out of his misery, just as happened in the 'Captain Eldeb' / 'Captain James' broadsides.[9] The songs reveal a litany of common abuses used by sadistic masters.

Captain Rogers was found guilty of murder in August 1857 and hanged in September, just a month before Robert Eastick's persecutor, Captain Doyle, was put on trial at the Old Bailey for aggravated assaults. On the day Doyle was committed, the *East London Observer* reported two other violent cases: the captain of a north country boat was ordered to pay compensation to a boy he had repeatedly struck on a voyage from Sunderland to London; and the first and second mates of the *Dominion* were charged with assaulting and beating two members of the crew on a trip from India to London.[10] In December of that year the paper noted the case of Captain Robert McEachim, master of the *Heather Bell*, for 'ill-using' a boy named Norris at sea, which the reporter compared to Eastick's case.[11] The sentiments in the recorder's summing-up speech at Doyle's trail echo those expressed in the Andrew Rose case: '. . . it should be known that every boy or other person engaged on board ship was under the protection of the law, and that every excess of authority would meet with punishment.'[12] These words will have struck a hollow note for the bereaved Eastick family.

Apprentice indentures for April 1856. Robert Eastick's name is crossed out, with a note written above: 'Drowned at sea 19-8-56'.

⌒

A warrant for the arrest of Captain Johnson Doyle of the *John Sugars* was issued in early September 1857, the death at sea of Robert Eastick having been brought to the attention of the Secretary of State for the Home Department by the Board of Trade. The boy had started his apprenticeship on the *John Sugars* by sailing from Sunderland down the coast with a cargo of coal for London. The next voyage was more challenging – a round trip of several months from Hartlepool across the Atlantic and Indian Oceans to Point de Galle on the coast of Ceylon. On return to dock from foreign travel, all ships were required to deposit the logbook at the shipping office. The manager of the Thames shipping office, Henry Pengilly, found the bald entry for 19 August 1856 disturbing: 'Robert Eastick fell overboard, and was drowned; his clothes were brought aft.' He was concerned that there was no explanation of the circumstances nor had there been any actions to save the boy and, when he summoned Doyle to explain this omission, the captain would only say that the boy fell overboard. Pengilly reported the case to the police.[13] The death of Eastick also came to the attention of a solicitor, Charles Young. He had been consulted by two of the crew who complained that the captain had not paid their wages, and also told him about the assaults. A barrister, Mr Bodkin, was appointed on behalf of the Crown Prosecution.

On 14 September 1857 the *Morning Chronicle* devoted a full column to the story of the 'Execution of Captain Henry Rogers', providing the grim details of Rogers's last evening, the distress of his wife and children, and the vast crowds that descended on the

Liverpool jail to witness his hanging – some had slept under hedges overnight to secure a good view. Next to this story and with equal prominence was the headline CRUELTY TO A SAILOR BOY carrying the detail of Doyle's appearance at the Thames Police Court 'to answer a charge of cruelty to a sailor boy named Robert Eastick, aged 15 years, and who it is alleged, committed suicide by drowning himself at sea, in consequence of the harsh treatment pursued towards him on a voyage from Hartlepool to Ceylon'.[14] Doyle was no stranger to the justice system – he had been a defendant in at least two previous minor court cases and had managed so far to keep his liberty – but this juxtaposition of Eastick's death with the report of the hanging of Captain Rogers would surely have sent a shiver down his spine. His barrister, Mr Sergeant Parry, was keenly aware of the danger that the Rogers case would influence public opinion, and the jury's decision on his client's guilt. During the summing-up at the Old Bailey trial a few weeks later, he pointed out that 'he did not at all complain of the government having instituted the present prosecution . . . because there was no doubt, from disclosures that had recently been made public, that very great cruelty was frequently practised in merchant vessels at sea' – but in a plea to the jury he said he was sure that they 'would not allow the disclosures to which he had referred to prejudice unfairly the case of the defendant'.[15]

Doyle was lucky. The prosecutor, Mr Bodkin, did not accuse him of murder. He stated that though the captain was responsible for the numerous assaults committed upon Eastick he was not legally responsible for the boy's death. This separation of cause and effect, between the numerous acts of violence and the boy's death by falling overboard – either accidentally, or as an act of suicide – provided a loophole. The case against Doyle was further weakened by Mr Parry's shameless play on existing prejudices, pointing out that the crew were 'composed partly of negroes and foreigners who were evidently actuated by vindictive feelings towards the defendant'. He accused the crew of trumping up the charges against Doyle because he had caused some of them to be imprisoned for bad conduct at the end of the journey to Ceylon; he had not paid others; and he had refused to give them 'characters' (references). In the end, Doyle was found guilty of just one common assault, on the morning of 19 August 1856, after he had accused Eastick of stealing a cheese, which the boy denied. It was after this beating that the boy fell overboard.

⌢

The death of boys at sea continued. In 1878 the captain, mate and boatswain of the *Meggie Dixon* were charged with conspiring to murder their apprentice Charles Cooper on a voyage to Penang. Like Eastick he fell overboard and was drowned after sustained ill-treatment such as sleep deprivation, dousing in cold water, starvation rations and frequent beatings.[16] Because these cruelties were not considered to be the direct cause of Cooper's death the captain (whom the jury considered the least culpable) was sentenced to twelve months' hard labour while his two subordinates were sentenced to five years' penal servitude. A further two well-publicised cases of sadistic killings on Hull-based fishing smacks in 1881 and 1882 led eventually (1893) to new rules which made sixteen the minimum age for apprentice-ships and provided the option of a six-month trial period before indentures were signed under supervision from a Board of Trade officer.[17] The trial at the Leeds Assizes of one of the captains, Osmond Brand, was widely publicised – it was probably this case that Frank Kidson (who lived in Leeds) referred to when he mentioned a 'particularly brutal case of ill-treatment'. Both Hull captains claimed that the boys had fallen overboard. Both were found guilty of murder and sentenced to death.

⌒

The Suffolk poet George Crabbe drew attention to the conditions for apprentices at sea in his narrative poem, 'Peter Grimes', published in 1810 and set in his home town of Aldeburgh.[18] It has been suggested in the past that the poem was inspired by the 'Captain Mills' ballad but the tale told in Crabbe's poem is not set on the high seas, but inshore, off the East Anglian coast.[19] Although he was no doubt informed by the plentiful stories available to him on the mistreatment of apprentices, it appears that the poet was inspired by local events heard about as a child. In the introduction to the 1834 edition his son wrote that 'the original of Peter Grimes was an old fisherman of Aldeburgh'.

In the poem Grimes obtains boys from the workhouse, because he 'wish'd for one to trouble and control':

> . . . there were in London then, –
> Still have they being! – workhouse-clearing men,
> Who, undisturb'd by feelings just or kind,
> Would parish-boys to needy tradesmen bind:
> They in their want a trifling sum would take,
> And toiling slaves of piteous orphans make.

Three boys are sent out of the workhouse, taken on in succession by Grimes; all three die through neglect and cruelty. One is found dead in his bed; one falls from a mast – which some believe was a case of suicide; the third is drowned in suspicious circumstances. The local population do not think to challenge Grimes's behaviour:

> . . . none inquired how Peter used the rope,
> Or what the bruise, that made the stripling stoop;
> None could the ridges on his back behold,
> None sought him shiv'ring in the winter's cold;
> None put the question, –'Peter, dost thou give
> The boy his food? – What, man! The lad must live:
> Consider, Peter, let the child have bread,
> He'll serve thee better if he's stroked and fed.'
> None reason'd thus – and some, on hearing cries,
> Said calmly, 'Grimes is at his exercise.'

The techniques of torture – the use of the rope, the exposure to freezing conditions, the withholding of food – are now familiar.

The story of Peter Grimes is better known today through the libretto of Benjamin Britten's opera of the same name. The Suffolk-born composer became aware of the poem in 1941 after reading an article on Crabbe by E. M. Forster in the *Listener*. At the time he and his partner, Peter Pears, were in the USA, but they returned the following year to live in Suffolk, close to Aldeburgh. Here Britten wrote the new opera inspired by Crabbe's verses. But there was a transformation: Grimes is portrayed as a victim, unfairly suspected of murdering apprentices. He is not intentionally cruel but is driven by the hope of making enough money from fishing to escape the claustrophobic world of the town. The third apprentice, 'Boy (John)', appears on stage but does not have a speaking part. He falls over a cliff to his death.

In Crabbe's poem Grimes goes mad with guilt, tormented by visions of ghosts and the eternal hell that awaits him. In Britten's opera the downfall of Grimes, hounded to death by local people, is presented as a tragedy. 'Dr Crabbe', the poet, is a drunkard. Mrs Sedley, the sole person moved to prevent Grimes from harming more boys, is an interfering busybody: 'When women gossip the result / Is someone doesn't sleep at night'. Eventually, Grimes takes his boat out to sea and sinks it, drowning himself. In writing their opera, Britten and his librettist Montagu Slater chose to take the outsider's view in a critique of the howling mob. The composer explained later that the plot reflected the tension he and Pears felt as conscientious objectors returning to Britain at the height of the Second World War: 'A central feeling for us was that of the individual against the crowd, with ironic overtones for our own situation.'[20] They were also a gay couple returning from the relative obscurity of the USA's big cities to a small conservative community, at a time when their same-sex relationship was still illegal. This is surely reflected in Pears's description of Grimes as 'an ordinary, weak person who, being at odds with society . . . offends against the conventional code, is classed by society as a criminal, and destroyed as such'.[21]

The adapted Peter Grimes verses were shaped by the composer's search for personal and moral relevance. The result is an avoidance of the real brutality that apprentices suffered, and an apology for hard men of few words. When Vaughan Williams used 'The Captain's Apprentice' melody as a theme in *Norfolk Rhapsody*, he put a tune which was the vessel for holding a tragic tale to another purpose. In both these twentieth-century adaptations the apprentices are silenced.

A New Ballad of Captain Doyle or 'The Unrepentant Master'

(by the author, to be sung to the tune of 'Dives and Lazarus')[1]

I am a man from Blakeney fair, on Norfolk's windswept shore.
My father was a Grocer, and I was never poor.
My parents reared me tenderly, good learning gave to me,
But as a boy of fourteen years, I sailed the raging sea.

Doyle was the son of a grocer in the fishing village of Blakeney on the north Norfolk coast. According to his 'Certificate of Master Mariner' issued in April 1851 he was born in 1818 and went to sea at the age of fourteen. For nineteen years he served as boy, mate and master, 'foreign and coasting', and had sailed all over the world by the time he received his certificate in his early thirties.

For nineteen years I made my way, as cabin boy then mate,
I knew the meaning of the rope; the marling spike was my fate;

I walked the deck for two long hours, in fear of that cruel whip,
And I learnt to be a sailor bold, and captain of my ship.

William Doyle's Master's Certificate of Service, 1851.

It is certain that as a cabin boy, Doyle observed and was subject to the various physical punishments inflicted by captains on their crew. No doubt this affected how he behaved as an adult in charge. During the Eastick court case in 1857, Captain James Scott, who had known Doyle since he was fifteen, was called to give him a 'good character'. In defending the punishments given out by the captain, Scott claimed that 'ordering an apprentice eighteen years of age to walk the deck with a capstan bar for an hour or two is a very frequent punishment, but I should rather have the rope's end, it is the soonest over'. The newspaper report recorded that there was laughter in the court at this remark.

At Wellington, New Zealand, all my crew deserted me.
To get the ship away I said, 'I'll pay an extra fee.'
I signed an oath I'd pay them, though it was a brave deceit,
Old Yardley in the courthouse said, 'It's a bad example indeed.'

In 1851 Doyle was accused of failing to pay the extra wages promised to Edward Seaman, a crew member on the *Fairy Queen* which Doyle had captained on a trip from New Zealand. He had promised each of the crew three shillings extra in compensation for the ship being short-handed. Doyle claimed that he signed the written agreement under duress as the crew refused to sail unless they were offered the extra money – he never meant to pay it. Mr Yardley, the magistrate at Thames Police Court, reprimanded Doyle for the 'jaunty' way in which he answered his questions, and for failing to conduct himself properly in the witness box. The magistrate noted that Doyle seemed to 'have changed his men very often', implying that crew under the captain's charge frequently deserted because of bad management. He was shocked that Doyle had signed an agreement under oath but had never intended to honour it, commenting that 'it is very bad morality indeed'. Although Yardley reluctantly accepted that the ad hoc agreement was not enforceable, he remarked, 'I do not at all approve of the conduct of the defendant.' Six years later, Yardley was still the magistrate when Doyle was charged with Eastick's assault, and it was Yardley who issued the warrant for his arrest.

That proud judge could not fine me, and soon I was on my way,
And I married my sweet cousin, Sarah, on a fine November day.

But I could not stay on shore, my boys, though Sarah was my dear,
It was 'all aboard the *John Sugars*' under sail to Australia.

Doyle married Elizabeth Emmery Sarah Howard in 1851. In the 1861 census she is recorded as 'Sarah' rather than Elizabeth. Her surname, Howard, was the maiden name of Doyle's mother who might have been Sarah's aunt – Doyle and his wife were probably cousins.

From Sunderland we made our way, to the docks of London Town,
As we sailed upon the river Thames, we mowed the *Neptuno* down.
It was my word 'gainst the Spanish crew. The court of the Admiralty
Ruled it was the foreigner's fault not mine, no blame was attached to me.

This accident happened on the maiden voyage of the *John Sugars* in 1853. The captain of the *Neptuno* (which was considerably smaller than the *John Sugars*) claimed Doyle had suddenly turned the ship and made collision inevitable. Doyle argued that it was the *Neptuno* that had disastrously altered course. The Spanish ship sank immediately, but the crew were able to jump aboard the *John Sugars*. Again, Doyle managed to avoid punishment.

So off we sailed to Australia, then Burma and Peru,
At Rangoon there was trouble again, when I went and lost my crew.

Some say they was deserters, but I say they had money for rum,
And to Calcutta went the message clear, to fetch Lascars to
   sail my ship home.

Doyle arrived in Rangoon in 1854. He later claimed that only one member of the crew deserted the *John Sugars* when they reached port, and that the others were paid their due, though this was disputed by the agent who was employed to find a replacement crew from Calcutta. 'Lascars' – a term originally used to describe sailors from the Indian subcontinent – were often employed on journeys back to Europe to replace sailors who had deserted or died on the outward trip.[2] They received lower wages than their white counterparts and were routinely mistreated.

Well, two weeks passed and two weeks more, and another
   fortnight went,
So I gathered a crew in old Rangoon, as no men from
   Calcutta were sent,
But as we sailed down the river wide, the steamer with the
   Lascars came by,
And now they say that John Sugars must pay, for the crew
   that I left behind.

The steamer between Calcutta and Rangoon sailed twice a month. The agent searching for a replacement crew intended to return on the first steamer but failed to complete recruitment before it sailed. The next steamer was commandeered by soldiers, and so the new crew were only able to embark on the third available one. In the meantime, Doyle managed to scrape a crew together in Rangoon and decided to leave. When the steamer from Calcutta and the *John Sugars* passed each other on the river, the agent hailed Doyle, but he refused to stop. The agent's employers, Messrs Macrae and Begbie, successfully prosecuted shipowner John Sugars and his partner, who were required to reimburse the £134.4s.8d spent by the agent. The case was tried while Doyle was already in prison.

> To Newgate Gaol I am condemned, for the death of my cabin
> lad,
> The boy was idle and wept for home, but I say I never treated
> him bad,
> Except for a thump or a lick of the rope, as captains will
> understand,
> And I starved him too when he didn't turn to, for to make
> him into a man.

At the trial in 1857, Doyle could have been charged with 'aggravated assault' or multiple assaults on Eastick but in the end he was given three months for the less serious charge of single common assault. The crew's testimonies against him were weakened by the suspicion that they bore him a grudge. On handing down the sentence of three months in Newgate jail, the recorder said that 'if the jury had convicted him upon any of the more serious counts in the indictment he should certainly have inflicted a much more severe sentence'. While in jail, Doyle's certificate of competency as master of a ship was suspended for twelve months. After his release he does not appear to have held the position of captain again. He and Sarah had a baby, Ada, in January 1859, but this family life was short-lived – he died in 1862 in his mid-forties.

You captains, warning take by me and do your mischief quiet,
Don't let the crew see the bruises blue, if you don't want a
    riot,
And Newgate Gaol, though a living hell, is better than the
    gibbet,
Make sure the cry is 'Boy overboard' and not 'It's the captain
    that did it.'

PART III

IN THE FEN COUNTRY

Magic Casements

The setting of Vaughan Williams's childhood home, Leith Hill Place, is extraordinary. You first sense this on the approach from the car park where the pale white exterior of the house is seen against a misty jumble of trees and distant hills, like a theatre backdrop for Arcadia. Set on the steep slope of Leith Hill, the back of the house faces almost due south towards the coast. The ground beyond the garden terrace drops away at your feet, a vale of woodland, hedgerows and compact fields rolling out into the distance. Inside the house, at every window, you are aware of being up in the air, as if you are flying above the surreal miniaturised countryside. Barely a sign of human habitation can be seen. Contemplating this view from the nursery windows in the attic I am reminded of how Vaughan Williams explained to a group of primary school children that music would enable them 'to see past facts to the very essence of things' and would provide 'the means by which we can look through the magic casements and see what lies beyond'.[1] The reference is from Keats's 'Ode to a Nightingale' in which the poet describes how, through the ages, the song of the bird has

> Charm'd magic casements, opening on the foam
> Of perilous seas, in faery lands forlorn.

To grow up with this view would affect the way a child saw the world, as with a shepherd or a fisherman whose eyes seem always to be focused on the far horizon.

Margaret Vaughan Williams brought her young family – Hervey, Meggie and Ralph – to live at Leith Hill Place when her husband, Arthur, died in 1875. The children had been born into a circle of upper-class, intellectual and liberal-leaning families centred around the Wedgwoods and Darwins; the house, set in the Surrey Hills south of London, was Margaret's own childhood home where her parents, Josiah and Caroline Wedgwood (*née* Darwin) and sister Sophie still lived.[2] Arthur had been the 'boy-next-door' at Tanhurst House. It was only on visiting that I realised quite how close the families had lived, only a narrow lane separating the two estates. For Margaret, walks around the gardens were full of memories. For Ralph, the move brought him an idyllic playground of parkland, woods and heath to explore at will.

When his older brother, Hervey, died in 1944 Vaughan Williams inherited the Leith Hill estate. Despite the frequent characterisation of him as a country gentleman he did not take

South-facing facade of Leith Hill Place and view

up the opportunity to become one, declaring that 'if I ran the place properly, I shouldn't have any time for my own work'.[3] Instead, he donated it to the National Trust, while he and his first wife, Adeline, continued to live in their more convenient bungalow at nearby Dorking. Opened to the public in 2013, visitors to Leith Hill Place can now walk through the 'dark passage' to the kitchen, which the young Ralph found frightening, experience the views his child-eyes saw, and walk in the gardens where he played, that airy vista the constant backdrop. When he was older he explored the wider heaths and woods of Leith Hill, up to the viewing tower built by a previous owner for people 'to enjoy the glory of the English countryside'.[4] During the composer's childhood this tower was already a visitor attraction – an old lady sold ginger beers, luncheons and teas to over six thousand tourists each year.[5] Thousands still climb to the top today to survey what feels like the whole of southern England. The bristling towers of the City of London are only thirty miles distant, St Paul's Cathedral a rounded white hump nestled at their roots – but in Vaughan Williams's youth it was the tallest landmark, a visible siren's call to the capital. In his late teens, when studying at the Royal College of Music, he sometimes walked between London and Leith Hill on his own kind of pilgrimage.

The countryside of the Surrey Hills is small scale, hedged in, soft with leafy heads of beech and oak, its undulating body cloaked with pasture. The Fens, in contrast, are laid bare – vast open fields of ploughed black soil, level as a board, relieved occasionally by the twisted willows along their ditches. This is the land Vaughan Williams moved to when in 1892 he left Leith Hill Place for good, and became a student at Trinity College, Cambridge.

☉

Returning to the banks of the Great Ouse, the difference between the Surrey Hills on a gentle summer's afternoon, and the Fens on a cold, bright March morning, was stark. I was looking for evidence of the engineering works that had such an impact on North Lynn and the North End during the nineteenth century. Starting at West Lynn, I turned towards the Wash, the expanse of shallow tidal waters formed by a notch in the coast between Norfolk, Cambridgeshire and Lincolnshire, where the North End fishermen made their living. Now that I understood the major landscape changes here in the Victorian period I realised that it was not the old Great Ouse I was gazing across, but the man-made Lynn Cut, built to bypass the natural meander in the river, and which transferred the settlement of North Lynn from the west bank to the east. Upstream, I could see the sea walls and familiar church towers of King's Lynn, while immediately opposite I looked for the remains of North Lynn, now an industrial suburb.

Buffeted by the stiff onshore breeze, I continued seaward until I could see the surviving barns set back from the bank, built for the cattle on this side of the river once the Cut had severed North Lynn Farm from its grazing land. How strange it must have been for the owner, no longer able to step out of the house and stroll down the track to check his livestock or have a quiet chat with the cattle man. Instead, the rhythm of the tide controlled when it was possible to row over to the fields. By the water's edge, with the eye of faith, I could see the remnants of a landing stage. Behind me the ground stretched away, divided into measured square fields, reclaimed from the sea and salt marsh. Four hundred years ago a boat would have been necessary to navigate the wild fen here, that dense network of waterways and reed beds which extended for miles and miles inland, as far as Cambridge and Peterborough.

For centuries, the Fens were considered dangerous wildernesses by incomers; places where both the landscape and the indigenous people needed to be tamed. For those who grew up in the place it was a larder full of fish (eels, pike, perch, roach and lampreys), fowl (goose, heron and duck), and eggs for which they foraged on wooden stilts. Reed and sedge provided thatch for their homes which in some areas were built and heated with peat bricks and, in summer when the flood waters receded, their cattle grazed on sumptuous common land.[6]

Organised drainage of the Fens began in the Roman period and continued in fits and starts from then on, accelerating in the seventeenth century. As well as draining the land, huge changes to the river systems were initiated, diverting them, joining them together and straightening them. Profitable arable crops could be grown on the reclaimed land – but the process destroyed a unique ecosystem and the fen dwellers' way of life. The result was considered by landowners to be 'improvement' and it was assumed that the local population would also be 'improved', as expressed in this contemporary poem:

> There shall a change of Men and manners be;
> Hearts, thick and tough as Hydes, shall feel Remorse,
> And Souls of Sedge shall understand Discourse,
> New hands shall learn to Work, forget to Steal,
> New leggs shall go to church, new knees shall kneel.[7]

As usual, the voices of the people affected by these changes are difficult to find except in the fragments of recorded oral tradition. The stories in *Tales from the Fens* and *More Tales from the Fens* were learnt by the young 'Jack' Barrett at the end of the nineteenth century.[8] Unlike most of the collectors of songs, dances and folklore of the time, Barrett was a local from a rural labouring family, who left school when he was eleven. He grew up with the stories told by his father and other Fenmen who used to gather in the Ship Inn on the banks of the Little Ouse at Brandon. As an old man in the 1960s, he retold these to Enid

Porter, curator of the Cambridge and County Folk Museum: '. . . during the first years of my working life, when out in the isolated areas of the Fens, crow-scaring or sheep-tending, I eased the loneliness by memorising the tales . . .'[9]

They are not quaint stories of love or fairies or wispy white ghosts. They weave stories around the violent resistance to the changes imposed by the Romans, the monasteries, the seventeenth-century 'Adventurers' and large land corporations. They tell of how the Romans came and tried to take their land, and how the fen dwellers dragged them off into the marshes and slit their throats. They tell of how the medieval monks came and raped their women and enslaved the poor, and how the fen dwellers took refuge on the marsh islands and launched guerrilla attacks on the fortified monasteries, picking off monks at random. They tell of how the marshes were drained from under them, and the old ways of living from the water and the reed all lost. There is a sense of outrage at the things that have been done to them over the centuries, a sense of collective psychological damage. Many skeletons are dug up from the mud – the slaughtered Romans and their horses, the raving rector drowned in a pond, crucified peasants, an old woman tied to a stake in the flood, buried in the clay. These were the tales that the Fenland communities grew up with, full of violence and revenge, retold by grandparents sitting by peat fires, or in the pubs and fields.

One of the best-known storytellers, with a characteristically angular Fen nickname, was 'Chafer' Legge. He is described as 'the last of the real old type of Fenmen', dressed in an otter-skin cap, moleskin waistcoat and 'Crabitt' trousers.[10] Legge and others like him were sought out by academics because of the many ancient finds they turned up as they dug out drainage ditches. His reminiscences shine a light on the relationship between the academic world of Vaughan Williams's Cambridge and the Fens' rural population.

In the severe winter of 1895, Legge was invited to Newnham College by Eleanor Sidgwick, the principal, to teach the female students how to ice-skate, for he had been a champion skater when young. He was led through the house which she shared with her husband, Henry, Fellow of Trinity College and Professor of Moral Philosophy. At the time he counted amongst his students both George Moore and Ralph Wedgwood, friends of Vaughan Williams. Legge was 'flabbergasted to see a glass case with all those bits of iron and brass from my shed in it, all laid out with bits of white paper stuck on them'.[11] After spending three happy days with the excitable students he was shown Professor Sidgwick's full collection of 'old iron'. This included a three-pronged rat killer which Bill Creek, the blacksmith, had made for Legge forty years earlier. 'I asked what the label said, and it was this: "Fish trident of the Iron Age, dug from Feltwell Fen."' Chafer's audience of Fenmen in the Ship Inn must have laughed uproariously at the foolishness of the upper-class Cambridge professors who earnestly collected these bits of scrap iron and revered them in glass cases. In the same way, labourers, fishermen and workhouse inmates might have chuckled amongst themselves when the Edwardian well-to-do came collecting their old songs.

'Chafer Legge at Newnham' is an amusing story about the potential for misunderstandings which arise from the collision of two cultures. Most of the stories in the two volumes of Barrett's tales illustrate the brutal outcomes of these collisions. Sadism is an everyday occurrence. One story in particular seems to share the gruesome attention to the details of torture found in 'The Captain's Apprentice'. In ' "Lamplighter's" Dream' the eponymous storyteller describes the punishment given to a Fenman accused of theft by the Romans, which he sees in a vision-like dream after digging up a piece of bog oak.[12] Someone bangs on a gong to drown the thief's screams as he is whipped until his bare ribs can be seen. He is brought round with freezing water before being nailed to the piece of oak. When the first spike is driven into his hand the man attempts to sit up before the second hand is nailed, his legs broken with hammer blows and his two feet fixed to the cross with a single spike.

Onlookers throw earth at the man, and then sit down to a feast. The thief's people are brought to watch him die as a warning, but they manage to wreak a violent revenge. The Roman guards are poisoned and the sleeping soldiers killed in their beds: '. . . those that didn't die outright were finished off by the women.'

The frequent violence in these tales, in 'The Captain's Apprentice' and in other folk songs, was retold by people living in a landscape that was ruthlessly shaped and manipulated over centuries. Living on the contended line where fens and open seas meet, the local inhabitants knew about hard struggle, the erosion of their way of life and of the land and rivers around them, drained, cut, truncated and transformed despite their protest. Vaughan Williams, alighting suddenly in their kitchens, and expressing interest in their songs, could not have known the depths from which these stories emerged. For the inhabitants of the North End he must have seemed 'a funny old customer'.

⌒

After retracing my steps along the bank of the Lynn Cut, I drove over the bridge at South Lynn, and back up the other side of the river to park by the mouth of the Fisher Fleet. It is little more than a cul-de-sac, a handful of fishing boats clinging to the mud-banks, against the wall of the dock. A couple of skeletal wrecks rotted in the rough grass amongst the litter. The wind whining through metal railings increased the sense of desolation. From here, on the OS map, a footpath appears to follow the curve of the old river that was drained when the Cut made it redundant. I found the path entrance in the car park of a warehouse, from where it continued, hemmed in by security fencing, between industrial buildings. The ground fell away either side of this nar-row tunnel and I realised with a shiver that I was walking along the defunct riverbank, a thin sliver of the 1850s landscape erupt-ing like the spine of a dinosaur into a twenty-first-century wilderness.

Beauty of the Plain Alone

In the Fen Country

The simple bleakness of the Fenlands, the direct experience of wind uninterrupted by trees, the brown, slapping waves in wide dykes, and the unremitting fields, present a challenge to conventional ideals of what is beautiful. In the 1930s Iris Wedgwood (wife of Vaughan Williams's cousin Ralph) wrote a travel book, *Fenland Rivers*, in which she points out that certain landscapes such as heath or golden sands can be found throughout England but 'the Fens are all their own': it is 'too little realized that there is beauty of the plain alone'.[1]

When, as students, Vaughan Williams and Ralph Wedgwood cycled about the man-wrought Fenlands north of Cambridge, it is possible they felt the same exhilaration of the alien that draws artists and writers in the twenty-first century to the blurred zone between urban and rural – the 'unofficial countryside' – as opposed to the 'enshrined, ecologically arrested, controlled garden space' of the 'official wilderness'.[2] In this modern narrative, mountains and moorlands that were elevated from the 'rubbish of the world' to their 'sublime' status by the Romantics are now seen as cossetted and artificial, while the edgy spaces, which develop with no consideration for aesthetics, are something like the new sublime.[3] The stripped-back Fens might have been experienced as a landscape of progress and industry by young Edwardian intellectuals who wanted to challenge conventions and who railed against the accepted beauty of the pastoral and sublime. In a letter to his cousin dated June 1899, Vaughan Williams made a list of things he would like to find in an ideal holiday spot:

(a) bracing air (b) quiet surroundings (c) hills (d) valleys (e) good bicycling roads (f) beautiful forest walks (g) trees (h) heaths (i) fens (j) downs (k) a river (l) nobody we know (m) salt marshes . . .[4]

Mountains do not appear in the list, but fens do.

Seatoller, March 1895

Standing on Combe Head, 735 metres above sea level, you can look north through the ragged Jaws of Borrowdale, to the grey sheen of Derwent Water in the middle distance. Below, the tiny hamlet of Seatoller lies at the edge of a green bowl of pasture and smoke-coloured woodland. Ribs of mountains, gathered at the back of stone houses, cast long shadows. It has been one of the coldest winters on record, with heavy snowfalls and weeks of hard frost. Now a partial thaw has begun.[5] Snow remains on the treeless tops and high flanks of the fells but down in the valley, where five friends wait outside an old farmhouse, the chill air is filled with the tinkling of meltwater in the runnels, the rushing of gills and waterfalls.

Ralph Vaughan Williams, Ralph Wedgwood, George Moore, George Trevelyan and Maurice Amos are earnest, bright young men. Three of them – Wedgwood, Moore and Trevelyan – are members of the elite group of intellectuals, the Cambridge Apostles. Moore, Wedgwood and Amos are reading 'moral sciences'. 'Trevy' is in his second year, studying classics, and Vaughan Williams is preparing for his history finals. Their minds are full of philosophy, poetry and novels and their plan is to spend the Easter vacation at the Lake District guesthouse reading, revising, debating, and hiking in the mountains.

They keep a diary of the trip. Each adopts the name of a classical philosopher. The book is filled with poems, drawings, cameos, and notes on the topics discussed each day – these include Thackeray, the parable of the unjust steward, the insufficiency of Natural Selection and the Universe in Relation to God.[6] Amos sketches them lounging in the dining room, gathered at the table or leaning on the mantelpiece next to the fire, each poring over a book.[7] One of them is reading *Treasure Island* so it is uncertain whether they are all studying hard. During the three weeks' stay Moore and Trevelyan make a pilgrimage to Wordsworth's houses, Dove Cottage and Rydal Mount, and meet an old woman who knew the great poet laureate – they are within touching distance of the Romantics.

On another day they climb the mountain behind the guesthouse: Glaramara. The approach is long and steep across

Sketch in Seatoller 'logbook' – Vaughan Williams bottom right corner

Thornythwaite Fell, up to Comb Head and beyond. Though the valley stream below is in full spate, thick snow and ice still lie in the shade, crackle under their heavy boots as they tramp along. Barring the way to the summit is a low cliff of rock, a wall of grey pillars that must be climbed. They each clamber up, fingers sore with cold against the stones, breath puffing in clouds of steam. From the top, rubbing their hands and stamping their feet, the party surveys a sweeping panorama of knotty mountain peaks – the masses of Great Gable and Green Gable to the west, to the south-east the ridges of Loft Crag and Pike o' Stickle, to the south-west the crumpled cliff face of Great End. These are the 'fantastic mountains' which Wordsworth describes south of Derwent Water, the lake '*surrounded* with sublimity'.[8]

They descend to the guesthouse, warm themselves at the drawing-room fire and reflect on the adventure. Vaughan

Glaramara

Williams responds to the sublime landscape he has experienced by writing a sexually suggestive poem in the manner of Swinburne:[9]

> I have clasped thee, O great Glaramara,
> I am weary of clasping thy slope
> And the passionate lips that press nearer
> Are foaming with fear and with hope.
> With furious desire to embrace thee
> My clothes are lascivious rags;
> But my love turns to fear when I face thee
> And I kiss, without wishing, thy crags.

He quotes directly from the controversial poet: 'I am torn by thy rock, Glaramara / And the "amorous blows" of thy stones'; and ends with intended bathos:

And – I must say I wish I was nearer
Some place, where I shan't break my bones.

Vaughan Williams – also known as Sir Behemoth – is the clown of the party.[10] He cannot help himself. As well as failing to appreciate the sublime qualities of Glaramara, he is frank about his interest in food:

There was a young man of Seatoller
Who did nothing but guzzle and swaller
For he found that the food
Was so tasty and good
That he frequently wished he was holler

By the second week, at least one fellow guest has tired of his frivolity.[11] Vaughan Williams is goaded into writing a sonnet – 'To a philosopher who complained that I was not serious enough' – in which he alludes to the criticism that he 'has not stored sweet wisdom' in his brain but 'clutched at shallow jest, and gained – a stone'. He argues that there is no point in him imitating 'crow-like' his friend who stands in the 'shining train' of 'great Philosophy'. On 29 March he leaves earlier than the others with what Moore characterises as 'utmost complaisance'.[12]

New Forest, June 1899

Four years after the Seatoller trip, much has changed. Vaughan Williams is married to Adeline Fisher, and they are holidaying in the New Forest. He writes to Ralph Wedgwood, still his dearest friend: 'We've had it grey and wet and fine and green and its [*sic*] always beautiful – not one of your horrid stern places where you feel you must discuss high themes but a warm comfortable beauty . . .'[13] He acknowledges the Romantic assumption that awe-inspiring landscapes should invoke higher levels of thinking, but then adds a moral dimension: 'Don't think me degenerate in my likes but you know I always <u>have</u> preferred soft scenery to stern uncomfortable scenery.' He knows he did not rise to the occasion when they stayed at Seatoller. He is like Kant's Savoyard peasant who 'lacking in the development of moral ideas' finds the Alps repellent.[14] He blames this 'craven spirit' on growing up in Surrey. His heart leaps, not when he sees a rainbow, as in Wordsworth's poem, but at the sight of a long low range of hills.

The subject of landscape crops up regularly in his correspondence with Wedgwood. In one letter prior to the Seatoller jaunt he suggests various destinations for a trip and mentions that it will make him 'positively ill to see anything more than 100 feet high'.[15] In another, he describes the surroundings of Valescure in the South of France as like 'a beautiful Cambridge plain',[16] and later he remarks that his favourite type of landscape is 'a long low valley . . . all arable and ploughed fields – and just one or two trees'.[17] He prefers countryside that is lived in, where nature is tamed. The sublime does not move him, and he sees this as a way in which he fails to measure up to the intellectual stature of his Cambridge friends. Landscape becomes a lens through which he judges his own moral character and finds himself wanting.

Cambridgeshire, 2018

As a student Vaughan Williams regularly travelled from Cambridge to Ely Cathedral on summer Sundays to hear the morning service:

> . . . the exciting moment when the towered hill appeared from the surrounding fens was one that never ceased to delight him. The train arrived in time for him to slip in just after the service had started and the sound of the choir's singing set new musical ideas flowing.[18]

I took this same journey on a late afternoon in October, hoping to see with Vaughan Williams's eyes the landscape that inspired *In the Fen Country*, the 'symphonic impression' he first completed in 1904. Cambridge railway station is recognisable as the building he knew, though the arches of the grand facade have been filled with glass. The flowering weeds by the tracks would have been familiar to him, but not the garish plastics of crisp packets and bottles entwined in their stems. The short journey passed through flat fields of sweetcorn, sugar beet, photovoltaic arrays and plastic-wrapped straw bales, neatly delineated by water-filled dykes. Just outside Ely the train paused, before the west tower and the central lantern of the cathedral were finally revealed over the blocks of industrial buildings and Portakabins.

In its pristine state a fen can be magical, with secret patches of bright water, feathery reeds incandescent in low winter light, and ripples left by invisible birds and water voles. It is not dramatic or awe-inspiring in the manner of mountain ranges but has something primeval about it – a quiet place that invites meditation. Sadly, little of this landscape survives – but the *idea* of it seems to linger. Reviews of *In the Fen Country* in recent decades have been emphatic about the imagery the piece is intended to conjure:

. . . the reedy lodes and droves of peatland . . .

. . . a spaciousness, a sense of the Fens' mysterious spell . . .

. . . this flat and watery part of England the sea is always near, the water seeps into the land, the tang of Holland stings the nostrils.

. . . the wide, flat vistas of the Fens, where land, water and sky blur together . . .

. . . that flat wind-swept East Coast, where the largest wild flowers in England grow and the most romantic wading birds inhabit . . .

. . . the spaciousness and tranquillity of the broad, flat countryside with which the composer was so familiar.[19]

These descriptions perpetuate a vision of the Fens as a wild, uncanny wetland, a broad, flat sheet inhabited by birds rather than humans, the land, sea and sky merging in shades of greys and blues. It is an idea originating in the seventh century, when early Christians came seeking isolated places sequestered from society to build monasteries, at Medeshamstede (now Peterborough, founded AD 655), Ely (AD 673) and Crowland (AD 716), this last founded by St Guthlac. His eighth-century biographer, Felix, described the Fens as they were then '. . . now consisting of marshes, now of bogs, sometimes of black waters overhung by fog . . .'[20] Charles Kingsley's popular Victorian novel *Hereward the Wake,* set near Ely in the eleventh century, took up this notion of a watery haven: 'dark velvet alder beds, long lines of reed-rond, emerald in spring, and golden under the autumn sun; shining river-reaches; broad meres dotted with a million fowl . . .'[21] Although these features were largely gone by the late nineteenth century, the sense of a strange watery land lives on in more recent literature, notably Graham Swift's *Waterland*; and Philip Pullman's Lyra novels, in which the Gyptians take refuge in the 'mazy waterways'[22] of the Fens. But this is a landscape of the literary imagination, a symbolic backdrop for exploring themes of the outsider – it is not the Fens that Vaughan Williams saw. When he was exploring the area, most of the true fens had been remorselessly drained. The reds and yellows I saw on the train journey, the shiny materials, the scale and shapes of buildings, even some of the crops in the fields, would have been alien to him. But the canvas of pitch-black soil, the dykes lined with willows, the embankments and the church steeples could all be seen from the train window in the 1890s. It is still a mystery in this low landscape how the towers of Ely Cathedral remain hidden until you are almost upon them, where they soar on top of that gentle hill.

Cambridge, 1895

There was a winter when the frosts were so hard it was possible to skate from Cambridge to Ely. Vaughan Williams skated one way and caught the train back.

This was the famously icy winter of 1894–95 when there were air frosts on almost every night between 26 December 1894 and 20 March 1895.[23] The rivers Cam and Great Ouse froze for weeks. It was the winter when Chafer Legge taught the female Cambridge students to skate. It was also the winter described in the children's book *Tom's Midnight Garden*, when Hatty and Tom skate from the fictional town of Castleford (Cambridge) to Ely in the gathering dark:

> They skated on, and the thin, brilliant sun was beginning to set, and Hatty's shadow flitted along at their right hand, across the dazzle of the ice. Sometimes they skated on the main river; sometimes they skated along the flooded washes. Only the willows along the bank watched them; and the ice hissed with their passage.[24]

At nearby Littleport a local farmer used to flood some of his fields – 'The Moors' – to provide a skating rink when the freezing weather came. A contemporary described how professors and undergraduates from Cambridge, clergy from Ely cathedral, bookmakers and pickpockets would mingle at these events but would give 'the speedy Fenmen a wide berth if they knew what was good for them'.[25]

Small-built and sinewy, the 'speedy Fenmen' lived hard physical lives in isolated cottages down long droves, cut off from each other by dykes and ditches. They suffered from 'the ague' – malaria – and the pervasive damp sank into their bones. Despite these hardships the toughness and independent spirit of the fen dwellers was legendary.

The staccato sounds of the skaters' nicknames evoke the cold and wet of the Fens winter – Fish, Gutta Percha, Turkey, Muckey, Traps, Ratty. Skating races, and the prizes that came with them, could compensate for the lack of work available when the weather was harsh. As soon as the waterways froze they would be out on the ice, practising their technique, improving their speed. If the moon was bright they could skate after dark. Then it was silent, only the sound of the skates crackling through the surface, the occasional screech of an owl. Modern fen skaters describe the feeling as 'freedom', 'floating on air', and those late Victorian men will have felt the same: an interval of magical beauty in their battling lives.

Numerous skating races were held in the Cambridge area, drawing huge crowds – a race on the River Nene above Wisbech was said to have attracted nine thousand spectators. On 13 February 1895 a race took place from Cambridge to Ely and back, which was enough of an event to be reported in the national newspapers. It was probably this exciting spectacle that inspired Vaughan Williams to attempt the trip along the frozen river himself, skating over the milky, mottled ribbon of ice, lined with the feathered silhouettes of willow. Perhaps it was then that the bleak Fen character first crept into his soul, the simple blocks of horizontal land and dark sky made brutally pure and simple by the frost.

Warboys, August 1899

A raised causeway carries the arrow-straight white road across unbroken fields of potatoes and corn, stretching to the horizon. Tracks and ditches run off at right angles in regimented parallel lines. The August evening is warm, the air soft. Two cyclists pelt along at high speed, one a young woman in a long skirt, her hair flying out from under her hat, the other, her brother, face thrust forward, eyes fixed on the road ahead. They skid to a halt as the road ends abruptly at a raised bank. On the other side a wide ditch cuts across the fields for miles.[26] Discarding their bikes, they scramble down the embankment. Tiny white moths flutter amongst tall rushes and plants that grow in the brown water.[27]

Adeline's cousins, Virginia (later Woolf) and Adrian Stephen, are in the middle of a two-month holiday in the Fens. Along with their siblings, Vanessa and Thoby, they are staying in the Warboys rectory twenty miles north-west of Cambridge. During the train journey from London the unbroken expanses of turnip fields had been so dull they stopped looking.[28] But on the omnibus between Warboys station and the village, something happened – a 'golden gauze streamer' of sunlight caught the spire of a church, making it glitter 'like a gem in the darkness and wetness'.[29] After this, the Fenland skyscape enraptures Virginia:

> Such expanse & majesty & illuminations I have never seen. Pure air for fathoms and fathoms & acres and acres; & then such lavish cloud conglomerations; there is a vast space of blue into which the gods are certainly blowing wondrous cloud bubbles.[30]

She and Adrian go for an hour of 'hard riding' every afternoon on their bikes, down straight roads with no hills to disturb them. She knows that only a few years ago the solid ground had been 'all swamp and reed' but she finds a hint of the old Fens in the ditches, and some 'picturesque element' in the harvesters, windmills and golden cornfields.[31] The monotony of the Fen plains gets under her skin – 'how great I feel the stony-hard flatness . . .'[32] As autumn comes, the atmosphere changes – the fields are ploughed into brown clods, the hedges along the roads are full of berries, there is 'a look & feeling of melancholy in everything'.[33] By the end of their stay, she declares, 'I shall think it a test of friends for the future whether they can appreciate the Fen country . . .'[34]

Cambridge, 1892–5

During term-time at Cambridge Vaughan Williams and his friends often cycle in the surrounding countryside. The town lies on the edge of the Fens that stretch northwards to the Wash. They see the same landscape as Virginia records in her letters: open expanses of arable fields, water-filled ditches, stunted willows, the occasional decaying windmill.

The future novelist John Cowper Powys is a contemporary of Vaughan Williams at Cambridge, though not a friend. A less sociable young man, he prefers to explore the Fens alone, on foot, tramping 'long straight flat monotonous roads for miles and miles, north, south, east, and west'.[35] As he travels along these 'unpicturesque, unromantic highways', every swamp-pool, rushy brook, weedy estuary, turnip field, grey milestone and desolate haystack becomes part of his spirit.[36] When on holiday in Wales with his father, he claims to detest mountains, and says the only scenery in which he feels really happy is the 'fen-country of Norfolk' where he visited his grandparents as a child.[37] For him, this desolate landscape reflects his inner self.

Cowper Powys's rejection of mountains in favour of the monotonous fens sounds like a rebellion. Virginia Stephen's championing of the stony-flat hardness is in the same vein, as if the stark lines and utilitarianism of the Fens are an antidote to the over-emotional sentimentalism of the Romantics and the Victorian age. When the Stephen and Fisher cousins socialised in the 1890s did she, Adeline and Vaughan Williams share their enthusiasm for the unsettling atmosphere of the Fens, that 'test of friends'? In this company, Vaughan Williams's rejection of the Lake District mountains appears similarly radical, even defiant. He composes *In the Fen Country* in opposition to the reverence some of his friends hold for the chaotic awe of the sublime. Despite the desolation, the flatness, the monotony,

Fenland road

this melancholy scene of straight roads, cornfields and ditches inspires him.

River Avon, July 1903

In the summer of 1903 Vaughan Williams and Adeline join Ralph Wedgwood on a boating trip, travelling down the Avon from Salisbury to Christchurch.[38] The composer is with the two people he loves most in the world. His attachment to Wedgwood is intense, deferential, guileless. In a letter to him written soon after leaving Cambridge Vaughan Williams describes himself as 'naturally of bestial, lazy, sensual, earthy, devilish nature but when I was with you a lot of that used to disappear'.[39] In another he writes, 'you mustn't think that because I'm married I don't hate not seeing you just as much . . .'[40] and later, ' I would rather be praised for my songs by you than by any one'.[41] As they glide down the river they talk of old times. Since the Seatoller trip, members of the group have gone their separate ways. George Moore's *Principia Ethica* is about to change the direction of twentieth-century philosophy; Trevelyan is a published historian; Amos is a judge in the Egyptian Ministry of Justice; and Wedgwood is District Superintendent at the North Eastern Railway. Vaughan Williams already talks of being 'middle-aged'.[42] Those youthful student days seem far away. In the months following the river trip he composes *In the Fen Country* and dedicates it to 'R.L.W.' – Ralph Lewis Wedgwood.[43]

Vaughan Williams does not stand outside the Fens as a passive spectator. He is 'In' the Fen Country, body and soul. For him, landscape is inextricably linked to feelings, whether they be stern, uncomfortable or soft. This 'symphonic impression' reflects his emotional relationship with the Fens. It is a place of stories as well as earth, water and sky – in it are layered old myths of Hereward the Wake, fragments of lost reedbeds seen at the edges of ditches, love, the choir in Ely Cathedral, sky, monotonous roads, old arguments between friends. I see Vaughan Williams on his bike, freewheeling down a fen causeway, long legs stretched out in front of the pedals. His companions swerve and weave around him. Wedgwood is amongst them, head thrown back, laughing at his cousin's antics. At that moment the Fens become for Vaughan Williams the locus of youth, friendship and love, the juncture in time and space when he is happiest: his landscape of memory.

Folk-Like

During the early years of the twentieth century Vaughan Williams was much absorbed with the idea of evoking place. In his creative response to the physical landscape, folk music was an intrinsic element: for him, the songs were an audible manifestation of the English soil. He began to experiment with the idea of 'folk-like' themes (unlike the direct use of folk tunes in the *Norfolk Rhapsodies*) with the intention of capturing but not replicating the melodic shape of folk songs he 'knew and loved' from printed collections.[1] In a letter to Ralph Wedgwood in 1898 he states that it is a good idea for a composer to 'get the spirit of his national tunes into his work <u>if it comes natural to him</u>'.

> . . . I very much believe in the folk tune theory – by which
> I don't mean that modern composing is done by

sandwiching an occasional national tune – not your own invention – between lumps of '2d the pound' stuff – which seems to be Dvorak's latest method.[2]

He was arguing at this point in his career that tunes should not ordinarily be lifted straight from a folk song and inserted into a composition, but that it would not matter if work 'occasionally corresponds with some real "folk tune"'. He was making excuses for himself in the letter, having just used 'a bit of Welsh tune' as his main theme in a piece, which he states boldly was 'unacknowledged of course – but then "I made it my own"'.[3] Vaughan Williams was never shy of what he called 'cribbing' from other composers – he considered it 'a legitimate and praiseworthy practice' as long as it was deliberate; and he came to use both direct quotes and folk-like phrases throughout his work.[4] In his series of lectures on folk music which he gave first in 1902 – before any direct experience of collecting songs in the field – he expanded on this theme, remarking that composers who used folk music as inspiration should not be accused of stealing as 'these great popular tunes were the property of all those who by nationality, friendship or analogous feeling found themselves in sympathy with them'.[5] Half a century later his position had not changed: 'If a composer can, by tapping the sources hidden in folk-song, make beautiful music, he will be disloyal to his art if he does not make full use of such an avenue of beauty.'[6]

One of his best-loved songs, and his first published work, 'Linden Lea', was written in this spirit. Composed around 1901 its subtitle is 'A Dorset Folk Song', although the folk-like melody is his own, and the text used is a poem by the nineteenth-century Dorset poet William Barnes.[7] This was followed by the setting of two further Barnes poems – 'Blackmwore [*sic*] by the Stour', described by *The Times* as the 'cleverest imitation of a genuine folk song', and 'The Winter's Willow' alongside other pieces that explored landscape through music – his 'Burley Heath' and 'The Solent' impressions.[8] These last two were intended as part of a larger work entitled *In the New Forest*. Though never finished, the choice of the New Forest as its subject is significant as it is where he and Adeline holidayed in 1899, and where he mused on his emotional response to landscapes. In this same period of experimentation he wrote *In the Fen Country*, dedicated to Wedgwood.

The composition and early revisions of *In the Fen Country* span the composer's transition from theoretical interest in folk songs when he 'only believed in them vaguely' to active engagement after hearing Charles Potiphar sing 'Bushes and Briars' in December 1903.[9] Though its premier was at the Queen's Hall in 1909, Vaughan Williams had completed the first version of *In the Fen Country* in April 1904, only four months after he embarked on his intensive period of folk-song collecting. He revised the piece in February 1905, immediately after his visit to King's Lynn; again, in December of that year; and for a third time in 1907, before the work was performed at the Queen's Hall two years later. By this time, he had been collecting for over five years and had written the *Norfolk Rhapsodies*, with their direct use of folk melody.

When Edward Evans assessed Vaughan Williams's work in 1920, the score for *In the Fen Country* had been 'lost', though it re-emerged after further revision in 1935.[10] Evans remembered the piece as 'not indebted to folk-song', perhaps because it did not directly quote any particular air, but he felt it was 'intimately associated with the English soil', a 'quietly poetic composition in the style of a landscape, without incident'. Significantly, he emphasised the composer's particular response: 'The melodic lines are such as one associates with a pastoral scene, but Vaughan Williams has endowed them with a rare personal quality.'[11]

The orchestral piece is subtitled 'symphonic impression' – the only clue Vaughan Williams provides for its interpretation. Reviews immediately after its premier in 1909 noted the folk-like flavour. Some critics took issue with the lack of programme notes to explain its meaning and structure while others attempted their own analysis.[12] For one, the piece was 'an endeavour to express the composer's emotions engendered by the specified portion of England' although he was not overly enthusiastic about the effect: 'the continued "greyness" of the tone-colour makes the music depressing'.[13] For another more percipient reviewer, 'The composer provides no key to the poetic basis of his musical thoughts, beyond that which the title indicates: and that listener was therefore more highly satisfied, perhaps, in closely noting the development, and appreciating the real [sic] pleasant musical pictures . . . than he who endeavoured to discover the inspiring cause or causes of the different pictures.'[14] Without direction, the listeners inevitably imagined their own 'Fen Country' – and Vaughan Williams would have been happy with that. Later in life he wrote about the interpretation of music: 'Each person may attach their own meaning if they like, but it does not follow that their meaning will have the same meaning to anybody else – music is too universal for that.'[15]

Despite some positive reviews of its first performance Vaughan Williams lost confidence in *In the Fen Country*, perhaps partly due to criticism of his folk-song experiments.[16] A critic, writing about *Norfolk Rhapsody No. 1* in 1906, argued that by using folk tunes as a source of inspiration Vaughan Williams and other composers 'shirked a great part, perhaps the greatest part, of the composer's responsibility'.[17] In the year of *In the Fen Country*'s premier, critic Sydney Grew wrote that folk music's 'beautiful simplicity would be tortured beyond recognition in the strain of bearing an unwieldy superstructure . . .'[18] And in 1910, in a review of *Fantasia on English Folk Song* (another piece based on traditional melodies which Vaughan Williams later suppressed) a critic wished that the composer 'would leave our folk-songs alone, and give us, as the saying is, music out of his own head!'[19]

In his late thirties, and still establishing his reputation, such direct criticism of folk-inspired work must have been disheartening. During the winter of 1907–8 he decided his output was 'lumpy and stodgy, had come to a dead-end' and he went to Paris for three months to study composition under Ravel.[20] *In the Fen Country* received its premier after this, but the piece no longer pleased its creator and was withdrawn afterwards. It shared a corner in the back of a cupboard with *Norfolk Rhapsodies Nos 2* and *3,* the unfinished *In the New Forest* (*The Solent* and *Burley Heath*) and the two 'impressions for orchestra', *Harnham Down* and *Boldre Wood*.[21]

The sights and sounds Vaughan Williams experienced as he travelled across England in the first decade of the twentieth century can be seen reflected in his composition of the period, a mixing and matching of traditional songs, 'folk-like' melodies and landscapes that held personal significance for him. After his crisis of confidence in 1907, these three passions became less entwined. His published work focused on arrangements of collected folk tunes for classical singers and choirs, either unaccompanied or with piano: there was no tinkering with the melody in these pieces, but an intention to share what he had found with a wider public. An exception was *Fantasia on Christmas Carols* (1912), an arrangement of four traditional carols for baritone soloist, mixed choir and orchestra. It was not until 1923 that he completed a more ambitious treatment of folk tunes, his *English Folk Songs Suite* for military band (published 1924), followed in 1925 by publication of the revised *Norfolk Rhapsody No. 1*. His best-known work based on a folk tune, *Five Variants of 'Dives and Lazarus'*, did not come until 1939. A preoccupation with landscape remained but was usually conveyed through the texts he chose to set, such as *On Wenlock Edge* (A. E. Housman) or *A Sea Symphony* (Walt Whitman), rather than through overt musical 'impressions': *In the Fen Country* remained unpublished until after his death. Experimentation with the 'folk-like' – the intended imitation of a traditional melody – became less self-conscious. The modal scales and melodic phrasing in the hundreds of folk songs he had heard were woven into the texture of his composition but embedded in a deeper layer of his creativity: in his own words, 'the spirit' of folk melody had become 'natural' to him.

After *In the Fen Country* the next orchestral work named after a specific place – *A London Symphony* – was his last until 1953

(*Sinfonia Antartica*). Finished at the end of 1913, Vaughan Williams later said it should have been called 'Symphony by a Londoner', with an emphasis on his personal relationship with the place.[22] In this exploration of the capital city in which he lived, he leaves behind the quiet corners of rural England and enters its urban heart, with its 'noise and scurry', the bright and the dark, the passing street cry of a lavender seller, and the chiming of bells.[23]

Monday 26 October 1857

(London, sunrise, c. 7.30)[1]

It is not difficult to imagine Matilda Rennart, restless and fidgety, in her bed, at 23 Stanhope Street early on this morning.

It is dark. Even in the middle of the day the bedroom is full of shadows, the three-storey houses looming at each other across the narrow lane. In late October the sun does not rise above the roofs until mid-morning. Before dawn there is no glimmer to illuminate the foot of her brass bed, the bare floorboards or the single chair in the corner, draped with her shawl and her husband's trousers.

Matilda is Robert Eastick's sister.[2] In 1857 she was thirty-four. She left King's Lynn before her brother was born, so they did not grow up together or see each other often. Even so, on this October day, she is summoned to visit the Old Bailey to testify on his behalf.

The owner of the trousers is Prussian-born William Rennart, a tailor and trimming seller. The combination of his country of origin and his trade suggests that he was Jewish – in the second half of the nineteenth century the textile industry in London included a high number of Jewish immigrants. At first glance it is surprising to find a mid-nineteenth-century Norfolk girl from a country town living in London and married to a Prussian Jew. But this story is full of journeys away from home to find employment and stability. Matilda's own mother, Elizabeth, emigrated to England from Ireland. Robert died on a ship travelling to Ceylon. The crew of the John Sugars *contained at least one member from Austria and another from Jamaica. And as a young woman Matilda travelled to London from King's Lynn to go into service and met her husband while working there. Sound asleep in the other bedrooms are their two children, fourteen-year-old Charles and eleven-year-old Isabella, as well as a 'Gentleman's servant', Maria Morgan, from Denver, near King's Lynn.*

Stanhope Street is close to Clare Market, the second-largest meat market in London after Smithfield.[3] It lies to the north of the Strand in the parish of Westminster and at the heart of the capital. In the early eighteenth century John Strype described Stanhope Street as 'a pretty broad, well-built and inhabited Street' but he also noted pockets of poverty in small courts off the main thoroughfares.[4] Nearly two hundred years later, at the end of the nineteenth century, Charles Booth produced his innovative Maps Descriptive of London Poverty *in which each street is coloured to indicate the income and social class of its inhabitants.[5] Most of the Clare Market area is dark blue, indicating inhabitants who were 'very poor, casual [workers]' and in 'chronic want'. Stanhope Street is outlined in black: 'Lowest class. Vicious, semi-criminal'.*

William Rennart has a trade, and the household includes a maid – even though she might be a relation who receives little or no wage. This suggests that when the Rennarts were living in Stanhope Street it was in decline but had not reached the depths of poverty suggested by Booth's analysis. Everyone in the parish went to Clare Market to buy provisions. As Matilda lies in bed she hears the daily noise of the costermongers setting up their stalls, the rumbling of carts over the cobbles.

The thought of going to the Old Bailey is frightening. The court-house is a place to which her neighbours and acquaintances are often taken but from where they do not return. The occupants of Clare Market are continually pursued for pickpocketing, petty fraud, malingering and skulduggery. The law is something which descends upon them, plucks them from the street and sends them to the dark recesses of the prison cell, the transportation boat or the scaffold. She wonders whether she will ever be allowed home to her family once she is caught inside the terrible portals of that stark building.

Out of bed, she does not need light to find the familiar way to her door and along the landing towards the stairs. In the back bedroom she puts her face close to the head of her son and listens to his steady breathing. Just about the same age as Robert, and yet warm and safe in his own bed.

Downstairs in the kitchen the maid has already lit the fire and made breakfast, but Matilda is too nervous to eat. To go outside her local streets, to such a formidable place, to be connected to a violent crime – such a break in her routine is deeply unsettling. Although the Old Bailey is a world away from Matilda's day-to-day life, it is physically nearby. She wears her best and most sober dress, decorated with some of William's trimmings, and a shawl wrapped around her head and shoulders as she sets off, turning into Wych Street, a narrow dirty lane lined with ancient timber-framed buildings three and four storeys high, jetties and bow windows swaying above her. Bells chime the hour – 'oranges and lemons' – and, looking up, she sees the church of St Clement's, its pagoda-like tower poking up behind the grimy tenements. Today of all days a prayer to the patron saint of mariners would help her through the coming trial. The church stands like an exotic white-iced cake in the midst of the Strand. Inside is cool and quiet. She kneels for a few moments and thinks of her murdered brother.

The Eastick family were thrilled when Robert became a ship's apprentice. It was a turn in their fortunes after the early death of their father, which had brought them low. Their mother had started to take in laundry to make ends meet. If only Robert had done well on the voyage to Ceylon he could have earned himself a secure future, married, rented a little house back in King's Lynn, maybe helped his old mother. How sweet a life it might have been! Instead, there had been the dreadful visit from the police.

Communication between sailors and their loved ones was diffi-cult in the mid-nineteenth century. A missive could only be sent from a port or, if a homebound ship happened to pass by close enough, correspondence could be exchanged at sea. The vagaries of the weather, and frequent damage to ships en route, meant that times of arrival were impossible to predict. Families at home did not know when to expect news. Robert had learnt to write but, as he never reached his destination, his family were left for many weeks with no word from him. The John Sugars lost her rudder during the voyage out, and on arrival at the port of Galle in Ceylon on 25 October 1856 she had to be repaired before returning. It was the manager of the shipping office in London who alerted the police to

Robert's unexplained disappearance. All those months when the family imagined him visiting foreign lands, having adventures and learning his new trade, he had been rotting at the bottom of the sea.[6]

After the cool silence of the church the noise of Fleet Street is unsettling. St Paul's Cathedral towers against the sky ahead as Matilda hurries up Ludgate Street and turns into the lane called Old Bailey. The courthouse looks like a castle with two great square blocks rising either side of its bleak facade, all rusticated stone and gaunt windows. It takes about fifteen minutes to walk there from St Clement's, and the Old Bailey bells are ringing the quarter hour – 'When will you pay me?' – as she arrives. She crosses the street and disappears through the narrow door of the court's outer wall.

When Matilda is eventually called to the witness box she hopes to tell them what a fine boy Robert had been, how loved by his mother, but she is asked only to confirm a few basic facts: 'I live at No. 23 Stanhope Street, Clare Market. Robert Eastick was my brother – he was an apprentice on board the John Sugars *– he was fifteen years old. He had been once before to Sunderland on a coasting voyage.'*[7]

Old Bailey Court, London 1824

Afterwards, Doyle is brought to the dock for sentencing. Matilda stares at the face of her brother's tormentor while the judge speaks about the gravity of the case and how he hopes the present prosecution will have a salutary effect on those in command of ships. She hopes for a hanging. The judge sentences Doyle to three months in prison.

The next case concerns a nineteen-year-old boy found guilty of stealing a number of small cheques from his employer. He is sentenced to five years' penal servitude.

PART IV

ON THE ROAD

The Hebrides Connection

Barra

On the last morning of our trip to the Outer Hebrides we drove the length of South Uist, across the causeway to Eriskay, and from there caught the car ferry to the isle of Barra. The sea crossing took a little over an hour past outcrops of rock where seals basked. Barra is small, shaped rather like a turtle on the map, very unlike linear South Uist, and less watery. On Barra the road encircles a series of mountains rising at its centre.

We stopped below the highest mountain, Heabhal, where I imagine that the singer of 'Kishmul's Galley' stood, gazing seaward, watching the ship sailing. It felt right to head for the summit, a steep climb past a gleaming statue of the Virgin Mary and the Christ child. The top is a few minutes' sharp scramble further up. From there you can see the whole island set in the turquoise sea, Kisimul Castle floating in the bay like a toy. I stood next to the trig point and sang the ballad at full pelt into the wind, and then spent a minute or two thinking about my mother, and what she might have said about my quest to find this spot: '*Did* you, darling? How funny!'

After ten minutes in the cold breezes, we made our way down, and drove into Castlebay, a huddle of white and grey terraced houses facing out to sea. I asked the young woman behind the desk at the heritage centre where I might be able to find some information on 'Kishmul's Galley', with scant hope she would know what I was talking about. 'Is it this one you mean?' she said and played a rumbustious instrumental version on her phone by the Vatersay Boys, a local band. I said that it was the right tune but that I knew it as a mournful ballad. 'Round here, they play it at the end of every gig. I've known it since I was a girl.'

The song that I had nurtured all these years as a rare flower was commonplace here. I mentioned my MacIsaac connection, how my grandpa had been proud of his Scottish roots and had been president of the Burns society in Walsall. 'Och, I don't know why Burns is the national poet, he didn't even speak Gaelic,' she scoffed.

We wandered into the exhibition on the herring industry that bloomed and died here in the late nineteenth century. In the background the young woman was talking in Gaelic to someone who had come into the reception area – a bespectacled woman with straight grey hair, who came over and introduced herself as Mairi. She had received the email from the museum in South Uist and brought out a large hardback book, published by Boosey & Co. in 1909: *Songs of the Hebrides*. There was 'Kishmul's Galley', pages 80–3. The ballad had been 'adapted' into

English and given a piano accompaniment by Marjory Kennedy-Fraser, but the original Gaelic words were from a Mrs Maclean of Barra, and the air from the singing of Mary Macdonald of Mingulay – an island next to Barra. The instruction was to perform it 'with exultation'. Mairi read through the Gaelic words, and pointed out that Ruari'n Tartair, is mentioned – 'Rory the Turbulent' – one of the MacNeils who built the castle and was arrested for piracy of an English ship in the later 1500s.

My response to the sight of 'Kishmul's Galley' printed in a book was confused. The song had been passed on to me in true oral tradition – I'd never seen it written down, or heard it sung by anyone but my mother. And yet here it was, set out in a publication, with only a few small differences in the words: I sing 'no hook, nor line, anchor, tackle or cable had she' when the printed version is 'nor hoop, nor yards, anchor, cable or tackle has she' – one of those lists of unfamiliar words easily rearranged over time. There was the same tune, and even the instruction to be slower and broader where the melody changes in the third verse: 'Now at last 'gainst wind and tide, they've brought her to . . .' – although I sing 'Now at last 'gainst Kishmul's walls, they hove her to'. I wondered how the Hebridean crofters felt if they ever saw their songs written down. These words and melodies were the same as the view from the window, the smell of the peat fire, the laying of the table – part of their everyday. I had felt that 'Kishmul's Galley' belonged to the everyday of our family. To see it there on the page was unsettling, both a confirmation that in origin it is the genuine article – a Gaelic song from the Hebrides – but also an opening up to the wider world. It is not *my* song any more.

The words I learnt match the published version so closely,

Edna (née Dean) and Harry Myatt, the author's maternal grandparents.
Harry was the son of Jessie Bell MacIsaac.

there can be no doubt that it was the 1909 translation that my mother taught me, nothing earlier. It must have been popular when my English grandmother sang it at parties in Walsall. Perhaps that's when my half-Scottish grandfather fell for her – an attractive idea, but not quite what I had dreamed.

☙

Latha dhomh am Beinn a' Cheathaich, the first Gaelic line as printed in 'Kishmul's Galley', translates as 'One day on the misty mountain'. The verses that follow tell a subtly different story to the one I had grown up with.

In the Gaelic account the ship is sailing *out* to the wide ocean, not coming back to the castle in triumph.[1] We hear about the feasting and ale-drinking that has taken place in 'Cíosamul's joyful Castle' but the singer is 'afflicted' because it seems that things are not well with the ship, its cable and best rope broken, its anchor left behind. When the Revd Kenneth MacLeod came to translate the words for Marjory Kennedy-Fraser he rearranged the order of events, omitted the detail on the ship's crew (who were real members of the piratical MacNeil family) and provided a heroic and happy ending. According to one modern critic, '. . . instead of providing a Gaelic counter-balance MacLeod proved himself able to rarify the earthiest stories and out-whimsy Kennedy-Fraser herself'.[2] In a contemporary newspaper cutting, kept by Lucy Broadwood, a reviewer retorted that for MacLeod's translation to have any scientific value, ' "Kishmul's Galley" would have to be tamed down to "MacNeill's [*sic*] Boat" '.[3]

This change in the meaning was the second adjustment I had to make in my understanding of the ballad. The third was the mood and the rhythm. I was taught to sing it as a solemn ballad. The Vatersay Boys' instrumental, played to me in the Barra museum, had already shaken that idea, and then I found an online resource of Gaelic recordings from the 1930s onwards.[4] Here were several versions of 'Kishmul's Galley', listed under its Gaelic first line 'Latha Dhomh's Mi am Beinn a' Cheathaich'. All were sung by women from Barra and, in every example, it was performed as a 'waulking' song.

Waulking was a finishing process for the locally made woollen cloth known as tweed. The cloth was soaked in urine and pounded by hand on a hard surface – this fixed the dye and shrank the fibres to produce a smooth texture. Groups of women gathered together for this arduous and pungent activity. A description of a waulking session at the turn of the nineteenth century describes the 'almost weird' scene: ten big, muscular women with bare arms and coarse aprons over their gowns, sat around a table of planks in a long low house, the peat fire burning on the floor, the thick air reeking of fish, hot sheep and urine, and filled with the sound of 'deep-toned and monotonous' singing.[5]

This singing was in the form of call and response – a soloist sang a couple of lines, and then the other women responded with a refrain, usually of meaningless words: in 'Kishmul's Galley' this is the recurring 'o-*hee* a *ho*, *fal*-oo-*o*'. Each song was sustained for several minutes and a variety of subjects were introduced by other soloists, to keep up spirits and energy. The text of 'Latha Dhomh's Mi am Beinn a' Cheathaich' collected by Donald MacCormick in 1893 (he listed it as 'La dhomh's mi 'm Beinn a' Cheathaich') starts with the story of MacNeil's galley sailing, but then changes direction abruptly as the singer confesses, 'When I was a girl 'neath the sheen of my tresses / I'd not lie myself down beside any mean fellow . . .'

The real shock is the rhythm of the piece – there is a relentless emphasis on every other beat – *DA*-di-*DA*-di – necessary to keep the waulking team in time; and the women perform it twice as fast as my version. It is no longer a mournful ballad but a jaunty sing-along with the occasional spontaneous 'whoop' from the chorus. A dramatic metamorphosis had taken place on the emotional journey from Barra to Walsall.

Kennedy-Fraser collected and published these Hebridean songs in the same period as Vaughan Williams, Sharp and other Edwardian collectors in England. She, too, has been criticised for the way she 'adapted' them to suit the rarefied tastes of middle-class parlours. She even wrote a booklet entitled *Hebridean Songs and the Laws of Interpretation* in which she discusses in detail how to sing 'Kishmul's Galley':

> . . . In singing the word 'wind' keep the sound of the wind in the mind, and for the word 'tide' let the exultancy of victory, victory over great odds, be the key to the situation; and on the open vowel ah of the diphthong ah-ee in 'tide' let this exultancy come through . . .[6]

This is the description of a different species of song to the pounding 'Latha Dhomh's Mi am Beinn a' Cheathaich' sung by the Barra women, who were not inclined to inject colour, experiment with phrasing, or think about how they sang the open vowel 'ah'. Kennedy-Fraser is no longer describing a folk song.

Despite this, since it was written down over a century ago, 'Kishmul's Galley' has taken on a life of its own. In 1913 the composer Granville Bantock used the air as a theme in his Hebridean symphony. The Scottish folk band, the Corries, can be seen performing it on YouTube in full folk mode during a 1983 television appearance. The Vatersay Boys play it as a rock anthem with bagpipes. The piece has achieved a kind of authenticity. Steve Roud, creator of the Roud Folk Song Index, emphasises the importance of a folk song's journey: 'It is not the origin of a song that makes it folk but the transmission within the folk tradition which makes it so . . . Folk songs are not necessarily very old, but they must have been around long enough to become part of this traditional transmission (two generations might be an acceptable rule of thumb).'[7]

'Kishmul's Galley' was not handed down to me by a MacIsaac –
there was no perfect drawing together of my threads. The version
I inherited is not the ancient ballad I hoped it was, but it has
been sung within the family circle for over one hundred years.
Without knowing it, we participated in this 'traditional transmission', the oral passing on of a treasured song from generation
to generation. When I sing it, I reflect the Edwardian mood, the
phrasing, and the slight variants that I learnt at home. It has
the power of time-travel, this connection through the breath of
our voices: my grandma, my mother, me.

One of Life's Free Pleasures

Performance

'Bushes and Briars' #1

In December 1903 Ralph Vaughan Williams meets Mr Potiphar in the village of Ingrave, Essex, and experiences an epiphany.

Nine years later, the composer gave a talk on English folk song in which he described this moment: 'I was invited to a tea-party given to the old people of a village in Essex, only twenty miles from London; after tea we asked if any of them knew any of the old songs, whereupon an old man, a shepherd, began to sing a song which set all my doubts about folk-song at rest. The song which he sang was "Bushes and Briars".'[1]

We can picture Mr Potiphar, a weather-beaten old man, wearing his traditional shepherd's smock, singing 'Bushes and Briars' in the full-throated country way while the guests in the rectory parlour listen, and then murmur their approval when he falls silent.

'Bushes and Briars' #2

In December 1903 Ralph Vaughan Williams meets Mr Potiphar in the village of Ingrave, Essex, and experiences an epiphany.

The composer was attending a tea party organised by the vicar's middle-aged daughters, the Misses Heatley. Earlier that year the two women had attended a series of lectures on folk song which he gave at nearby Brentwood. At this point in his career he was fond of the folk songs he had learnt from books, but was not fully convinced of their value: his 'faith was not yet active'.[2] Despite this, he inspired Georgiana Heatley (also known as Locksie) to collect together detailed information about singers in the area, with lists of the songs they could sing, and directions on where to find them.[3] She passed these on to the composer and asked him to the tea party to be held on 3 December. Although Vaughan Williams was 'shy of a Parish Tea' he accepted the invitation.[4]

It is an iron-grey winter's afternoon when the village guests take the short walk along the lane to the rectory, dressed in their best Sunday clothes and wrapped up against the cold. Amongst them are Mrs Humphreys, who knows songs her grandparents sang in the late eighteenth century; Mrs Turner, mother of a maid at the rectory; and Charles Potiphar, a retired labourer of seventy-four. As they make their way along the rutted track, they discuss how peculiar it is that Miss Locksie has suddenly become interested in their old ditties.

They are led into a room where there is a good fire alight to warm their toes. Although the guests have known the Heatley sisters since they were babies, they do not know the tall young gentleman standing by the mantelpiece. Miss Locksie introduces him as Dr Vaughan Williams and says he is very interested to hear some of their old country songs. The villagers begin to feel uneasy. Tea at the rectory is a rarity for the likes of them, who have laboured in the fields all their lives or worked in the kitchens of such houses. They expect the occasion to be formal – a little polite chatter about their health and the weather. Some of them look down into their laps, others exchange glances. They all know that the songs they sing at home, or in the pub, or at the old harvest suppers, are not suitable for a rectory parlour in front of two spinsters. The story about their father, the vicar, is well known in the village – how he made his daughters promise not to marry, after his wife died giving birth to a ninth child.[5] None of them can think of a ditty suitable for the ears of these innocent old maids. Mr Potiphar speaks for all of them when he says he can't sing at this sort of party, but if Mr Vaughan Williams would like to visit him next day, he would be delighted to sing to him then.[6] In their well-meaning enthusiasm the sisters have overlooked the complications of class and propriety. The poor of the parish can only assert themselves by remaining silent – it turns out to be an awkward little gathering.

Vaughan Williams stays on until the next day when he visits Mr Potiphar at his cottage in the village. The first song the old man sings is 'Bushes and Briars', with a melody Vaughan Williams recognises as universal; he felt it was 'something he had known all his life'.[7]

'Bushes and Briars' #3

In December 1903 Ralph Vaughan Williams meets Mr Potiphar in the village of Ingrave, Essex, and experiences an epiphany.

When the composer jotted down the 'Bushes and Briars' tune, he described Mr Potiphar as a labourer – not a shepherd.[8] The same note shows that he recorded the song on 4 December, the day after the tea party, when he also collected material from other village residents.

This fits with the story from his biography. But in 1905 – only two years after the party – he published a song called 'The Cruel Father and the Affectionate Lover', with a note that it was collected from Mr Potiphar, 'shepherd', on 3 December, which *was* the day of the party.[9] Did Mr Potiphar sing in front of the spinster sisters after all?

In the years immediately after hearing 'Bushes and Briars', Vaughan Williams's account of its discovery acquired a romantic gloss – a shepherd is more bucolic than a labourer, a

Vaughan Williams's manuscript of 'Bushes and Briars'

performance at a tea party more dramatic than a quiet meeting in a cottage, and 'Bushes and Briars' the better tune. The first version is the story of the party unfolding in the way Vaughan Williams and the Heatley sisters had hoped it would. The third version is the beginning of the story being spun. Version two, the story told by Ursula in her husband's biography, is probably the truth, remembered under the stark north light of old age.

⌢

By the evening of 4 December 1903 Vaughan Williams's life was set on a new course. While he sat with the country people at Ingrave, and heard them sing in their homes, he experienced a supernatural thrill – as if he had stepped through an invisible veil and entered a liminal world: 'I am like a psychical researcher who has actually seen a ghost, for I have been among the more primitive people of England.'[10] Within days he contacted Henry Burstow (a well-known singer from whom Lucy Broadwood had previously collected), and brought the old man the ten-mile journey from Horsham to Leith Hill Place. There, on 7 December Burstow sang at least eight songs to Vaughan Williams, some of which he recorded with a phonograph.[11] Burstow remembered, 'I was amazed beyond expression to hear my own songs thus repeated in my own voice.'[12]

At this stage Vaughan Williams was learning the skill of noting by ear. Along the top of the manuscript page for 'The Storm', sung by Potiphar on 4 December, he wrote, 'I doubt if I have this down right.' Although classically trained and able to recognise intervals between notes, and note values in a conventional setting, it was a different thing altogether to take down melodies which travelled in unexpected directions, varied in rhythm from one line – or one bar – to the next, were set in unfamiliar modal scales, and sung by people whose voices were affected by age and illness. Throughout his career he continued to note 'doubtful' after encountering a more than usually difficult performance. Broadwood may have suggested practising with a confident singer like Burstow with phonographic recordings as backup.

A few weeks later, while staying at Leith Hill Place over Christmas, he set off on his bike 'equipped with notebook and pencil' to find songs 'almost at his own doorstep', from Isaac Longhurst and Henry Garman – both locals, who were easy to contact and who knew Vaughan Williams from 'the big house'.[13] In fact, Mr Garman was another Broadwood connection: he had previously sung to her uncle.[14]

After this there was barely a month in 1904 when Vaughan Williams did not collect material from somewhere. Usually, a trip began with a contact from his own class – local gentry, a clergyman, or another collector – who introduced him to rural working people he would have found difficult to locate or approach.[15] Once this intermediary had breached the social barrier, Vaughan Williams could tap into a community of singers who then recommended each other. This was the pattern at Ingrave and was repeated in King's Lynn. Networking like this reduced effort wasted on people who knew few interesting songs or sang badly.

Having found a good source, like a bee to a flower he visited again and again to ensure he had taken up all the nectar – and so he returned to the Ingrave area for a day in February 1904, and then for almost a fortnight in April, when he cycled from village to village, assisted by Georgiana Heatley's directions, to revisit known singers and new contacts.[16] Some he found at home, some in local pubs, and one man in the workhouse.[17] These institutions for the old, sick and impoverished could have been designed with the folk-song collector in mind – they offered him meetings, mediated by members of staff, with groups of elderly people gathered in one place who could potentially offer material from the early nineteenth century and beyond. Workhouses became a regular destination. He recalled that the workhouse residents 'were delighted to sing to him and to find a visitor interested in the music they loved and which belonged to their happier times'.[18] He also returned to Leith Hill and its vicinity, taking down songs from more local people – Mrs Berry of Leith Hill Farm, Mr Ansfield the gamekeeper, and Mrs Harriet Verrall at Monk's Gate, near Horsham.[19] Over the coming years he revisited Mrs Verrall, her husband (who was also a singer), and Henry Burstow, knowing they always had something new to offer – he gathered over eighty songs from these three alone.[20]

During the summer months of 1904, while on holiday at Cookham Dean, the North York Moors and Salisbury, Vaughan Williams ventured into pubs and local workhouses, and he continued these more impromptu forays in the following years. Occasionally, encounters were fleeting – at Sheringham, a 'B. Jackson' sang him 'Come Nancy, Will You Marry Me' at the level crossing. But his most fruitful collecting trips were usually planned and accompanied – by Revd Huddle in King's

Lynn; Ella Leather in Herefordshire; and on Norfolk/Suffolk trips by Ivor Gatty (1908)[21] and George Butterworth (1910 and 1911). With these last two men a good number of the songs were collected in pubs. Like most of us, Vaughan Williams found entering an unfamiliar inn easier when he had a friend in tow.

⌒

Singing was for entertainment and for solace. In 1787 Thomas Wilkinson, travelling near Loch Lomond at a time when tourism was still rare, 'passed a female who was reaping alone: she sung in Erse [a Scottish variant of the Gaelic language] as she bended over her sickle; the sweetest human voice I ever heard: her strains were tenderly melancholy, and felt delicious, long after they were heard no more'. On reading Wilkinson's manuscript Wordsworth was moved to write 'The Solitary Reaper':

> Behold her, single in the field,
> Yon solitary Highland Lass!
> Reaping and singing by herself;
> Stop here, or gently pass![22]

In his essay on 'Making Your Own Music' Vaughan Williams uses the figure of the singing solitary reaper as an example of self-expression – she performed for herself alone.[23] Singing lightened the long hours of arduous labour. James Knights, born near Woodbridge, Suffolk, in 1880, recalled, 'When I used to be following the plough all day long, I used to be singing all day long. I've heard 'em say this – "Know where you've been aploughing today, I know the field you've been in." '[24] Harry Cox, born in 1885, and a celebrated Norfolk singer (it was he who gave the version of 'The Captain's Apprentice' to Ernest Moeran in 1921), said he used to sing all day long to amuse himself when working on the farm.[25] Mont Abbot, growing up in rural Oxfordshire before the First World War, remembered, 'How welcome all they songs be that sweetened my harsh work all they years out in the fields, warming my frozen fingers and toes and making the long drudging hours to pass much more quickly.' His father also sang while making shoes outside his workshop: 'You often heerd a man a-singing at his work in they days; singing was one of life's free pleasures. A man 'ud sing out unabashed as he strode down the village street. If thee was to sing out like that down Enstone nowadays they'd think thee'd just come out of the Bell and lock 'ee up in Oxford Castle.'[26] If you have no device on which to play music how else can you hear your favourite tune, unless you sing it out?

Singing also went on in the home. Walter Pardon, born at the outset of the First World War in north-east Norfolk, knew more than a hundred and eighty ballads but rarely sang in public – they were learnt from relatives and performed in the house, only revealed to the wider world in the folk revival of the 1970s.[27] Cyril Poacher from Blaxhall in Suffolk started to learn his repertoire sitting on the knee of his grandfather, who had 'a stone jug of beer, and he used to give Cyril a swig and a puff of his pipe and he used to sing the old songs to him . . .'[28] Duggie Carter's granddaughter remembered Sunday evenings when the family were together and her grandfather would sing 'The Captain's Apprentice' and another old favourite, 'The Dark-Eyed Sailor'.[29] This was unselfconscious singing, very unlike the solo performances required by collectors. Sharp observed that during the 'invariable ritual' of such formal occasions the singer usually kept their 'eyes closed, their head upraised, and a rigid expression of countenance maintained' until the final verse. Then they relaxed and repeated in their ordinary voice the last line of the song or its title.[30] Vaughan Williams noted the 'personal detachment' of traditional singers as well as 'the tightly shut eyes' which he thought was not a sign of 'mystical exultation' but the 'effort of memory'.[31] It was the 'impersonal' aspect of traditional performance which made him adamant that classically trained musicians should not attempt to dramatise folk songs: '. . . a fine ballad tune only begins to show its quality when it has been repeated several times . . . this cumulative effect must obviously be lost if the tune be cut up by continued pauses, rallentandos and "dramatic" ejaculations'.[32]

Vaughan Williams's prime interest was in the melodies, but this did not prevent him from identifying the importance of words in performance, placing 'clearness of diction' in front of 'perfection of melodic outline and beauty of phrasing' in his list of requirements.[33] Between 1974 and 1976 Ginette Dunn interviewed a group of singers from Snape and Blaxhall in Suffolk, mostly born between the 1880s and the 1920s, who were able to provide insights into this question of what made a successful performance. The most frequent reply was someone who sings 'clear' so that the words could be understood: Frank Reeve reported that Ben Ling, born 1891, would 'stand very erect when he sang and you could always hear every word that he said'; for James Knights a good singer 'should pronounce every word distinct' so that anybody 'down at the bottom of the yard, can hear you and understand it'. For these singers, who were also members of the audience, the words were the most important part: Bob Hart, aged eighty-two, said, 'I listen to every word, and that's why I don't like, you know, this 'ere guitar, in't it . . . well, that's not singing if you can't understand what they say.'[34]

Some of the singers Dunn interviewed in the 1970s are present in a glorious film of an evening in 1955 at the Ship, Blaxhall.[35] The main bar of the pub is packed with men and some women, squeezed together on high-backed benches, or leaning on the wall, or clustered around small tables, sipping beer and smoking pipes and cigarettes. The men wear flat caps and jackets and most look over fifty. The film opens with a rendition of 'Good Luck to the Barley Mow' led by Arthur Smith, pint in one hand, his lapel held in the other, his expression concentrated as he recites the growing list of drink measures to which he wishes good luck, including the barrel, half barrel, gallon, half gallon, quart pint, half pint, nipperkin and brown bowl: while the crowd join in with the repeated chorus, 'Good luck, good luck, good luck to the barley mow!' The proceedings are led by 'Wickets' Richardson who calls, 'Order, please, ladies and gentlemen,' before inviting Cyril Poacher to sing, 'What few nuts that poor girl had, she threw them all away' ('The Nutting Girl'). This bawdy song tells of a girl gathering nuts in the wood, who is so mesmerised by the beautiful singing of a 'brisk young farmer' as he sits on his plough – another example of a worker entertaining himself out in the fields – that she lies down with him under the shady broom, saying, 'Young man, I think I feel the world go round and round.' One of the younger men there – he was forty-five at the time – Poacher stands up, hands in pockets, with a nonchalant 'Hare go, 'en' ('Here goes, then'). A melodeon provides the first note. He looks into the half-distance, concentrating on the words, but occasionally looking at his neighbours for affirmation, and they call back in response:

'It's of this fair young damsel was nutting in the wood.'
'*In the wood!*'
'His voice was so melodious it charmed her as she stood.'
'*As she stood!*'
'She could no longer stay and what few nuts she had, poor girl,
She threw them all away.'

Everyone joins in the chorus with gusto, some miming the action of throwing away the nuts:

'*With my fal-lal to my ral-tal-lal
Whack-fol-the-dear-ol-day
And what few nuts that poor girl had
She threw them all away.*'

By the final verse he is in full throttle, almost shouting the last lines, with a laugh in his eyes:

'For if you should stay too late to hear this ploughboy sing,
You might have a young farmer to nurse up in the spring.'

After this, Wickets Richardson sings 'Fagan the Cobbler', seated, while miming cobbling actions – again, everyone joins in with the chorus. Bob Scarce strikes a more serious tone as he stands up to sing 'General Wolfe' which commemorates the British taking of

Bob Scarce and 'Wickets' Richardson singing in the Ship, Blaxhall

Quebec in 1759 at which Wolfe was killed. With two world wars still fresh in the memory, the song retained its relevance. Getting on for seventy, Scarce has a strong voice, but he holds his body still and his face expressionless, as if the ballad is emanating from him like a spirit. The crowd repeats the last lines of each verse while he draws on his cigarette, preparing for the next one.

'Be a soldier's friend, my boys, be a soldier's friend, my boys
And the boys they will fight, fight for evermore.'

In *Lark Rise to Candleford* Flora Thompson describes an evening in the Wagon and Horses in the Oxfordshire village where she grew up in the 1880s. A session usually started with the 'boy-chaps', the unmarried younger men, who sang novel songs of the day such as 'Two Lovely Black Eyes'.[36] The older men followed these with mournful ballads of 'thwarted lovers, children

buried in snowdrifts, dead maidens and motherless homes' – but
were interrupted by more uplifting old favourites such as 'The
Barley Mow' (as sung in the Ship) before the cry went up, 'Let's
give the old 'uns a turn.' And then Master Price rose from his
corner of the settle, 'using the stick he called his "third leg" to
support his bent figure', as he launched into 'Lord Lovell'. There
is a mix of bawdy lyrics, choruses to join in with, and elderly
men performing old standards that had become 'their' songs. It
sounds very like the evening in the Blaxhall Ship seventy years
later.

Some families developed reputations as singing families – such
as the Hurrs in Southwold, the Lings in Blaxhall or the famous
Copper family of Rottingdean. Children from such families
grew up – like Poacher and Pardon – imbibing the repertoire of
their parents and grandparents and other relatives. Georgiana
Heatley, the Ingrave vicar's daughter, wrote to Vaughan Williams that in her village it appeared that songs were 'looked upon
as personal property or at least are sung only by individual [*sic*]
or a family perhaps'.[37] Once family members were of working
age – whether on farms or at sea – and were old enough to go to
the pub, their knowledge widened through listening to other
performers, memorising words and joining in the choruses. If
considered good enough they gradually established themselves
as soloists and became associated with certain songs. By the time
they grew old these were regarded as 'their' songs, which other
members of the pub audience did not perform.

Duggie Carter's rendition of 'The Captain's Apprentice' is
likely to have developed along this trajectory: if the death of
Robert Eastick was the cause of the song's popularity in the

town, Carter's father, who was also a fisherman, would have heard it in the pub and brought it home, or crew members might have sung it on the boat out on the Wash. Each verse was sung by a lead voice before the rest of the group responded with the last two lines – Carter repeated them when he sang the song to Vaughan Williams. The gruesome lyrics and their association with Eastick's death remained vivid in Carter's mind and he took the song into his repertoire. Many years after Duggie Carter died, when his daughter, Lottie, was asked if she recalled his singing, it was 'The Captain's Apprentice' that had stuck in her mind.[38]

Exchange was No Robbery

Late in 1904 Vaughan Williams was working at home in Barton Street, Westminster, when he was interrupted by an unexpected call at the door. Mr Dearmer, 'a parson who invited tramps to sleep in his drawing room', had come to ask the composer to be the music editor for a new hymn book.[1] Although Vaughan Williams was an atheist at the time (he later became more agnostic) he decided to accept the role, which he anticipated would take two months to complete, but took two years. He saw that it was an opportunity to introduce 'the finest hymn tunes of the world' to church congregations across the country.[2] In his previous job as organist at St Barnabas church in South Lambeth (1895–9) he had come to the conclusion that for many people 'the music the Church gave them each week was the only music in their lives and that it was all too often unworthy both of their faith and of music itself'.[3]

The meeting with Dearmer came towards the end of Vaughan Williams's first twelve months of folk-song collecting. Acceptance of the editorship provided him with the opportunity to 'give [folk songs] back to the world': this rich source of material went straight into the new hymn book. [4] In December 1904, soon after the hymnal's commission, he collected Harriet Verrall's melody for 'Our Captain Calls', which he matched with Dearmer's adaptation of John Bunyan's 'Pilgrim's Hymn' to create 'He Who Would Valiant Be'. The air of Joe Anderson's song 'Young Henry the Poacher', noted down a couple of weeks later, was named 'King's Lynn' and matched with the words of G. K. Chesterton's 'O God of Earth and Altar'.

The chance of finding potential hymn tunes must have added piquancy to the composer's early collecting forays – over thirty 'English Traditional' airs were used in the first edition published in 1906. [5] Words and melodies from many sources (including Wagner, traditional tunes from other countries and Tudor music) were mixed and matched by Vaughan Williams in much the same way as folk singers manipulated their material. Usually, he was able to pair existing tunes and words but if he found a beautiful tune for which no words were available, he asked someone to write them. If a set of chosen words did not fit any known air, he commissioned one of his friends, such as Holst or Nicholas Gatty, to produce something appropriate. Occasionally, he composed the melody himself: in a touching tribute to Ralph Wedgwood, he set the words of 'God be with you till we meet again' to a tune he named 'Randolph' – the nickname of his cousin. The singers of the traditional airs, such as Anderson and Verrall, were not credited, as they were performers rather than composers of the songs. Collectors were aware of the grey area between these two roles – the embellishments, variations and inventions of experienced singers could turn a common-place tune into what Vaughan Williams would describe as a 'good' version – but there was no room for these individual contributions to be acknowledged. For him it was clear that the transaction was the other way round: in the *English Hymnal* he was returning folk music to the nation.

It is easy to see why Vaughan Williams was reluctant to reveal the names of the folk songs used for some of these settings. The de-coupling of earthy words from their tunes did not always erase the connection in the ears of the audience. For some critics, pairings such as Longfellow's words – ''Tis winter now; the fallen snow / Has left the heav'ns all coldly clear / Thro' leafless boughs the sharp winds blow / And all the earth lies dead and drear' – with a secular melody once sung to 'A brisk young farmer courted me / He stole away my liberty / He stole my heart with my free good will / I must confess I love him still' were incongruous, even indecent, akin to hearing a psalm sung to the tune of a rugby song. Vaughan Williams remained bullish about mixing secular and religious music; on the fiftieth anniversary of the book's initial publication he wrote, 'I have been blamed for using adaptations of folk tunes for hymn purposes but this is surely an age-old custom', and he repeated the well-known remark sometimes attributed to John Wesley that 'he did not see why the Devil should have all the pretty tunes'.[6] As always, his attention was on the music – a fine melody held its own 'moral atmosphere' and bad tunes were 'positively harmful to those who sing and hear them'.[7] It was the musical soul of the congregation that he aimed to save.

The adoption of the *English Hymnal* in churches across the land meant that folk melody became part of the week-to-week life of churchgoers, at a time when attendance was still relatively high.[8] Some hymns are so familiar now it is difficult to believe they are not part of an ancient tradition. Perhaps the best known is 'O Little Town of Bethlehem', the setting of a nineteenth-century American poem to one of the tunes Vaughan Williams collected from Mr Garman near Leith Hill Place during the Christmas holidays of 1903. It accompanied the lyrics of 'The Ploughboy's Dream': 'I am a ploughboy stout and strong as ever drove a team'.

Initially worried that this two-year-long project took him away from original composition he later realised that 'close association with some of the best . . . tunes in the world was a better musical education than any amount of sonatas and fugues'.[9]

⌒

In an impassioned speech at the inaugural meeting of the Folk-Song Society, its vice-president, Hubert Parry, described popular music as the 'repulsive and insidious' enemy that would drive out folk music unless something were done. The chairman, Sir Alexander Mackenzie, changed the tone somewhat in his closing speech: 'We musicians like to rob the fruits of the amateurs and make use of the tunes they pick up: we can always use them in our so-called original music.'[10] Did other composers in the room shift uneasily in their seats?

The accusation of stealing folk songs was a concern for collectors. Conscious of this, Charles Marson, who worked alongside Sharp, wrote in the preface to *Songs from Somerset* (1904), 'We do not rob the poor man when we take his song. It is not like buying away his ancestral chest or his grandmother's tea-pot. Rather we enrich him by making him more conscious that he owns treasures.'[11] When Sharp gave Louise Hooper a book of songs, after recording her own repertoire, he remarked, 'Exchange was no robbery.'[12] But when he writes that he is trying 'to run to earth' a singer called William Shelton and will move on as soon as he has 'caught him and emptied him',[13] there is something vampirish about his appetite – I imagine Shelton left by the side of the road, a bloodless zombie, as Sharp rushes on to sink his teeth into the next victim. The people engaged in these encounters were not necessarily blind to the inequality of the transaction. While Sharp was taking notes from a singer in her wash-house, a neighbour came in and remarked, 'You be going to make a deal o' money out 'o this, sir?'[14]

In their reminiscences, collectors speak of rewarding singers with drinks or tobacco or sometimes a ten-shilling note, but the performers were not formally paid or credited for the songs they contributed whereas, once they were published, the collectors received fees for reproduction and performance rights. Vaughan Williams was adamant that this was just: 'In my opinion, both legally and morally the transcriber of a folk-song or dance ought to be treated as if he were the original author of it.'[15] He argued that these 'transcribers' had made possible a revival in folk music through their skills and insights and that their copies, transcripts and versions of the original material were distinct from the 'original, traditional stuff'.[16] None of them made a fortune out of publishing folk songs. Even so, the lack of financial reward to the singers, who were usually poor, from the collectors, who were well off, is questionable at best. Some of them sang many songs over several sessions, wrote down words, and helped with contacting other singers, while continuing to work or while running overcrowded households with straitened income. In such circumstances, when no fee was offered, it might be expected that the collector would make the effort to note the singer's name and occupation correctly – something Vaughan Williams did not always do well.

There are other forms of stealing. In arranging and orchestrating the songs for the parlour and concert hall the words were frequently edited or entirely rewritten to suit polite tastes. Lyrics sung from the point of view of the sailor or the farmer's daughter were performed as art songs in conventionally trained soprano/alto/tenor/bass voices by people who had no inkling of the lives described. Percy Grainger disliked this approach: 'The greatest crime against folksong is to "middle-class" it – to sing it with a "white collar" voice production and other townified suggestions.'[17] The roughness of tone, raw emotion and idiosyncrasies of individual folk performers were squeezed out to create sanitised, reproducible standards. Vaughan Williams understood this: 'Our traditional melodies are, I am aware, no longer traditional . . . they have in fact been stereotyped.'[18] He felt that the 'art of the folk-singer' was dead (he was writing in the early 1930s) but that folk song had now taken its place 'side by side with the classical songs of Schubert, the drawing-room ballad and the music hall song'. For him this was part of the evolutionary process and he had few regrets.

A Great Fancy for the Old-Fashioned Songs

Collection

Here will I sit and wait
While to my ear from uplands far away
The bleating of the folded flocks is borne
With distant cries of reapers in the corn –
All the live murmur of a summer's day.

'The Scholar Gipsy', Matthew Arnold[1]

Vaughan Williams cycles into a rural village in the spring of 1904, pausing at one of those triangular patches of green where three roads converge, a couple of cottages at the corners, one or two more strung along the dusty track. What do his finely tuned ears hear? Birdsong – a constant twittering in the hedgerows and callings from wood copses – sheep bleating, cows hooting, the rhythmic thud of horses' hooves pulling carts along unmade roads, the distant whistle of a steam train, and voices: in fields, men holler at horses and cattle, women murmur together as they hang out the washing, dig the vegetables, call to their children through open windows, and greet each other in the lanes. No aeroplanes overhead, no rumble of cars on a bypass, no grind and beep of reversing agricultural machinery, buzz of chainsaw or drone of lawnmower – and no music, not from an open window, or a passing car or escaping from the headphones of a jogger. If he pedals down the road to the pub and steps inside for a pint, there will be no soundtrack; in the shop where he buys chocolate, no radio.

Compared to modern times, the palette of musical sounds to which country people were accustomed was quite limited. They heard local singing and whistling: a Suffolk farmworker recalled, 'The boys used to whistle – you don't see the boys go whistling about now – they were always awhistling tunes.'[2] At dances there might be a fiddle or melodeon; at church the organ or harmonium, choir and bells; the occasional brass band at a fete or travelling fair; a piano in the schoolhouse or the pub. In Mont Abbot's village the daughter of the pub landlord ordered sheet music by post for new songs to play on the piano: ' "Mary's got the latest!" 'ud travel like pop-fever round the village, and that same night a fair crowd would gather around the piano in the smoke room . . .'[3] Scarcity made music a precious commodity.

The phonograph's ability to record sound, in a form that could be listened to multiple times, was the start of a radical change in the range of sounds available to our ears. Invented in the late 1870s and more widely available by the early twentieth century, they were used occasionally by most folk-song collectors and at least two were purchased by the Folk-Song Society for use by its active members – at its inaugural meeting Hubert

Parry identified the machines as the only way to take down material with absolute accuracy.[4] Percy Grainger, an early adopter, set out the advantages of mechanical recording in the 1908 *Journal of the Folk-Song Society*. He was particularly concerned with capturing individual performances, which could not be reproduced by pen on paper – a difficulty Vaughan Williams acknowledged after hearing Mr Potiphar perform 'Bushes and Briars': 'It is impossible to reproduce the free rhythm and subtle *portamento* effects of this beautiful tune in ordinary notation . . .'[5] A record of detailed differences in singing styles, breath control, pronunciation, rhythmic sense and dynamics became possible with the phonograph. In the *Journal* Grainger provides potted biographies of three Lincolnshire singers and describes their performances in an attempt to convey how the music is infused by 'the charm of their sweet, pure, quaint, breezy, lovable personalities'.[6] Joseph Taylor has 'effortless high notes, sturdy rhythms, clean unmistakeable intervals and . . . twiddles and "bleating" ornaments'; George Gouldthorpe breathes 'a spirit of almost caressing tenderness into all he does, says or sings'; while George Wray uses 'means of all kinds of swift touches of swagger, heaps of added meaningless syllables, queer, hollow vowel-sounds (doubtless owing to his lack of teeth) and a jovial, jogging persistency'. Grainger's attention to the individuality of these singers shows that it was not inevitable for a collector's relationship with performers to be aloof, although a patronising tone seems to have been unavoidable.

There were further practical benefits to the phonograph. It enabled singers to perform a whole song without interruption by a harassed note-taker trying to recognise a particular phrase or interval; and they only needed to sing it once, enabling more songs to be captured before the singers were exhausted. Once recorded onto a wax cylinder, a song could be listened to at will by a collector, who could reduce the speed of rotation so that ornaments and 'twiddles' could be analysed note by note. Grainger was conscious that 'one is so distressingly liable to think one hears what one is expecting to hear' – for example, a flattened seventh. The phonograph provided the means for careful analysis.

Despite these advantages, the phonograph was not used as standard. Grainger's presentation of his transcribed material usually included a full set of all verses as they were sung (not just a standardised first verse) with each change and development in the melody meticulously documented. This could include multiple time-signatures, ornamentation and key changes. Prominent collectors within the Folk-Song Society believed that this amount of detail obscured the core melody and made performance impossible. Sharp wrote that many of the notes Grainger transcribed would not be audible to normal hearing, and that the ordinary collector would correctly ignore them – he wanted to find the 'characteristic' tune separated from the variants and 'twiddles'.[7] Sharp was evangelical about introducing folk song into schools 'to effect an improvement in the musical taste of the people, and to refine and strengthen the national character'.[8] He was after 'ditties' that were 'natural, pure and simple', the kind of material that could be adopted in schools to engender in each child a knowledge and understanding of 'their country and countrymen'; tunes that would 'purge' town and country of 'coarse' music hall songs as a way of 'civilizing the masses'.[9] This could not be achieved by Grainger's complex and technical representations. He was absorbed by the detail of each individual performance while Sharp was fixated on the general sense of the song. Although other members of the Folk-Song Society believed their methods were scientific, they did not fully grasp the value of phonographic cylinders (if recorded and conserved properly) as objective evidence – raw data in modern parlance – that could be freely available for analysis and adaptation by future generations. In understanding this, Grainger was percipient.

There were obvious practical drawbacks which prevented the frequent use of the phonograph. It was heavy and unwieldy – the whole kit consisted of a wooden box with a recording cylinder on top, which weighed about ten pounds (four and a half kilograms), plus detachable recording and playback horns and a supply of wax cylinders, each of which could only record about two and a half minutes of material, and was easily broken.[10] As a result it was usually simpler to bring singers to a place where the machine was set up – Grainger recorded much of his material at the house of his friend Lady Elwes, in Lincolnshire. Although he felt that singers were not unduly disturbed by a visit to the big house or by singing into a recording horn this kind of setting surely influenced who was invited – would Gypsies have been regulars? – and what material they chose to sing. Even when set up in a suitable room the sound produced in these early recordings was often distorted or faint.

Vaughan Williams used the phonograph for specific reasons – when he was practising notation early on; occasionally to make an archive recording of particularly valued singers (such as Verrall and Burstow); on trips with Butterworth (they were on bikes so perhaps they hired the machine locally); and, in particular, to support Ella Leather with her research in Herefordshire.[11] Leather had access to local singers but was unable to note tunes by ear so she sent her recordings on to Vaughan Williams for him to transcribe. This successful partnership produced, amongst other things, a collection of Herefordshire carols, published in the *Journal* for 1910. But, as a rule, the phonograph was too cumbersome and did not fit with his desire for spontaneity: attaching the whole kit safely to a bicycle was well-nigh impossible. A notebook and pencil in his rucksack, and the company of a friend on two wheels, remained his preferred method.

⌢

It is a brilliantly starry night, frosty and still. The light of a half-moon stripes the lake's surface, silhouettes the straggling bushes and stunted trees. No breeze laps the water or rattles the reeds.[12]

Three men emerge from the wood. Two of them are pushing bicycles, the third leads them to a rowing boat moored on the bank. He climbs in while one of his companions, slight and athletic, grapples with the bicycles, lifting and dropping them into the bottom of the vessel before stepping nimbly into the boat. The third man follows, arranging his long legs awkwardly around the handlebars and pedals. The skipper takes up the oars and a swift jab at the bank sets them gliding across the black-and-silver water. His passengers listen to the splash of the blades slicing the lake surface, the rhythmic creaking of the rowlocks. They dream of warm beds and congratulate themselves on this short-cut adventure across the Broad. The skipper lifts an oar momentarily and points. 'See them lights? – Southwold.' He rows on. The men notice a change in the rhythm, it falters, speeds up, slows down.

They see the lights again. The oar is raised. 'See them lights? – Lowestoft.' The oars splash back into the water but the rhythm is slower, it decreases, it stops. 'See them lights?' he says drowsily. The two passengers exchange glances. 'I tell you what, old man, why don't we take over for a bit.'

There is a precarious dance as the three men rearrange themselves in the unsteady vessel, the skipper finally slumped in a drunken stupor at the front, the others squeezed together in the middle, an oar each. They row towards the bank, keeping close to the water's edge until at last a jetty emerges from the reeds. While the boatman snores they tie the boat securely to the moorings, lift out the bicycles, and pedal away as fast as they can across the marsh.

Vaughan Williams's account of this escapade with George Butterworth while on a collecting trip in Norfolk includes all the elements you might look for in an episode from *Three Men in a Boat* – extended carousing in a pub; slapstick shenanigans between men, bikes and boats; and confused communications with an amusing, drunken rustic. Although some sort of rowing trip took place, the yarn became stretched and tangled over the years. In Ursula's retelling the incident happened in Norfolk in December 1911 but Southwold and Lowestoft are in Suffolk. The two men did briefly visit Southwold that year on their way back from a trip near Diss in south Norfolk – but neither place is near the Broads. In the previous year, the pair had visited Southwold for a few days where they collected several songs from the Hurr family, before going north into Norfolk to revisit Mr Locke of Rollesby, who they knew had some good material. Rollesby is next to a Broad, and if the men had visited the Fox and Hounds at Filby to hear another singer, Mr Goble, there might have been a reason for taking a short cut across the water – although perhaps you would only agree to it if you were drunk. Only if you were very drunk would the lights of Southwold and Lowestoft in Suffolk be visible from a Broad in Norfolk. It looks as though these 'arduous and hilarious expeditions' from a care-free pre-war age were conflated in Vaughan Williams's memory.[13] I can hear the composer telling the tale to Ursula with laughter and tears, as he remembered his dear friend Butterworth, who did not return from the trenches.

⌒

Although Vaughan Williams told a few stories about collecting moments that made the hair stand up on the back of his neck, or made him laugh, he wrote little about his day-to-day methods. Cecil Sharp is more forthcoming. While he used the same tech-niques as Vaughan Williams and other collectors – local contacts, recommendations from singers, and visits to workhouses – he was bolder than his friend, driven by a zeal for the cause of folk-song salvation and promotion that left no room for diffidence or self-consciousness. He was happy to walk into a pub on his own and engage a crowd of drinkers. He describes how he would find a village inn where a dozen men and women might be found at midday, order milk and biscuits, and then engage the group in a 'mild argument' about the comparative merits of milk and cider.[14] Then he would introduce his interest in singing: '. . . I have a great fancy for the old-fashioned songs. Perhaps you can tell me of a singer I could get one or two from.' After some toing and froing and the purchase of more cider for his new companions, he might manage to persuade a man to sing a verse. If it was 'a fine tune' Sharp would ask the man to sing it again, so that he could write it down in his pocket-book; and then again to double-check it.

Pubs were not Sharp's favourite locations as he found that drinkers too frequently preferred modern 'music hall'. He liked to collect ditties 'in cottages, in barns, by the roadside or in the open fields'.[15] Like Vaughan Williams his usual form of transport was the bicycle and he was always on the lookout for a 'chance encounter with a stone-breaker, a farm-labourer returning home from work, or a gypsy encampment'.[16] This is reflected in his collection of photographs where men and women are shown sometimes in the kitchen or parlour but more often outside their cottages or workshops, in the lane or the garden, by a haystack, perched on a low wall or bank or, in the case of Betsy Holland, in the shelter of her bender tent.

The images reflect his interest in the people he collected from – he sent singers tobacco and other small presents at Christmas and got to know some well enough to socialise with them. Louise

Betsy Holland and her children

Hooper recalled how she went to Ilminster Fair with him to hear the old people sing; that she and her sister, Lucy White, attended one of his concerts, where he bought them tea; and that after singing at his house they occasionally had supper with him and his wife.[17] Although frequently patronising and gauche he seems to have been genuinely interested in the people he met.

Vaughan Williams was careful to thank singers in general when he published their material, but there is no evidence that he sought any further interaction with them. He may have possessed a copy of the picture of James Carter, Joe Anderson and the Revd Huddle[18] but, even in this case, he does not seem to have engaged the fishermen in deeper conversation. How simple it would have been to ask Carter where he had learnt the melody for 'The Captain's Apprentice' and whether it was truly about a particular case. He liked the *idea* of a cosy rural pub full of singers, all swigging beer and full of bonhomie, but a comment he makes about Leather's ability to discover a lovely melody 'in the usual unpromising circumstances' hints at a less romantic reality. Anselm Hughes reported Vaughan Williams's occasional irritation with the collecting process: he accompanied the composer on trips to pubs where they would identify a potential singer, buy them a drink, and then be forced to endure 'A Bicycle Made for Two': 'Ralph would start to get crusty and say "Come on, Hughes, we'll do no good here."'[19] The composer's biographer and friend, Michael Kennedy, wrote candidly that 'nothing can convey what must have been the sheer tedium of many of the folk-song collectors' forays'.[20] His later assertion, that Vaughan Williams did not enjoy the act of collecting songs and was awkward in the company of the country people who sang for him, is even more surprising.[21] To feel justified in these comments, he must have received at least a hint from Vaughan Williams (perhaps via Ursula) that this was the truth.

Vaughan Williams's collaboration with Ella Leather was one of his most fruitful. They were brought together by Lucy Broadwood when Leather was researching what became *The Folklore of Herefordshire* (1912).[22] He made his first trip to that county in the summer of 1908 and returned several times before the outbreak of the First World War. Though engaged to take notes from recordings he also went out into the country with Leather, including a memorable evening in 1912 when, accompanied by Adeline, he travelled to the village of Monkland near Leominster.[23] Leather remembered that they found the camp of hop-pickers

in a little round field at dusk, on a fine September evening. There were several caravans, each with its wood fire burning . . . Alfred Price whom we were seeking was with his wife under an awning near one of the fires (his wife was very ill). He agreed to sing, so we all sat down on upturned buckets, kindly provided for us by the gypsies . . .[24]

She describes a homely scene and a friendly welcome. Vaughan Williams recalled the same occasion in his obituary for Leather in 1928. There are no buckets or ill wives in his version:

It was a cold, clear September night and we stood by the light of a blazing fire in the open ground of the gypsy encampment; the fire had been specially lighted to enable us to note down tunes and words in the growing darkness.

Then out of the half light there came the sound of a beautiful tenor voice singing 'The unquiet grave'.[25]

Perhaps affected by Leather's death, in his memory the ethereal words rise up – *Cold blows the wind o'er my true lover's grave and cold blow the drops of rain* – beautiful but disembodied, as if from the funeral pyre.

Elsewhere in Leather's obituary he asserts that a 'good folklorist' requires to be scientifically accurate, artistically imaginative and humanly sympathetic: 'As to [Leather's] human sympathy, one only had to accompany her . . . on a folk-song collecting expedition among the gypsies of Herefordshire to be astonished at her friendly reception by these proud and suspicious people.'[26] This characterisation of her rings true – she names the singer, notices his wife's illness, acknowledges the hospitality given. Vaughan Williams's astonishment suggests he was not used to

Ella Leather

such a welcome, as if empathy with his singers did not come naturally. For her, the collecting trip was intimate and domestic; for him it was allegorical.

⌒

It is closing time on a damp September's night in Ledbury High Street, Herefordshire. Men and women stand outside in groups, shout goodbyes, amble unevenly down the high street.[27] A girl sings a ballad outside a saloon door while two men listen. Light from the pub falls onto their faces, creating a fleeting *tableau vivant*. The composer, notebook and pencil in hand, watches the trio from the other side of the street. As the song ends he walks up to them.

Composer:	I beg your pardon, but do you know any more songs?
Man:	My old father does. Would you care to come with us now to visit him?
Composer:	Oh, no. Perhaps another day would be more convenient. It's rather late . . .
Man:	[interrupting] Come with us, sir. It's not far.

He indicates the way. With a shrug of his shoulders, the composer goes with him, the other two follow. They head out of the town along wet country lanes, dimly lit by moonlight. The lane turns into a muddy track. It gets darker. They stop outside a barn.

Man:	The old folks' tent is nearby. If you wait here, I'll see if they're awake.

The trio leave and the composer steps inside the barn doors to take shelter. He strikes a match, holds it up high to light the interior and reveals two shabbily dressed men sitting on hay bales. They take no notice of his arrival, and he does not speak to them.

First tramp: [to the other tramp] Did you ever hear the harmonium?
Second tramp: No.
First tramp: It's sweet music.

The match goes out. The composer leans on the barn door looking out into the night. Time passes. At last he hears footsteps and the man appears.

Man: My folks are in bed and don't feel like singing tonight. Perhaps you could visit in the morning? I'll take you back to town.

The two men return to the hotel where the composer goes to bed.

This anticlimactic episode from Ursula's biography is meant to illustrate her husband's recklessness in pursuit of a good tune, but it gives us nothing about Vaughan Williams's emotional state. While he was waiting in the barn did his thoughts turn to the possibility of being ambushed in the shadowy lane? Did he really ignore the two men in the barn even when they discussed the sweet sound of the harmonium? An unintended outcome of the story is a sense of the composer's detachment from the people he met. Who were they? Unlike Grainger, who might have provided a vivid picture – such as his description of Mr Perring who had 'a briny fragrance about his personality, and is a bold figure to behold in his jersey, vehemently swinging his arms and clenched fists to the lilt of his extra impassioned deliveries' – Vaughan Williams's story is reticent.[28] All we are told is that he went back in the morning to meet the old couple, who were friendly but had no material worth collecting. These tales are mediated through Ursula's retelling, of course, but in his lifetime he was moved to write down the songs he heard rather than impressions of the people he met.

In his editorial notes given to Sharp on the draft of *English Folk Songs: Some Conclusions*, his attitude to the people he recorded becomes clearer.[29] He objects to Sharp's use of the word 'peasantry' or 'the folk' to denote poor rural communities (he prefers 'country people'), and he does not like them being described as illiterate, 'which has a certain odium connected with it'. In response to Sharp's description of 'the peasant' approach to song he writes that 'this way of putting things – which one loves to hear so much when you <u>tell</u> it – somehow looks wrong in cold print – to those who do not know you it might seem a little <u>patronising</u> . . .' When Sharp characterises 'the Englishman's love song' as 'of the adventurous, open-air order, with love at first sight, hastily reciprocated, to the accompaniment of nightingales and the breaking into blossom of buds at Spring time . . . It is the Englishman's way to look on the bright side of things . . .'[30] Vaughan Williams attempts to bring him back down to earth: 'I don't quite agree about the optimism of the English folk-song – I think how popular "Died for love" sort of songs are & "A maid again I shall never be" etc – and also how about . . . all the transportation and murder ballads.'[31]

He expresses similar concerns in a note to Harold Child on the first drafts of their collaboration, *Hugh the Drover*, when the librettist appears to be laughing at country folk: 'Now what I want in the opera is that the English peasant shall not be looked on as a mere <u>clown</u> but a person capable of such beautiful song (and all that is implied by them) as we now know of.'[32] But when he meets such people he seems to stand outside, looking in on their domain. He moves 'among the more primitive people of England' rather than communicating with them, an invisible anthropologist silently moving through the crowd, looking for that something he first encountered at Ingrave, and which he continued to search for throughout his collecting years – the sense of a psychical researcher in the company of ghosts. Sometimes, in his haste, he forgot to raise his eyes and apprehend the singers as living beings, rather than vessels for songs. Sometimes, perhaps, he felt too awkward to raise his gaze – to look from his world of privilege into the eyes of a tramp taking shelter in a barn. He may have felt as Stephen Graham did in his book *The Gentle Art of Tramping* (1927) that 'Class . . . puts barriers between man and man . . . You cannot get rid of that absurd, unwanted, kind look – that "tell me, my dear man" expression.'[33]

His face-to-face meetings with country people did not match up to his theoretical views on their rights and causes. As well as 'more primitive', 'unlettered, unsophisticated and untravelled', he described them as people who 'make music which is often beautiful in itself and has in it the germs of great art'.[34] He is not unsympathetic and wants to avoid condescension, but although his Victorian upbringing was liberal, and he was a declared Fabian, the agricultural labourers and Gypsies who sang to him remain unfathomable, other-worldly and almost magical. If this mixture of guilt, admiration and bafflement was at the root of his awkwardness, he did not choose to discuss it in writing – schooled in 'amused detachment' at Cambridge, his instinct was to tell a light-hearted tale.[35]

The people sleeping in tents and barns were hop-pickers who travelled annually to the Ledbury area in late summer to harvest the crop. Ursula does not give a date for this adventure, but Vaughan Williams was there in September 1913, which would have been a good time to catch this itinerant workforce, many of whom were from Romany and Traveller communities.[36] If it *was* 1913, this was his last trip before the onset of the First World War and it ended a decade of intensive collecting. After the war, such trips became rare; he never returned to the task with the same vigour.

Hop-pickers, Herefordshire

A Wind on the Heath

Give to me the life I love,
Let the lave go by me,
Give the jolly heaven above
And the byway nigh me.
Bed in the bush with stars to see,
Bread I dip in the river –
There's the life for a man like me.
There's the life for ever.

'The Vagabond', Robert Louis Stevenson

In between the collecting trips throughout 1904 Vaughan
Williams continued to compose. For his song cycle *Songs
of Travel* he selected nine poems from a collection of forty-
four by Robert Louis Stevenson.[1] Through the composer's
arrangement of these verses, a loose narrative emerges in
which the central figure – 'The Vagabond' of the first poem –
rejects wealth and friendship for the open road and a 'nobler
fate':

Wealth I seek not, hope nor love
Nor a friend to know me;
All I seek, the heaven above
And the road below me.

Despite the protagonist's commitment to the vagabond life, the following songs reveal there is room in his heart to remember with regret lost love and his childhood home, now abandoned – 'Birds come and cry there and twitter in the chimney'. He is a singer of 'boyish staves', of songs that 'only I remember, that only you admire / Of the broad road that stretches and the roadside fire' and he muses on the power of song which endures after the singer is dead. It is thought that Vaughan Williams intended the cycle to end with a ninth song, a kind of 'goodnight', his journey done:

I have trod the upward and downward slope;
I have endured and done in days before;
I have longed for all, and bid farewell to hope;
And I have lived and loved, and closed the door.[2]

First performed in December 1904, Vaughan Williams had been working on the piece for more than a year – his setting of 'Whither Must I Wander' (placed seventh in the cycle) was first performed in November 1902.[3] Of all the songs, this one, with its melancholy description of an abandoned and ruined croft, set to a melody that reflects the fashion for sentimental Scottish art songs, is the one that touches my own childhood and brings tears to my eyes. It is no surprise to find that Stevenson suggested it should be set to the tune of 'Wandering Willie', the old setting of a poem by Robert Burns. But it is the first song, 'The Vagabond', that sets the mood, of a man out in all weathers, lingering in fields and tramping the byways, on an existential quest for his place between heaven and earth.

⌒

There is a photograph I like, of Vaughan Williams and his close friend Gustav Holst, strolling down an unmade track, their backs towards us, hills ahead. The lane runs straight through the middle of the image with the hint of a bend in the distance. Vaughan Williams wears a jaunty boater, a rucksack on his back, and grasps a walking stick – the camera has caught him mid-stride with purposeful movement towards the bend.

Holst and Vaughan Williams, September 1921, Malvern Hills

Holst, slight and round-shouldered, with a floppy white sunhat, is in front and holds the map. There is a sense of destination.

The picture was taken in September 1921 in the Malvern Hills, on a walking holiday after both composers had conducted one of their own works at the Three Choirs Festival in Hereford.[4] The two men often walked together, sometimes just for a day, at other times on longer excursions 'doing a little mild sightseeing, not making rigid plans but feeling free to follow their fancies' which was 'entirely to Ralph's taste'.[5]

He also loved to cycle. The bicycle enabled collectors to get around the countryside, assisted by the railway network.[6] In his letters bikes crop up regularly. In 1895 he tells Wedgwood that he is about to get a bicycle and that he has joined the Cyclists' Touring Club.[7] Five years later he reports that he will be getting a new bike for Christmas, 'a Lee-Francis with a very high gear (82) . . . I wish I could go some rides with you on it.'[8] Planning a trip to Ireland with his cousin in 1913 he writes, 'I like walking v. much – but will bring my bicycle – only I'm afraid my old machine won't go quick enough for you – only I'm afraid my legs won't either so its [sic] much of a much-ness.'[9] There are plans for further cycling holidays, comments about inconvenient burst tyres, and directions given for arrival by bike. He claimed the activity stimulated composition although usually, when he dismounted, he could not remember the tunes he had invented.[10] In his essay 'How Do We Make Music?' he compares the difference between reading a score and hearing it performed by an orchestra, to reading a map and cycling through the landscape:

The expert map reader can tell fairly exactly what sort of country he is going to visit, whether it is hilly or flat, whether the hills are steep or gradual, whether it is wooded or bare, what the roads are likely to be; but can he experience from a map the spiritual exaltation when a wonderful view spreads before his eyes, or the joy of careering downhill on a bicycle or, above all, the sense of rest and comfort induced by the factual realisation of those prophetic letters 'P.H.' [Public House]?[11]

His preoccupation with the open road was sparked at an early age, after reading George Borrow's *Lavengro*, and Bunyan's *The Pilgrim's Progress*. At their heart is the wayfarer who seeks meaning and purpose, the walk an allegory for the journey of life. His first musical exploration into the world of Bunyan was the setting of the 'Pilgrim's Hymn' to the tune of 'Our Captain Calls', the song collected in December 1904 and called 'Monk's Gate' by Vaughan Williams when he included it in the *English Hymnal*. There followed a lifetime of sketches and revisions – by way of the *Shepherds of the Delectable Mountains* produced in the 1920s – culminating in the opera of *The Pilgrim's Progress*, first staged in 1951.[12] For this work he wanted a backcloth that represented 'a road stretching straight out into the distance'.[13]

In 1902 Leslie Stephen (Virginia Woolf's father) published an essay 'In Praise of Walking', an activity which he asserts 'is among recreations what ploughing and fishing are among industrial labours: it is primitive and simple; it brings us into contact with mother earth and unsophisticated nature; it requires no elaborate apparatus and no extraneous excitement'.[14] These words 'primitive' and 'unsophisticated', which contemporary folk-song collectors also habitually used when referring to singers and songs, held talismanic power for Edwardian city-dwellers who yearned for the simplicity of a pre-industrial life. Stephen, who talks fondly of the network of paths on Leith Hill (paths that, through their family connection, he may have explored with Vaughan Williams), alludes to both Bunyan and Borrow as authors who celebrate walking: 'You share for the time the mood in which Borrow settled down in the dingle after escaping from his bondage in the publishers' London slums. You have no dignity to support, and the dress-coat of conventional life has dropped into oblivion, like the bundle from Christian's shoulders. You are in the world of Lavengro . . .'[15] He ends the essay with an appreciation of walking which has taken him 'from the amusements of *Vanity Fair* to the *Delectable Mountains* of pedestrianism'.[16] This connection between creativity, walking, the simplicity of rural life, and the cult of the open road was a trope well established in Vaughan Williams's circle, brought up on the poetry of the tramping poets, Wordsworth and Coleridge as well as Bunyan, Borrow and Stevenson (remember, he and his friends read *Treasure Island* when staying in the Lake District).[17] Added to this was the poetry of Walt Whitman, which Vaughan Williams discovered while at Cambridge and 'never got over'.[18] His settings from Whitman's *Leaves of Grass* during this pre-war period – *Toward the Unknown Region* and *A Sea Symphony* – take up existential themes of exploration and the voyage of the soul:

Darest thou now O soul,
Walk out with me toward the unknown region,
Where neither ground is for the feet nor any path to follow?
No map there, nor guide . . .[19]

Fully saturated in the romance of the wanderer, both as a poetic figure in the landscape and as a metaphor for life's spiritual journey, the theme seeps into his earlier works. *Songs of Travel, Toward the Unknown Region* and *A Sea Symphony* were all in different stages of development during 1904, the same year that he was engaged in his most intensive collecting.[20] The poetry circling in his head surely coloured his idea of himself as he went out into the countryside to seek 'the more primitive people' of England, in Whitman's words, 'Caroling free, singing our song of God / Chanting our chant of pleasant exploration.'[21] The character of a pilgrim (though not necessarily a Christian one) suited his idea of himself as a noble traveller on a quest for the soul of England's national music.[22] As he freewheeled down a gentle Essex incline towards the village pub on a fine spring day he may well have sung out loud, 'There's the life for a man like me!'

⌒

Vaughan Williams's memories of the walking holidays he took with friends in Wiltshire and Dorset[23] were of 'the green roads and open skies of the Great Plain with its summer flowers, thymey smells, and an infinity of larks rising above the bleached grass and the pale coloured chalk country' which 'was still almost the world Borrow had known . . .' In Borrow's work the romance of walking and the Gypsy life combine. *Lavengro* was Vaughan Williams's favourite book, and he and Ursula reread it in his old age.[24] The eponymous narrator ('Lavengro' means 'word-person' in Romany) spends part of his childhood in Norfolk, where he witnesses a boxing match and celebrates the art of pugilism.[25]

After moving to London for employment he soon becomes disaffected with city life and begins a long tramp west into the wild countryside, mending pots and pans for a living. Camped in a 'dingle', he fights his competitor, the 'Flaming Tinman' and wins the affection of 'Belle' (Isopel). Borrow makes a direct link between the narrator and the author of *The Pilgrim's Progress* when a preacher points out there is no shame in Lavengro's occupation as a wandering artisan, because John Bunyan had been 'a mighty speaker of old [who] sprang up from that family . . .'[26] Vaughan Williams assimilated the common themes in these tales – the transformational journeys, the symbolic characters encountered, and the struggles between good and evil, life and death.[27] A significant – and real-life – Romany character in Borrow's book is Jasper Petulengro, who persuades Lavengro that life is worth living because: 'There's night and day, brother, both sweet things; sun, moon, and stars, brother, all sweet things; there's likewise a wind on the heath.'[28]

From the 1880s and into the early decades of the twentieth century the 'Gypsy' figure appears regularly in paintings and literature, and was a lifestyle aspired to by bohemian artists and writers rebelling against the stifling conventions of the Victorian age. A 'Gypsy anthology' entitled *The Wind on the Heath* reflects this body of literary interest. Published in 1935 it includes extracts from Vaughan Williams's contemporaries such as Edward Thomas, W. H. Hudson and Vita Sackville-West, as well as earlier authors: Matthew Arnold, Borrow and Bunyan.[29] The editor, John Sampson, was friends with the artist Augustus John, who became so entranced he bought himself a caravan and took his family away in it for long periods, and later became president of the Gypsy Lore Society. Part of the attraction was the idea that Gypsies were entirely separate from society, 'pure blooded' and untarnished by 'civilisation': 'The Gypsies represent nature before civilisation . . . the last romance left in the world.' [30] This concept of a separate group or 'race' with pre-industrial values and a 'pure' culture was applied to both the Romany people and to old 'peasant' singers sought out in rural places – collectors were excited to gather songs from both, as a way of sourcing material they considered to be unsullied by modern society.

The Romantic idea of the untrammelled wanderer, and his own quest for the old songs produced in Vaughan Williams a creative flurry in the years before the First World War. *Hugh the Drover*, said by Michael Kennedy to be 'the culmination of his folk-song enthusiasm', began its long journey from concept to first performance when Vaughan Williams decided he wanted to 'set a prize fight to music'.[31] He proposed that the opera would be 'folk-songy' in character with 'a certain amount of real ballad stuff thrown in' and would 'hinge around a scene from Borrow's "Zincali" which describes a gypsy and a prize fight' – events that also occur in *Lavengro*. In fact, the composer wrote to the librettist Harold Child that 'our next opera might be Lavengro – I've always had this in my mind . . .'[32] Correspondence with Child began in 1910, and in 1922 the composer wrote that the opera was finished although it was not performed until 1924. Set in a nineteenth-century Cotswold village, the opera opens with a noisy fair, where a ballad singer sells his wares: 'The Deeds of Napoleon', 'The Murder of Maria Martin' and 'Tuesday Morning'.[33] Mary, daughter of the pompous Constable, is due to marry brutal John the Butcher against her will, but is beguiled by Hugh, a horse drover – not a Gypsy, but still the outsider. He 'fascinates Mary with his description of the joys of the road' – just like the Lady in the folk song:

> What care I for my goose feather bed
> What care I for my riches, O?
> What care I for my silken gown?
> I'll away with the raggle taggle gypsies, O!

The two men fight for Mary's hand, Hugh wins, and after some twists and turns in the plot, she leaves with him:

> Now for the road again
> The blessed sun and rain

– the words harking back to the Vagabond's 'heaven above / And the road below me'.

⌒

The texts preoccupying Vaughan Williams as he embarked in earnest on folk-song collecting in 1904 were of metaphorical landscapes, Whitman's 'unknown region', Bunyan's City of Destruction and Delectable Mountains, Stevenson's infinite shining heavens. As the protagonists – Pilgrim/Christian, the Scholar/Lavengro, the Vagabond, the Poet himself – travel through these fabled lands they encounter other symbolic characters and embodied ideals: Bunyan's Charity and Envy (and, significantly, Shepherds); Borrow's 'Scholar, Gypsy, Priest', the Flaming Tinman and Belle; Stevenson's Vagabond and Beauty; Whitman's Soul, or Adam and Eve, 'Wandering, yearning, curious, with restless explorations . . .'[34] I can imagine Vaughan Williams as he sets aside his copy of *Leaves of Grass* – along with a sheet of scribbled notes that would become *A Sea Symphony* – to walk out alone into a rural England he believes will soon be gone for ever: he encounters unknown shepherds, fishermen and Gypsies who sing to him of the sailor, the poacher, the bold robber, the ploughman, lovely Nancy, and the captain's apprentice: something of the metaphoric affects his gaze, so that, though the singers have their own stories to tell, to him they become symbols of the songs themselves.

On a one-off visit in 1922 Vaughan Williams and Leather revisited Alfred Price Jones and heard him sing a different version of 'Cold Blows the Wind' (or 'The Unquiet Grave').[35] Though the quality of the man's tenor voice, the memorable experience of hearing him at the encampment in 1912, and his performance of two versions of 'The Unquiet Grave' might have made him notable, the composer wrote down his name incorrectly as 'Arthur Jones'.

I would walk alone,
In storm and tempest, or in star-light nights
Beneath the quiet Heavens; and, at that time,
Have felt whate'er there is of power in sound

To breathe an elevated mood, by form
Or image unprofaned; and I would stand,
Beneath some rock, listening to sounds that are
The ghostly language of the ancient earth,
Or make their dim abode in distant winds.
Thence did I drink the visionary power.

William Wordsworth,
The Prelude: Book 2: School-time

Despite his commitment to the idea of the open road, Vaughan Williams was not a great walker – his flat feet were a problem, and he needed to rest regularly on longer walks.[36] In a parenthetic note to Scholes about Mary's preference for a free life on the road with Hugh the Drover he admits that 'we used to imagine we liked that kind of thing before the war when we had not experienced it'.[37] Even so, he remained fascinated with the idea of the outdoor, wandering life. His last known folk-song collecting trip was in 1955 when he and Ursula, with friend Frank Hollins, drove to the New Forest to meet a Romany girl in response to a letter she had written: 'I have a version of the *Raggle Taggle Gypsies, oh* . . . I can dance like a peacock but I like some port to get started on.'[38] They found her and her husband in a strip of field in an old-fashioned 'Gypsy' caravan with a 'splendid' horse. The woman had invited 'all the other gypsies' to the nearby pub to sing, but 'no tunes of any quality emerged'. Things got too rowdy for the publican and they were all 'bundled out into the night'. Afterwards they picnicked on the heath in brilliant moonlight.

Things were not quite as they seemed. The woman was Juanita Berlin (born Joy Barlow) who led an extraordinary life – as an artist, writer, sailor, zoo keeper, and horse-master in a circus – but had grown up in a wealthy family, and was educated in a series of boarding schools.[39] Her husband at the time was the painter and sculptor Sven Berlin. Vaughan Williams came armed with his dream of Gypsies in the night and was met by Juanita and her husband playing out their own bohemian dream of the Wanderer.

Is it a coincidence that some of Vaughan Williams's most retold stories are of nocturnal adventures? The texts he chose for his early works often conjure up the overarching sky of a starry night: Whitman's 'teeming spiritual darkness / Unspeakable, high processions of sun and moon, and countless stars above' (a faint echo of Petulengro's 'sun, moon and stars, brother'); or Stevenson's 'Unaccountable angel stars / Showering sorrow and light'.[40] Roaming free under a night sky was a vision he returned to: there was something in it that inspired him to reach 'beyond sense and knowledge' to 'see glimpses of the heart of things' and crystallise them into 'earthly sound'.[41]

A walk in the countryside at night is timeless, lit only by the stars and moon: modern detail and colour fade or disappear into the shadows. Your mind is diverted from trivia and impelled to contemplate the infinite. At night it is possible to travel through time: your feet on the road could be those of a medieval pilgrim, an eighteenth-century tinker, or a smuggler. Your sight may be dimmed but your power to listen is enhanced. You hear unfamiliar sounds, the bark of a fox, the shriek of an owl; and the absence of sound, a heavy, turning silence. Hidden in the dark, you may step outside convention and off the public road. At night you are more likely to see ghosts.

The Dream of John Sugars

(Hastings, 1885)[1]

John Sugars lies in his bed listening to the push and pull of waves on shingle beyond his window. In his heart he knows that the salt air of Hastings cannot cure him. The sea has been a fickle friend all his life, bringing both joy and horror. Drifting on the edge of sleep, memories pop up like corks in the water. When was it, what day, what hour when things began to unravel?

It was the moment he dreamed of owning a ship. A beautiful barque, sleek and fast, sails billowing from her three masts, her bow slicing through the waves. Once she was built, the Lloyd's under-writer had not hesitated to class her A1. Yes, that was the proudest hour, when he'd watched her leave London docks. The Thames glittered in spring sunshine, passengers waved from the decks as they set off for new lives in Australia. Beneath the bowsprit, a figurehead carved in his own likeness gazed towards the horizon; and across her bow in large letters, for all to see, was the name: John Sugars.

What a day! It had put him in mind of his boyhood, watching crowds of ships sailing up the Great Ouse with the tide. He'd liked to see the men unloading the cargo, foreign voices on the air, the smell of wet rope and tar. He could have been a sailor, but there was no money to be made that way. Bricks and mortar were more solid. He'd started off a joiner, grafted at it, learnt the building trade, made his own luck, no one could doubt that. Before he was thirty, barely more than a boy-chap, he'd been appointed life governor of the West Norfolk Hospital, 'in consideration of his having fulfilled his contract to the complete satisfaction of the committee and the subscribers'. Words to remember! Afterwards, they'd asked him to build the Ely workhouse and he'd never looked back. 'The greatest ornament the city can boast', the papers said, if you didn't count the cathedral.

Lizzy used to collect the newspaper cuttings. She'd liked to walk through the streets of Lynn on his arm, past the hospital, the school, the fine residences he'd built. Fine enough to call himself 'architect'. Local people sought his opinion. They persuaded him to stand as town councillor. His name appeared in the papers in the same company as Sir John Boileau, High Sheriff of Norfolk, no less, when they campaigned for the new railway. He was trusted. On one occasion he was sent to London to argue against increased charges to the King's Lynn Union. When it was proposed to make the great cut from Lynn out to the sea, the mayor turned to him to negotiate with the Norfolk Estuary Company. The name John Sugars stood for honesty, quality, reliability. His reputation had been his most precious possession.

It was around then that the dream of the ship took hold. Great wealth could be made from such an endeavour. He had not considered the possibility that all might be lost in a single storm. The dream took him away to the north and to London for long periods. There'd been much business to oversee – he'd visited the Sunderland shipyard frequently to watch the vessel take shape; he'd ensured that the workmanship was of the finest quality and the passenger cabins well appointed; there'd been trade routes to discuss, imports and exports. And he'd interviewed shipmasters and apprentices. Once the ship was out in the world, he'd kept a close eye on the sales of goods brought back from far-flung places; cutch from Rangoon; guano from Peru; coffee, cinnamon and coconut oil from Ceylon – the smells from other realms captured beneath her decks. The matter of tides and winds had taken possession of him. Bricks and mortar became Lizzy's domain.

The ship brought him trouble from the start. On her maiden voyage, carrying a cargo of coals from Sunderland to London, she'd collided with a Spanish vessel. It was the foreign ship that came off worse, lost with all its cargo. What was the name of it, the brigantine that wilfully sailed into his own? Neptuno, *god of the sea. It had surely been an omen. At the time his heart had been too full of the dream to notice.*

After sending off the John Sugars *to Australia on her first long-distance voyage, he had not returned to the loving arms of his wife, but to lonely lodgings in Shoreditch. They'd sustained the pretence for some years that business kept him frequently from home, from her. What had gone wrong between them? There was a day, long ago, a fine day, when they were still young. She had hurried with him to the field just outside Lynn, eager to observe the spectacle of a hot-air balloon in flight. Its coloured silk swelled upwards as the gas roared, rising from the ground like a gigantic pearl. They had never seen anything so beautiful. When members of the crowd were invited to join in the ascent, Lizzy was the first to step forward, cheeks aflame, unafraid of the risk. He'd loved her then. But in the end, there had been insufficient gas, and the invitation was withdrawn. They were not taken up in the basket, and they never did see the Great Ouse sparkle beneath them.*

At some point she'd lost her taste for the adventure. Perhaps if they'd been blessed with children, little hands and sweet voices might have bound them together. He had striven to do good elsewhere; no one could accuse him of being mean with his money. He'd begun by giving coal to the poor of South Lynn at Christmas. Some ungrateful people muttered afterwards that it was to atone for the death of the boy, but it was not true. He had learnt long before that his wealth came at a price.

The boy had often been in his mind. Of course he had. He was a handy lad, keen to make a life for himself, grateful for the opportunity to become an apprentice. It was done for the best of reasons, to keep him out of the workhouse, provide him with a trade. People forgot that afterwards. He'd never believed the lad was driven to suicide. Captain Doyle said it was an accident, the boy had slipped, fallen, nothing to be done. The crew said different, but they were a rough lot, and hated Doyle. If he had thought the captain used unnecessary harshness, he would not have stood bail for him. He told the magistrate at the time: he had no desire to screen the man from justice if he was guilty of cruelty. He wished always that his apprentices should be kindly treated and he would not countenance any inhumanity. He had made that quite clear.

It was the ship that had dragged his name through every paper in the land. Underneath the headline 'CRUELTY AT SEA', the

John Sugars *appeared next to the news of Eastick's suicide, and the horrifying torment he'd suffered at Doyle's hand. There'd been talk of little else in Lynn. The fishermen sang about it in the pubs. Men who'd looked up to him sneered behind his back. A bit too high and mighty for his own good. Should have stayed a builder. They didn't say it to his face, but he knew their world and how they spoke about their betters. There'd been no choice but to leave Lynn for ever. In Hackney his new neighbours were self-made men – butchers, shopkeepers – who did not question where he came from. In London he was a gentleman.*

The ship no longer brought him pleasure. She was sold and he'd hoped to hear nothing more of her. But, no, the fates were not done with him. A few months later the John Sugars *was in the papers again. She'd been shipwrecked. At first, he'd worried for the crew – he could not have borne more death associated with the name* John Sugars. *Press reports confirmed they were all saved, but still he was not allowed to rest. Once returned to shore, the crew alleged that the captain had deliberately caused the ship to go down. He was put on trial and found guilty. A few weeks later members of the crew were charged with perjury, having given false evidence against the captain. The case of the* John Sugars *appeared repeatedly in the papers for over four months. Though he'd tried to ignore it, he could not avoid seeing his name. The ship was lost near Portugal when heavy seas opened up the bow, and water gushed into the hold. No doubt the figurehead bearing his likeness had been split asunder as the wave hit and went down, along with the leather boots, farm tools and beer barrels, to lie at the bottom of the sea.*

If only he'd called the ship Elizabeth *or* Victoria *– anything but* John Sugars. *There'd been no choice but to pay the price and try to* *salvage his name. He'd bestowed the new south transept window at All Saints' back in Lynn. It was a depiction of the Transfiguration – Christ turned into a creature of radiant glory – with 'ERECTED BY JOHN SUGARS' painted in the glass below. He'd built a row of almshouses for aged and needy masters and mates of merchant vessels – if he'd learnt anything from the court cases it was that the common crew were mostly undeserving. In his new local church at London Fields he'd paid for more stained glass and a painting of the Lamb of God decorated with two thousand leaves of gold. He had not lost his appetite for quality. How it gleamed in the gaslight!*

The click of the door wakes him. In the thick darkness of the winter morning he forgets for a few confused moments that he is not at home in Hackney, but in Hastings by the sea. Mrs Brown enters quietly, opens the curtains an inch, briefly takes his hand, then places her warm palm on his forehead. Yes, he is still alive, but he is

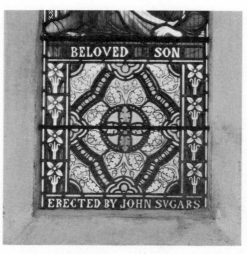

John Sugars's window, South Lynn church

ready to meet his maker. Before travelling to Hastings, his business affairs had been put in order. Legacies will keep his name alive for years to come. He has left money to a benevolent pension fund, to the West Norfolk hospital where his reputation was established all those years ago, and to a new charity that will dispense coal in perpetuity to the poor of Lynn. More than this: a substantial sum has been put in trust to build another row of 'Sugars Alms Houses' in Lynn for six poor widows. John Sugars will be for ever remembered for good works: vicious captains, perfidious sailors and the drowned boy will surely be forgotten.

PART V

GROWING UP, WITH WOMEN

'The effect of music upon the minds of children . . .'

My mother died at the age of ninety but had been fading away from us for several years, beset with a version of dementia which befuddled her mind, but crystallised the unconquered optimism at her core. Almost to the end, if I sang familiar songs to her, she would join in:

'Jackie boy.'
'*Master.*'
'Sing you well.'
'*Very well.*'
'Hey down.'
'*Ho down.*'
'Derry derry down.'
'*Among the leaves so green, O.*'

'The Keeper', with this call and response chorus, was part of our family repertoire. I didn't know it then, but versions of 'The Keeper' were recorded by Vaughan Williams and Sharp throughout the early years of the twentieth century, with the best-known melody collected in 1909 in Warwickshire. My mother, my aunt and my two sisters knew the words of a wide selection of these arranged folk songs which we sang at parties. Being around ten years younger than my sisters, Sally and Ann, I had heard the material less and tended to learn only the first verse and chorus but would join in with 'dee da dee' for the rest. It wasn't until I began looking for the origins of 'The Captain's Apprentice' that I became conscious of this childhood infusion of song, and that it was an outcome of an esoteric dispute with the Edwardian Board of Education.

When the Folk-Song Society was in its first flush – between the second Boer War (1899–1902) and the First World War – consecutive governments were concerned with improving the physical, mental and moral strength of the British population in order to sustain the structures of Empire and compete with other rising economies, especially the USA and Germany. In their desire to inculcate love of country, the authorities adopted the country*side* as the symbolic heart of national identity. Folk songs were used to introduce the idea of a cohesive, simpler, rural 'Old Albion' to schoolchildren. The Board of Education's 1905 handbook, edited by Sir Charles Villiers Stanford (Vaughan Williams's former tutor) and commonly known as the 'Blue Book', was akin to a national curriculum for music. It was designed to actively encourage the singing of folk songs as a way of expressing 'unaffected patriotism, zest for sport, the simple pleasures of country life'.[1] Cecil Sharp agreed wholeheartedly with the principle of the scheme but was horrified that the list of recommended songs did not discriminate between 'folk' songs – passed down through the oral tradition – and 'national' songs which were composed and 'popular'. He tried to get the Folk-Song Society to condemn this approach, but committee members passed a milder resolution, which welcomed the teaching of folk songs in schools, but regretted that a greater number of genuine folk songs were not included in the list.

This was not enough for Sharp. His book *English Folk Songs: Some conclusions* (1907) is his manifesto, written as a riposte to the Board of Education. Ostensibly a 'scientific' analysis of folk song, at its heart there is another agenda entirely, a disputation on patriotism and national character. The chapters on folk-song origin, the emphasis on the oral tradition, the evolutionary theory and the contrast between folk music and art music, prepare the ground for the final chapter, 'The Future of the English Folk Song'. Here he asserts that genuine folk music in education could lead to the development of a National School of English Music, as well as 'a beneficent and enduring effect' on national character – but this will only happen if popular songs are discarded: 'The effect of music upon the minds of children is so subtle and so far-reaching that it is impossible to exaggerate the harmful influence upon character which the singing of coarse and vulgar tunes may have.'[2] By coarse and vulgar, he meant songs such as 'The Roast Beef of Old England' and 'Hearts of Oak' to be found on the Board of Education list – composed songs performed in music halls.

In a note on Sharp's draft of the book, Vaughan Williams implored him to remove anything that looked like a personal vendetta: 'I think it is most important in this book to keep the high level and not to descend to details as to who said this & who said that . . . And finally I <u>do beg</u> of you to leave the B. of E. [Board of Education] wrangle out of this book . . .'[3] Despite this plea Sharp includes a warning that if the Board of Education does not recognise that folk song 'stands in a category of its own . . . and must be given a special place in the education system', its project will be 'foredoomed to failure'.[4] Through the vociferousness of his very public campaign, Sharp lost the support of most of the Folk-Song Society committee – he and Lucy Broadwood were never on good terms again.

Vaughan Williams supported Sharp despite holding some opposing views. He was relaxed about the sources of inspiration for great art which he felt could include 'the lilt of the chorus at a music-hall joining in a popular song, the children dancing to a barrel organ, the rousing fervour of a Salvation Army hymn, St Paul's and a great choir singing in one of its festivals, the Welshmen striking up one of their own hymns whenever they win a goal at the international football match, the cries of street pedlars, the factory girls singing their sentimental songs . . .'[5] He was also suspicious of jingoism: when Sharp argued that 'every English child . . . will love [folk songs] more, realize that he is united to them by subtle bond of blood and of kinship, and become, in the highest sense of the word, a better citizen, and a true patriot', Vaughan Williams responded bluntly: 'I entirely disagree with all this . . . – indeed all about patriotism – but that's neither here nor there.'[6]

Vaughan Williams was not interested in promoting ideological nationalism through folk song. From at least 1939 he was an outspoken and active supporter of a federal union of Europe and established a local Dorking branch of the Federal Union. After the war he joined with other eminent artists in calling for world federal government and a 'merging of sovereignty by all the peace-loving nations of the world'.[7] His motivation for collecting and publicising folk song was to provide the source for a new English national music: in another comment on Sharp's draft book he argues that folk song 'though old is also <u>new</u>' and could provide inspiration for forward-looking art.[8] He goes on to rail against sentimentality about the past:

I suppose I'm prejudiced – but I lose all self-control when I see the expression 'Merrie England' (at all events why not 'merry'?) – it seems to my mind connected with Ruskin-ianism and 'Home industries' and all the worst kind of obscurantism – if the folksong has nothing to say to us <u>as we are now</u> – without a sham return to an imaginary (probably quite illusory) arcadia of several centuries ago – if the folksong means this then I would burn all the collections I could lay my hands on and their singers with them – please forgive this splenetic outburst but that particular expression . . . connects the folksong (and, if you use the word, yourself, by implication) with the worst of its hangers on and camp-followers – Amen.[9]

Despite this background, he is often associated with flag-waving patriotism, his music cited as the epitome of Englishness and sepia-toned nostalgia.

In 1914 Vaughan Williams (then in his forties) joined the Royal Army Medical Corps Territorial Force, and worked in the Field Ambulance service, evacuating wounded and dying men from the battlefields of France. In the aftermath of the war, nationalist ideology grew in strength and influence across Europe. In these circumstances, Vaughan Williams's choice of 'National Music' as the subject for a series of lectures in the early 1930s was provocative – but he was careful to point out that his desire for the flowering of English national music based on the revival of folk songs did not mean a rejection of, or competition with, the music of other countries: 'I hope you do not think that I am preaching artistic chauvinism. That purely negative attitude of mind is, I trust, a thing of the past.'[10] For him it was clear that promoting a national school of music had little to do with nationalism. He did not care for 'mixing propaganda and art' and considered it a bad idea to 'advertise through music any particular brand of political opinion'. These were the fraught inter-war years: set against the rise of fascism, any campaign for nurturing national music was liable to be seized upon by political ideologues; and while British cultural imperialism was still in full spate it was naive to suggest artistic chauvinism was over – but he continued to argue for the rest of his life that 'political internationalism is not only compatible with cultural patriotism, but that one is an essential concomitant of the other'.[11]

While delving into this dispute over folk song, nationalism and the arcane question of which songs children should learn for the good of the country, I realised my family had been participants in a social experiment. Gathering together songbooks from the era, I came across *A Selection of Collected Folksongs*, published in 1909, with vocal parts arranged by Sharp and Vaughan Williams. It was second-hand from the library of

Chelsea College of Physical Education, where the songs were taught to improve moral character alongside a sound body. As well as 'The Keeper' I was intrigued to find other titles learnt at family sing-songs, such as 'O No, John' and 'Dashing away with a smoothing iron', which I had often sung with my mother when she was ill. I also obtained a copy of *The National Song Book*, the official Board of Education publication which included some of those 'national' songs – from Wales, Ireland and Scotland as well as England – which Sharp abhorred and which I have been singing all my life: 'Drink to me only', 'Early one Morning', 'There's nae Luck' , 'All through the Night', 'Auld lang syne' and many more, all absorbed by ear at family gatherings. In direct competition with *The National Song Book*, Sharp collaborated with seasoned collector Sabine Baring-Gould to publish *English Folk-Songs for Schools* – which included familiar childhood favourites such as 'This Old Man', 'A Frog he would a-wooing go', and another I've never heard sung outside my childhood home, 'The Tailor and the Mouse', which I had presumed my grandpa wrote because it was so silly: 'The tailor thought his mouse was ill; Hi diddle unkum feedle!; He gave him part of a blue pill, Hi diddle unkum feedle!'

My parents and older siblings learnt these songs at school, along with stories from the Bible and the Kings and Queens of England. They were part of the warp and weft of twentieth-century education until the 1960s (an updated version of the 'Blue Book' was published in 1958). When we sang them robustly around the piano at Christmas we had no idea we were part of a propaganda exercise, but innocently accepted these melodies into our lives. We did not become nationalists, but we absorbed a shared musical culture which to our ears sounded like 'something entirely new yet absolutely familiar'.[12] Vaughan Williams wrote in 1954 that folk tunes 'are again common property, and every English child must know them as well as he knows his own language, whether he likes it or not'.[13] For our family, this was true.

Separate Atoms

Adeline and Ralph

When Vaughan Williams's first wife died in 1951 there was no trace of her 'early beauty, her lively mind, her austere discipline, her tenderness and edged wit . . .'[1] This is how Ursula described Adeline on her deathbed.

When someone dies in old age – Adeline was eighty – it is easy to forget that they were once vibrant, creative, supple beings. Progressive arthritis had eventually limited Adeline's mobility to such an extent that in 1929 the couple moved from their house with many stairs in central London to a bungalow in Dorking, where they lived for the next twenty-two years. Ursula thought that Adeline's illness had inhibited the composer's immersion in the musical life he deserved: after the move he 'accepted the new life and tried not to regret the old'.[2]

Much of what is known about Adeline was written by Ursula, who was in an extramarital relationship with Vaughan Williams

Adeline Vaughan Williams, 1908

from 1938. They married two years after Adeline's death, when Vaughan Williams was eighty and Ursula forty-two. Much later on, Ursula admitted to being '*madly* jealous' of the woman who had wedded Vaughan Williams in his prime and shared his life for over fifty years; in her autobiography she is candid about the difficulty of coming to terms with the missed years of his youth.[3] She never asked her husband whether he had been happy in his first marriage: 'If the answer was yes, as the best part of one would like it to be, would one be wise enough not to feel the anguishing tentacles of jealousy?'[4] Once they were married, Ursula wanted to rescue the composer from his parochial life in Dorking – she was insistent that he thought of himself as a Londoner [5] – and they moved back to the capital in 1953. But while his first wife was alive, Vaughan Williams was immovable and Ursula was forced to acknowledge 'the inter-dependence, the shared interests, problems, friends, memories and fabric of living that made up their marriage'.[6] Despite Ursula's support after Adeline's death, Vaughan Williams wrote to friends, 'My wife died about a month ago, so now I'm all alone.'[7] No wonder that his second wife wanted to establish her influence, later remarking that 'all the symphonies from No. 5 onwards were mine'.[8] In her role as his official biographer, she could not be an objective witness. In his conversations with her at the end of his long life, perhaps Vaughan Williams did not dwell on the happiness of the early years with Adeline.

Ralph and Ursula Vaughan Williams on their wedding day, 1953

Ursula described Adeline as 'always aloof, even frightening to those who did not know her well: partly from shyness, reserve, and a capacity for silence which could be alarming'.[9] Adeline's looks influenced first impressions – a cousin to Virginia Woolf (whose first name was also Adeline), they shared a similar severe beauty with their languid eyes, long oval faces and high cheekbones. Her brother, Hervey, included her as a thinly disguised character in one of his short stories: 'a flaxen-haired girl . . . with heavy-lidded grey eyes and the light of June in her cheeks'.[10] Ursula, who took a great interest in clothes, could not understand Adeline's indifference to her appearance – there is implied criticism in her remark that Adeline made 'no concession to fashion, or the choice of anything which would enhance it'.[11]

An area of friction Ursula describes between husband and wife was the depth of Adeline's commitment to her family, the Fishers. She was one of eleven children who grew up intimately involved in each other's lives and these bonds continued into adult life. Inevitably, in such a large family, misfortunes arose, and everyone would rally round. Adeline was often called away to look after whichever one of the siblings was sick. In 1901 her brother Jack returned 'wrecked and destroyed' from the Boer War and died some months later.[12] During the First World War her brother Charlie was killed at the Battle of Jutland, and her mother died in a road accident.[13] Hervey suffered from tuberculosis of the spine for many years in addition to mental-health problems, and Adeline would nurse him when necessary, before he died in 1921.[14] Ursula's reaction to these family commitments which took Adeline away from her husband are barbed: '. . . the need to nurse Hervey . . . made her presence at her parents' home a great comfort and, *it seemed to her*, an urgent need'; '. . . she did not allow illness to interfere with her life, *perhaps unwisely*, for her mother's diary notes her almost daily visits . . .'[15] She suggests that Adeline was to blame for the start of her long illness in 1909: 'While she still had a high temperature she went, *against all advice*, to look after her mother who was recovering from a fall . . .' Though two of her sisters were caring for Mrs Fisher, she insisted on visiting. 'This *unwise action* was thought to have been the first cause of her own long suffering from arthritis: Ralph certainly believed it to be so.'[16] Adeline's behaviour might have been exasperating but there is something disquieting about this statement. It implies that Vaughan Williams felt in his heart that his wife had brought misfortune on herself. Ursula, looking back on the limitations this placed on her husband, frames Adeline's impulses to care for her siblings as a kind of selfishness.

Vaughan Williams had been acquainted with Adeline's family from childhood – their fathers were old friends, and the Fishers would regularly take a holiday house near Leith Hill Place during the summer. He knew Adeline at sixteen (he was two years younger), when she 'played hide-and-seek sometimes, read aloud fairy stories, caught newts and butterflies, paddled in the river, sailing boats with the boys'.[17] When he was a student at Cambridge, Vaughan Williams continued this relationship, by

Adeline Fisher, aged about ten, painted by her mother in 1880

regularly calling in at the home of Adeline's older sister Florence, who was married to Frederic Maitland, a professor at Downing College.[18] It was here that the romance with Adeline developed – she was a frequent visitor and would play cello at their musical gatherings. By the time he proposed, in 1897, he was fully aware of her sense of familial duty. Ursula notes that one of the reasons the couple went to stay in Berlin for six months soon after their marriage was because he wanted to separate her from the family.[19] Yet he must have known that they would continue to be an important part of her life, and therefore part of his.

⌒

The Fisher cousins, including Adeline, appear often in the teenage journal and letters of Virginia Woolf (*née* Stephen).[20] Through her eyes we see Adeline's relationships with her family, with Vaughan Williams and with Virginia herself.

Adeline was twelve years older than Virginia but similar in age to Virginia's half-sister, Stella Duckworth: the two older girls were close. [21] The Fishers lived in Hove, next to Brighton, so it was a short train journey to visit Stella at the Stephens' London home. The young women went on shopping trips into town, visited museums and galleries and attended evening dinners, concerts and dances – on one occasion they stayed out until 5.00 a.m.[22] Virginia notes how Adeline entertained them with her stories of 'the cabmen and the Vaughans', 'their dog, and of Tom and Boo', 'her dear Miss Roden', and 'Kittie's engagement once upon a time to Lord Morpeth'.[23]

In April 1897, when Virginia was fifteen, the Stephens holidayed in Brighton and saw the Fishers most days, walking over to have tea with them on the evening of arrival. On one occasion the Stephens children, Adeline and her brother Herbert took their bikes on the train to Dyke up on the South Downs, and cycled home in the pouring rain; on another Adeline accompanied them to the Parade in Brighton where they were entertained by a magician and musicians, while all the time she was 'nursing a poor half-starved mouse of Toms [*sic*]' in her pocket.[24] Later, they repeated the trip to Dyke, this time blown off their bikes by the high winds. Undeterred, they cycled twenty-two miles on another day, to Arundel Castle, before catching the train back.

It was on this holiday that the romance between Adeline and Vaughan Williams was first confirmed although Virginia writes 'we already knew'.[25] At the same time Stella, who had recently returned from her honeymoon, fell ill. When she had not recovered by June Adeline travelled to London, to help look after her. Then, on Thursday 10 June Virginia headlines her journal entry

Vaughan Williams and Adeline, 1897, the year they became engaged

with 'Adeline Fisher engaged to Ralph Vaughan Williams' and writes excitedly about Vaughan Williams coming to call, taking Adeline out for a walk at 11.00, not returning until 3.30 and then: 'Adeline was engaged! . . . A most exciting afternoon . . . Good heavens – what a whirlpool – No room for more!'[26] There follows a series of stifling hot days when Virginia feels irritable while Adeline, seemingly oblivious to the weather, '*bicycle rides* [Virginia's italics] & prints photographs'.[27]

Virginia's initial impressions of Vaughan Williams are of a 'tall stout solemn young gentleman – very stiff & proper at first sight . . .'[28] After discussing the engagement with Stella she echoes a comment her half-sister had made: 'Poor Ralph is a *calf* – according to her – & also, I am afraid, to us – However, they are very much in love, & there is a chance he is a genius' – the scathing perspective of a teenager, embarrassed by mawkish grown-ups but impressed by the potential for greatness.[29] In early July, Stella still being unwell, Adeline visited again. Virginia accompanied her to an afternoon concert at which Vaughan Williams was performing. They waited for a train that did not turn up and Adeline 'burst into tears on the platform, bewailing her fate, cursing the trains, & altogether miserable'.[30] That same evening there were further emotional scenes when Adeline's sister Emmeline and young brother Charles came, and 'Emmie' 'behaved very badly to Adeline . . .'[31] Virginia's half-brother, George, defended her and there was a scene: 'All the bawling & squalling & tears & attempts at peace making, & Adeline's sneers, & Charlie's roars of laughter, cannot find room here . . .'

In the next entry about her cousin there is a marked change in Virginia's tone: '. . . Ralph came to lunch – Adeline terribly irritating. An unselfish martyr – oh for arrows & stones to throw at her!'[32] This outburst might be explained by a diary entry two days later in which Virginia implies she has been criticised by Adeline for spending too much time with the sickly Stella and tiring her out. These diary entries highlight an aspect of Adeline which both Virginia and later, Ursula, found provoking: although she was moved by a tender heart to care for ill people, her good intentions could be undermined by what others saw as her self-appointed role as the long-suffering chief nurse. Even so, Virginia cannot help noticing her cousin's kindness: 'Poor Aunt Mary [Adeline's mother] looks like a washed out ghost . . . and no one but Adeline thinks of helping her.'[33]

Virginia continued to be fascinated by the couple's soppiness – 'Adeline and Ralph came and were rather irritating – Such a couple never was seen!' and 'Adeline and Ralph went with us and sat holding each others [*sic*] hands . . .'[34] In October 1900 she wondered if Adeline might be pregnant: 'We thought there were possible signs, but I don't know. I wish there could be, she drifts about rather aimlessly with that great Ralph, who goes on writing unpublished masterpieces, and grows his hair longer and longer.'[35]

The fact that the Vaughan Williamses had no children has given rise to speculation about their sex life. Stella died on 19 July, only a few weeks after they had agreed to marry. Ursula wrote that 'Adeline's grief and despair excluded everything else, and nearly brought the engagement to an end . . . the happiness of the first bright days of their engagement was never wholly recaptured.'[36] At the time it was rumoured within the family that Stella's death was linked to the sexual relationship with her new husband. Ursula later told a friend that after Adeline's death Vaughan Williams found a photograph of Stella and tore it up in a rage, saying she had almost ruined everything between his first wife and himself. Ursula was convinced that Stella persuaded Adeline that 'all men are brutes' and turned her against sex, but then undermines her own theory by stating that Adeline would have liked a large family.[37] It is impossible to know, but perhaps Adeline's devotion to her mother and siblings was partly in compensation for the children that never came along. Her husband's reaction to Stella's photograph might have been prompted by the memory of Adeline's intense grief when the couple should have been at their happiest.

Vaughan Williams's letters to Ralph Wedgwood, on hearing of his friend's engagement in 1906, do not imply that the early years of his marriage were sexless. He is thrilled that Wedgwood will no longer be living a 'lonely life' and becomes incoherent when discussing his cousin's fiancé, the nineteen-year-old Iris: '& now I must say – though you won't like my doing so – that I consider that the woman who has won you – well there I can't say what I mean but you know – and you can read between the lines – because I'm not saying anything I want to . . .'[38] He ends the letter by saying, 'This is quite illegible but my hand shakes from excitement.' In his next letter he speaks of his 'vicarious engagement' which is preventing him from sleeping or working: 'The more I think of that photograph [of Iris] the more I realise "la séduction même" – Do marry at once and don't wait that beastly 3 months – let all your knowledge of each other come after marriage and not before – that is so much better.'[39] Later that month he writes, '. . . I've got nothing to say except that I like thinking of you so much . . .'[40] Apart from the raw intensity these letters reveal of his feelings for Wedgwood, the overwhelming sense is that he is alive to the pleasures of sex with his own wife.

Virginia's relationship with Adeline did not recover. In 1903 there was a major falling-out which began at Salisbury station – both families were staying in the town: 'I saw Adeline and Ralph at the station on the day they arrived, but Adeline stared so that I rushed past without a word.'[41] What circumstances would cause one cousin to ignore another? I picture the couple on the platform, Ralph organising luggage, Adeline smoothing her skirts, as Virginia steps down from her carriage. Doors bang; the guard shouts, the whistle blows. Through the steam Adeline spots Virginia advancing towards the exit; their eyes meet for a moment before Virginia sweeps past, face averted. Adeline's stare is intriguing. Was it an expression of surprise, rage or sorrow? Did she really stare, or is this Virginia's gloss – or an unconscious counterpart of her own behaviour? Her next line – 'Then we heard nothing whatever for 10 days . . .' – appears disingenuous or obtuse: having been so blatantly snubbed it is not surprising that Adeline stayed away.

Eventually Aunt Mary wrote them a querulous note – 'Am I never going to see you?' – and so Virginia and her sister dutifully visited. The description of the Fisher household who 'would have made Eden un-inhabitable' is unashamedly partisan and written for laughs. Virginia conjures up a comically comfortless room of hard chairs, cushionless sofas, and 'half a fire' in the grate – but it is August and a roaring fire would surely have been more odd. She sets up a narrative of Fisher eccentricity which does not quite stand up to scrutiny: Hervey is lying on a blanket in the garden, which is not unusual in summer; Emmy is in a temper possibly because Virginia has been rude; Charles – unwashed – just sounds like a teenager. Virginia is a funny but unreliable witness. Even so, the picture of Adeline's stare remains in the mind. It chimes with Ursula's description, '. . . always aloof . . .' Yet a few weeks later Adeline – 'the little attitudinising woman' – calls to discuss the rift.[42] She and the family are hurt at the lack of interest the Stephens have shown in seeing the Fishers. The meeting does not go well, and contact is broken for a year until once again Adeline makes the first approach – Virginia writes that 'the ice cold Adeline has descended from her heights and has left a card on us'.[43] But her cousin had at least made an effort which Virginia did not: '. . . *I* have climbed my heights and stay there at present, calmly indifferent.'

In the context of Virginia's earlier letters and journals where Adeline tells amusing stories, cycles across town and country in all weathers, tenderly nurses a sickly mouse, breaks down in frustrated tears on a station platform, is nearly broken with grief over the death of Stella, and demonstrates embarrassing affection towards Vaughan Williams in public, 'ice cold' is an unexpected characterisation. It is a more accurate description of Virginia herself.

⌒

Ursula implies that Adeline spent too much time with her family, and Virginia suggests she drifted aimlessly in her husband's wake. There is another way of looking at their relationship. Right from the start Vaughan Williams worried that after he and

Adeline were married, friends would treat them as one entity instead of two individuals. Announcing his engagement in a letter to Wedgwood, he wrote about Adeline, 'You know, I think, that for many years we have been great friends.'[44] He wishes Wedgwood could get to know her before the wedding because otherwise 'you may get into the way of thinking of me and my wife instead of getting to know both as separate atoms'.[45] Their marriage was not the outcome of a giddy romance but of a slowly developed friendship and mutual respect. He did not want Adeline to be seen as an adjunct to him – instead, he hoped that they would be treated as autonomous beings and that Wedgwood would be equally friends with both.

In such a relationship it is not expected that each will be permanently living in the pocket of the other. They had their own passions to pursue. Adeline may have spent a lot of time with her family, but equally Vaughan Williams was deeply absorbed in his developing musical career and was often away. He collected over eight hundred songs between December 1903 and September 1913 from all corners of England.[46] He would regularly isolate himself to focus on composition. In July 1904, he was away for Adeline's birthday, staying in Yorkshire to work on the piece that was to become *The Sea Symphony*. He found that this 'solitary and concentrated attack was immensely valuable' and it became part of his creative practice. [47] In the winter of 1907–8 he spent three months in Paris to study under Ravel, leaving his wife in England. She visited on a couple of occasions, but they did little sightseeing because 'he worked for the greater part of the day'.[48] When they stayed with their friends, the Gattys, Mrs Gatty 'found Vaughan Williams's preoccupation and sudden absorbed silences at meals a little worrying'.[49] Ursula wrote about him that '. . . it seemed, to an onlooker, that there was a sub-conscious saving of all emotion for the deeper needs of creation'– the music in his head could make him difficult to reach.[50]

Another spouse might have complained about such a single-minded pursuit, which for the first years of their life together brought in little income, but instead Adeline was supportive and proud of her husband's dedication to his art. In her surviving letters from between 1898 and 1906, her enthusiasm for his work shines through. She writes mostly to René Gatty (he and the other two Gatty brothers, Nicholas and Ivor, were close friends of the Vaughan Williamses) and to Ralph Wedgwood, who had been best man at their wedding.

In the letters she chats about Vaughan Williams's writing and any performance or publication successes: 'He has set Matthew Arnold's "Dover Beach" to music and has got an article accepted by the *Londoner*'; 'Did he tell you there is a chance of his extension lecturing on music . . .'; 'He sold 2 songs the other day for £2.12.6! the first money he has earned in that way.'[51] The couple share in the emotional experience of attending live performances of his work: 'I had the excitement of hearing one of his songs sung at a party the other day – a sort of folk song to the very breezy words of Barnes . . .'; 'We have had the excitement of hearing my husband's 4tet . . . I think we were both too nervous to listen much!'[52] She discusses his creative process – '. . . he is entering on a new phase of composition & is getting "complicated" like the Russians'[53] – and those of their friends: to Holst she writes, 'I had no need of restoratives or of poisons after listening to yr tune. It has a haunting quality in it that I like – Ralph has come to the conclusion he was not made to write opera – & I think so too – but I hope you will.'[54]

Gatty's health is a source of worry – 'do not keep us out of your difficulties' – and she sends him money when he is ill: 'The only thing I will beg of you is not to employ that worst of economies a bad Doctor . . . please give Ralph the pleasure of using the £5 for that purpose . . .'[55] To Wedgwood her letters are affectionate and open – 'I hope we may have you here again – if you did not find it too horribly uncomfortable – you shall always be as erratic as you like. We miss you very much.'[56]

Usually, she intends to amuse. She writes about their housekeeper, Mrs Temple, who reappeared after a four-month absence having been in Holloway jail for 'threatening to brain a fellow lodger with a coal hammer . . . she denies the story & says "brain" as a verb has never formed part of her vocabulary'.[57] A holiday in the Quantocks 'necessitated a lot of Coleridge & Wordsworth from which I am only just recovering'.[58] In a letter to René Gatty she describes how his brother, Ivor, is painting her portrait: 'I always come out like a charwoman in photographs and portraits! I feel I have missed my true calling . . .'[59] She pokes fun at her husband too – they had recently moved to a new house at Barton Street and 'Ralph gives himself very important airs as a householder, turning off his gas & locking every window & door every night.'

Often, the mildly mocking tone is directed at herself, and she appears ready to examine her own behaviour. After writing critically about Maurice Amos, a friend from Cambridge days, she comments, 'Am I making too many desultory remarks about him? . . . lest you think I am trying to be ill-natured . . . I got on quite comfortably with him . . .'[60] In a letter to Wedgwood in February 1905 she is particularly confessional. The words feel wrenched from her, the difficulty in expressing herself reflected in the dashes and lack of punctuation: 'I am so touched at your writing – & glad to have such dear words from you – I was so hard & matter of fact at York I felt very unhappy afterwards but it wasn't that I was not feeling things. I can say so little & can never say what you are to us – & whatever the circumstances it is so lovely to see you.'[61] Here she is explicit that her outward 'hard' appearance is a protective layer, a way of keeping her inarticulate emotions under control. It is almost a love letter.

At this time, she was interested in photography – which she had been taught by her aunt, the renowned photographer Julia Margaret Cameron. This was not a dilettante hobby – she carried out the messy work of developing and printing her own plates.[62] She sent René one of her images taken from a steamer on the way to Kew – '. . . there seems to be something early Victorian about it & it looks as if it were a photograph from an oil painting . . .' – and others from a visit they made to the Gattys' family home in Hooton Roberts, South Yorkshire: 'Ralph irreverently suggests that under the one of Ivor should be written "what do you say God?"'[63] These holidays in Hooton were regular, and one of the younger Gatty children, Margot, loved Adeline for including her in the grown-up activities during their stays: 'Adeline won her heart for life . . .'[64]

Adeline continued to practise the piano and cello. During their engagement she and Vaughan Williams played duet arrangements of Wagner's operas together and, once married, her husband continued to write piano music for her.[65] Adeline mentions a happy afternoon at home when she was one of a string quartet whose other members were her husband on viola, Nicholas Gatty on violin and Gustav Holst on second violin – this is exalted company, and confirms that she was, at least, a competent player.[66] She was also learning Russian, although she mentions to Wedgwood (1899) that she should really be learning to cook and that her husband 'has tried to lead me in the right path by buying me a penny book called "Making the home" which contains a recipe for making a mattress . . .'[67] Another gift from her husband was a school atlas: 'My want of geography was bringing disgrace upon us both.'[68] The tone of the letters is light, amused, self-deprecating, ironic. The impression is of a couple busy with their independent interests, enjoying a varied social life and having fun together. It is tragic that those occupations which she loved – the photography, the piano and cello, the social visits – all slipped away from her as the arthritis took hold.

Although to Ursula and Virginia, Adeline appeared cold and aloof, it is clear from her letters that she felt things deeply. There is a poignant story which Ursula tells, of a party Adeline organised for the couple's friend, Martin Shaw, in 1910. On returning from the shops where she had bought further refreshments, she heard the guests talking animatedly upstairs. When she entered the room, they fell silent. Later that evening she said to Margot Gatty, who was staying at the house, 'I shall give a party some day and not be there.'[69] This is an enigmatic statement, but Margot loved Adeline and would have reported it as a friend who sympathised with her situation. For Ursula it indicated detachment. Vaughan Williams's more recent biographer believes it was a sign of her becoming 'socially withdrawn'.[70] It is, perhaps, an expression of something more complex. Adeline was an educated woman with creative impulses who, despite her marriage to a liberal-minded man, was confined by the expectations of her class. The room at the party for Shaw was full of men who may have felt obliged to end their noisy conversations when the lady of the house entered. She was not one of them. Her serious interests in music and photography and her family commitments provided Vaughan Williams with the artistic space he required to follow his musical calling but was interpreted by some as neglectful. Her 'cruel' criticism was probably just criticism,[71] her 'edged' wit just wit, her lack of attention to appearance only the same as her husband's well-known

Ralph and Adeline Vaughan Williams photographed by Ursula in 1950

indifference to such things. At this stage in her life, painful arthritis was already limiting her ability to walk long distances. Her world was contracting. It is not surprising that she predicted her own invisibility.

By the time Ursula wrote her autobiography, published almost forty years after the biography of Vaughan Williams, her assessment of his first marriage had evolved. She had the grace to acknowledge the positive role Adeline had played in her husband's creative process, even after arthritis had affected their life together: she had, Ursula admitted, been 'a centre for him rather than a curb'.[72]

⌒

Vaughan Williams married Adeline in October 1897, a few days before his twenty-fifth birthday. It was forty years since the conviction of Captain Doyle for common assault on Robert Eastick. The cabin boy's mother, Elizabeth, died the year before, after spending the rest of her days in the house off St James' Street in King's Lynn. She had lived long enough to see all her surviving children rise in the world. Matilda had moved with her husband to Hoxton in north London where, by the 1880s, she was the proprietor of a chandler's shop. After some years as a housemaid in the borough of Lambeth, Mary Ann married a 'boatman' and went to live in Devon. Sarah did not marry but made a career as a school matron in Downham Market, not far from King's Lynn, before joining Mary Ann in the south-west after retirement. Frances married a businessman, and the couple were retired and living in a 'villa' with a servant in 1891. Later, Sarah came to London to keep Frances company, and they grew old together in a Tottenham apartment. James, Elizabeth's other son, left King's Lynn for Hackney, where he worked as a stationer. From the 1860s until his death in the late 1890s he owned a terraced house in Appleby Road where he lived with his wife and a growing family of nine children. The house was within two minutes' walk of John Sugars's home in Richmond Road. If he had been a churchgoer, James would have shared the same congregation of St Michael's and All Angels with the former shipowner. Every Sunday he would have seen Sugars's name inscribed in the stained-glass window and the painting which had been gifted to the church. It is striking to find the two men resident in such close proximity and tempting to suggest a connection between James's good fortune and another of Sugars's charitable acts.

In the same year that Vaughan Williams collected 'The Captain's Apprentice', he and Adeline moved into Cheyne Walk, Chelsea, where they lived for the next twenty-four years. Although the composer assumed the song was connected to an event from King's Lynn's distant past, Robert Eastick's sisters were still living out their lives only a few miles away in a London suburb.

A Firm and Generous Friend

Lucy Broadwood

In a letter to Lucy Broadwood in April 1923 Vaughan Williams wrote, '. . . I remember years ago at St George's Square when I was v. raw how you shewed me Purcell & Bach & many things I did not know & as to Folksong – it was you who 1st introduced me to it.'[1]

Biographies of Vaughan Williams do not dwell on his friendship with Lucy Broadwood, but her role was fundamental to the development of his career, through her social network, and her knowledge of music. In this letter Vaughan Williams recalls visiting the Broadwoods' London home in St George's Square – perhaps while he was a student at the Royal College of Music between 1890 and 1892 – when, as he admits in his later memoir, he was 'painfully illiterate' and in need of musical education.[2] The letter implies a friendly and established relationship between the young man and the older woman (there were fourteen years between them) – she in the role of mentor, exploring with him the works of great composers, exchanging ideas and, most significantly, introducing him to folk song.[3]

Vaughan Williams wrote that he experienced his folk-music epiphany when he played through the song 'Lazarus' and realised that 'this was what we had all been waiting for – something which we knew already – something which had always been with us if we had only known it'.[4] It was published in *English County Songs* in 1893, when he was twenty-one.[5] Also known as 'Dives and Lazarus', the song tells the story of a rich man, Dives, who repeatedly ignores the pleas of the poor man, Lazarus, as he lies starving outside the door (an earlier angle on the sentiment expressed in that 1904 song sung in Southwold, 'It's the Poor that Help the Poor'). When Lazarus dies he is taken up to heaven by two angels, but when Dives dies two serpents take him down to hell. The words of the song were widely available on ballad sheets and in books, but the melody was chosen by performers. The tune used for 'Lazarus' in *English County Songs* was clearly popular – in this book alone two other songs use a similar tune with alternative words, and the editors point out its resemblance to three more examples from previously published collections.[6]

Vaughan Williams found several more versions of the air across the country in his collecting career, and it appears as a theme in a number of his later works, most famously in the popular orchestral piece, *Five variants of 'Dives and Lazarus'* (1939). He included the air under the title of 'Kingsfold' in *The English Hymnal* of 1906 and as 'Job' ('Come all you worthy Christian men') in *The Oxford Book of Carols* (1928), and used it as a theme in a number of later works – *Fantasia on Sussex Folk*

Tunes (1930); *Festival Te Deum* (1938); and in the film score for *The Dim Little Island* (1949).[7] This archetypal folk tune is used in modern times to evoke a nostalgic, rural past – as the foundation tune for the song in the theatre production of Michael Morpurgo's *War Horse*, or for the 2019 radio dramatisation of Edna O'Brien's *Country Girls*. Most people will have heard it as the melody for 'Star of the County Down':

> From Bantry Bay up to Derry Quay
> And from Galway to Dublin town
> No maid I've seen like the sweet colleen
> That I met in the County Down.

It is one of the threads running through Vaughan Williams's musical life.

He writes that he 'lighted' on the tune when a copy of *English County Songs* 'came into my hands'.[8] His possession of the book sounds like a lucky chance, a matter of finding it left on the seat of a train or passed quietly under a table. In fact, it would have been odd if he had not been one of the first to read the book, as Lucy Broadwood was its co-editor.

⌢

Vaughan Williams's awakening to folk music when he heard 'Lazarus', and his acknowledgement that Broadwood introduced him to folk song, appear to neatly align in her role as co-editor of *English County Songs*. But in the letter of April 1923, I think he is referring to an earlier, more personal and direct connection than this – Broadwood had known him from a young age.

Six miles down the road from Leith Hill Place, the Broadwoods – world-famous for their eponymous piano-manufacturing company – kept a country house in the village of Newdigate. They were long-standing friends of the Vaughan Williams and Wedgwood families and frequently met at social events.[9] In a letter to Cecil Sharp in 1909 Broadwood writes that Vaughan Williams 'was born with a quite unusually sensitive impetuous temperament (which in childhood naturally was remarkably apparent)', and asserts her 'literally life-long regard for R.V.W.' – she was about fourteen years old when he was born – as well as 'the whole of the huge tribe of Darwins, Wedgwoods, Allens etc.: with whom it has been my privilege to be intimate all ones [sic] own life'.[10] Once he was older, she and the teenage Vaughan Williams met at more formal gatherings – she notes in her diary that he was a fellow party guest at Abinger Hall in September 1887 when he was fifteen, and she was in her late twenties.[11] The hall, within five miles of Leith Hill Place, was the seat of Sir Thomas Farrer and his second wife Katherine Euphemia Wedgwood, cousin of Vaughan Williams's mother, and a distant relation of Broadwood.[12] Through such social gatherings a friendship grew up between the schoolboy and the young woman, based on a shared passion for music.[13] Ursula wrote that Broadwood interested him in the subject of folk song: as a result Vaughan Williams was familiar from an early age with how they were collected.[14]

This local link with folk-song collecting had its roots in the 1840s when Broadwood's uncle, John, brought together a collection of songs he had heard sung by country people in the counties of Surrey and Sussex and published them privately for

Lucy Broadwood

circulation amongst family and friends. In this volume, known as *Old English Songs*, tunes and words were presented together, and he was careful to ensure that the airs were set down 'exactly as they are now sung'.[15]

After John Broadwood's death in 1864 his brother Henry inherited the Newdigate house and moved in with his young family. Lucy was only six when Uncle John died but his *Old English Songs* collection was part of the family inheritance – Henry sang the tunes around the house and occasionally collected songs himself.[16] Young Miss Broadwood's interest in folk music was further encouraged by Alfred Hipkins, trusted long-term employee of the piano company. He suggested she should protect her uncle's legacy and write down the old Sussex songs from around her home, as 'in these days of rapid change many good airs will be lost that ought to be preserved'.[17] Broadwood took up this challenge, working with her cousin, Herbert Birch Reynardson, to produce in 1890 a revised public edition of John Broadwood's private collection, this time entitled *Sussex Songs: Popular Songs of Sussex*.[18] She added nine songs, brought together from material in the family archive, from printed sources, and from the knowledge of locals.[19]

Broadwood's key technique – developed further while researching her next book, *English County Songs* – was to enlist people to collect for her, including a baker from Sussex, a cornet player from Surrey, her sister-in-law in Hertfordshire, and an old friend in Cumberland along with well-known collectors such as Sabine Baring-Gould and Frank Kidson.[20] This approach enabled her to extend the search country-wide, and to gather material from places that were not accessible to a well-to-do young woman, such as pubs or out in the fields. Even when she found a willing performer, they would often censor songs considered 'unfit for ladies' ears'.[21]

It was in the years leading up to publication of *Sussex Songs* in 1890, when Broadwood was gathering new material from her local contacts, that the young Vaughan Williams was first inspired to actively collect folk songs himself. A former Leith Hill Place employee, J. Ellis Cook, remembered that during holidays from Charterhouse school (attended 1887–90), the teenager would ask workmen on the estate to sing to him and he would write the notes down, ask for the same song again and write down any difference.[22] At a time when the collection of folk tunes was a relatively rare and obscure activity, the timing of his interest is surely no coincidence. Broadwood directly influenced his decision to start collecting.

A photograph of the workers employed during Vaughan Williams's childhood shows his nurse sitting in the centre of the group, and on her right, the sort of man who might know old songs, dressed in thick woollen trousers and waistcoat, a sturdy jacket over. He sits with his legs apart, hands on knees, feet together, looking into the distance, his eyes small, his nose sharp. Most of the other men have moustaches or beards, but his slightly jutting chin is clean-shaven, a spotted neckerchief around his neck. From under his brimmed hat white curls protrude like an eighteenth-century wig. Of all the staff gathered there, he is the one I can imagine sitting down with young 'Ralphy' in the kitchen garden to sing an old ditty or two. This is very likely – the man is Mark Cook, the gardener who lived in a cottage still referred to as 'Mark Cottage', across the lane from the big house. A couple of other photos of him survive, both taken by Adeline in 1897.[23] In one he stands in the walled garden; the second depicts a staged scene with his granddaughter on the lawn of the house. He leans on a walking stick; his granddaughter, in white pinny and straw hat, shows him a basket, presumably containing produce picked from the garden. These images suggest an affectionate relationship with the old employee. His son, John Ellis, took over the role of gardener when Mark retired and it was he who recalled how Vaughan Williams collected songs as a boy. When Vaughan Williams returned in 1904 as an adult to find folk songs locally, he visited two people with links to his teenage collecting days, perhaps because he remembered that they both knew good songs. The first, Mrs Berry of Leith Hill Farm, was surely Phillis, wife of Edmund Berry, groom and coachman, who sits on the far right

Leith Hill Place staff, June 1885

of the front row (he was still the coachman in 1901); the second, Isaac Longhurst, was probably related to Anne Longhurst, lady's maid, who sits next to Berry.[24]

While at Charterhouse Vaughan Williams organised a 'Welsh Concert' based on Boosey's *Songs of Wales*, a collection of Welsh 'airs' set to English words. He composed a march for the event using these tunes and later points out that '. . . this must have been my first essay in "folk-song" composition'.[25] At sixteen, folk music was already his inspiration.

☙

At about the same age that Vaughan Williams began to take an active interest in folk song, Robert Eastick died at sea. The two boys shared one life experience in common – they were both infants when their fathers died. As a widow, Margaret Vaughan Williams returned to her childhood home where she was

Ralph Vaughan Williams, 1888

supported by her family and a household of servants. Elizabeth Eastick, bereaved in her early forties and with five children still at home, struggled to replace the income her husband had earned as a cooper – a maker and repairer of casks and barrels, often for ships, and a good skill to have in a port. She embarked on the hard, physical work of laundering other people's linen. Her daughters went to London to make their way as servants, and Elizabeth took in a lodger. When James was old enough, he earned some pennies as an errand boy. In 1853 he signed up as a captain's apprentice, but three months later his indenture was cancelled. No doubt he reflected on this abrupt change in his life's direction when, as a father, he sat in the comfortable Hoxton house with his children around him and remembered the fate of his brother. Had he survived, Robert would have become the adventurer of the family, the youngest sibling who escaped the backwaters of Norfolk and the suburbs of London to return with songs and stories of the world.

⌒

Vaughan Williams spent much of the 1890s working towards his preferred career as a composer: although he started a history degree at Cambridge in 1892, he took regular composition and organ lessons while there, and continued weekly lessons with Hubert Parry at the Royal College of Music (RCM) in London.[26] After completing his degree he returned to the capital, to pursue a doctorate at the RCM and to work as organist at St Barnabas church, South Lambeth. Two years later, in late 1897, he married Adeline and they went to Berlin, where Vaughan Williams took composition lessons with Max Bruch for several months.[27] In the meantime, following the death of her father, Lucy Broadwood moved permanently to London and developed a busy musical life. On visits to Sussex and Surrey, she continued to collect songs for which she wrote piano arrangements, and she began to compose her own pieces.[28] In London she sang at private soirées or provided piano accompaniment for others and attended numerous concerts and parties. Her social circle of performers and composers included influential figures in the capital's musical world such as Fuller Maitland and Hubert Parry.

By the time Vaughan Williams and Adeline returned to London in 1898 Broadwood was in a position to support his fledgling career. She and Fuller Maitland were prominent members of the Purcell Society, founded in 1876 with the aim of publishing the seventeenth-century composer's music. Through these connections Vaughan Williams was invited by the society in around 1900 to edit a series of songs known as the *Welcome Odes*.[29] This led to further commissions from Fuller Maitland to write entries on 'fugue' and 'conducting' for *Grove's Dictionary*.[30] Broadwood also provided Vaughan Williams with opportunities to air his new compositions at her regular private musical parties – at one of these in 1901 he performed his settings of poems by Dorset poet William Barnes.[31] This advocacy for the young composer was part of her wider activities to promote young musicians – her friend Mary Venables later praised 'the helping hand she was always willing to give to many young artists'.[32]

Broadwood's opinion on music was important to Vaughan Williams – in July 1902 he responded to a card from her which congratulated him on a performance of his work. He wrote, 'I expect you know yourself what a great pleasure it is to receive praise from those whose opinion you value.'[33] In October of that year he sought her advice on whether his composition 'Willowwood' might be appropriate for performance in a large hall – it was subsequently sung in 1903 by Broadwood's close friend Campbell McInnes at one of the Broadwood concerts – a series of events run by the piano-making company.[34]

In 1898 Broadwood was involved in the founding of the Folk-Song Society – she sat on the inaugural committee of twelve which included Fuller Maitland and Kidson. Vaughan Williams did not join immediately. He reports in his memoir that in around 1900 Broadwood asked him to 'see the songs she had collected in Sussex' where he saw 'the flattened cadence in all its glory'.[35] This is puzzling as it was five years since *English County Songs* had 'come into his hands'. Although during this period the young composer had focused on the music of Wagner, Purcell and Bach, his tutors were exasperated by his 'passion for the flat seventh': 'I went berserk on the flat seventh and the sharp sixth and the Mixolydian cadence'.[36] Perhaps Broadwood had sent him her newly collected material with the intention of rekindling his interest. If so, this ruse worked because not long after, in the autumn of 1902, Vaughan Williams delivered the first of his series of lectures on folk music.

The subject was his choice even though, as he admitted later, he knew 'precious little about it and the little knowledge I had was entirely out of books'.[37] During his preparation he turned to Broadwood for advice on Scottish folk song and to her published works, including a copy of the *Journal of the Folk-Song Society* that she had recently sent him. [38] This edition from 1902 consisted entirely of songs she had collected with an introduction describing her methods and sources.[39] In a letter to her, Vaughan Williams declares that he is going to use songs from the journal and large parts of her preface in his upcoming lecture at Bournemouth: 'I hope you do not mind.'[40] Her response to this brazen admission of plagiarism is not on record but, in the event, she attended his lecture in November on 'Characteristics of National Songs in the British Isles' and sang illustrative songs from her collection.[41] It is worth noting that there was a 'crowded attendance' for this lecture in anticipation of Broadwood's contribution – her reputation as an established folk-song collector and performer went before her. Even so, the event marks the moment when the balance of their relationship shifts. As the presenter of six talks on aspects of folk song Vaughan Williams establishes himself as an authority – *he* is giving the lectures, while Broadwood quietly listens to him expounding her research and takes the spotlight only when she is asked to sing.

In December of the following year, while lecturing in Essex, Vaughan Williams heard the second life-changing song, 'Bushes and Briars' – the one which set all his doubts about folk song at rest – performed by Mr Potiphar.[42] In the same month Cecil Sharp wrote to Broadwood. He had collected forty songs in Somerset and was impatient with the Folk-Song Society's moribund state.[43] Only two months later, in February 1904, Broadwood and Sharp dined at the Vaughan Williamses' house to discuss the Folk-Song Society and make 'a scheme for reviving its dying embers'.[44] In March, Broadwood became secretary and editor of the *Journal of the Folk-Song Society* while Sharp was elected to the committee, joined by Vaughan Williams in June. The society's annual report for that year declares, 'No time must be lost, for every day carries off some old singer with whom some precious tunes may die for ever unrecorded.'[45] The society's revival and the new impetus to collect songs was a pivotal moment in Vaughan Williams's life: he fully committed himself to the cause of folk song and embarked on a decade of intense collecting. On the journey to this point Lucy Broadwood had been his guide, leading the way. Now Vaughan Williams strode ahead, with Sharp at his side.

Both men grew increasingly frustrated with Broadwood's scholarly approach to collecting and research which made her slow to publish material. Vaughan Williams's valedictory piece written when she stepped down as the *Journal*'s editor in 1927 reflects this. Although he praises her as a pioneer and acknowledges her long service to the society, he hints at the difference between them: 'She loves the songs with an almost personal affection, and she has naturally shrunk from bringing into the glaring light of publicity these songs . . . which it has been her delight to ponder over in the quiet of her study.'[46] Though couched in flattering terms the implied criticism would have been clear to her.

She acknowledged her reputation as a 'pernickety fogey' in response to a bad-tempered letter from Vaughan Williams, sent after she had made negative comments about *The Oxford Book of Carols* (1928) which he co-edited.[47] His annoyance caused his writing to be 'specially illegible', which required Adeline to make a clean copy for Broadwood.[48] After thanking her for writing, he begins, 'I wish you had sent your emendations to me as I originally asked you – and could you specify your rather vague condemnation of Dearmer's methods?'[49] The transformation in the balance of power is stark – once deferential towards her greater scholarship, he now feels able to express his irritation and assert his own more practical approach: 'Suppose for example you found from one singer a very beautiful version of the tune and from another . . . a beautiful version of the words of a ballad – would you not put them together for singing purposes? Is this cooking? If it is may I often sit down to the meal.'[50] She writes an equally robust critique in reply, remarking that if the book had been a purely popular publication she would have said nothing but 'as coming from the Oxford University Press . . . That shocked me!'[51] This correspondence reflects the frankness that was possible between them after their lifelong relationship but also painfully exposes their different attitudes. Both must have been left smarting after the exchange.

Broadwood died less than a year later. In a 'portrait' published in 1948 Vaughan Williams wrote that 'to all those who were fortunate enough to gain her sympathy' – of which he was one – 'she was a firm and generous friend', but it is clear that the differences between them continued to rankle.[52] Shortly before his own death in 1958 he received a letter from Broadwood's niece, Joan Bray, who requested a memorial article to be published in the *English Folk Dance and Song Society Journal* to mark the centenary of her aunt's birth. She complained that Sharp 'following in my aunt's footsteps, & using her methods of folk song researching etc., stole much of the limelight that should have been rightly hers'.[53] This reflected Broadwood's own feelings, laid bare in a letter to her sister in 1924:

> Mr Cecil Sharp unfortunately took up old songs & old dance-collecting as a profession, &, not being a gentleman, he puffed and boomed and shoved and ousted . . . so that, although we pioneers were the people from whom he originally learnt all he knew of the subjects he came to believe himself to be King . . .[54]

Vaughan Williams may have felt personally attacked by Bray's allegations – he had, after all, been a close ally of Sharp's – or perhaps at the age of eighty-five he no longer had the patience to spare feelings: his response was forthright. He did not think an article was necessary, and defended Sharp against the snobbery that Broadwood and other committee members had displayed towards him for not belonging to the 'right musical set': 'Miss Broadwood was mistaken in keeping the Folk Songs as a study for the few, and also misunderstood Cecil Sharp's attitude towards our duty to disseminate Folk Song as broadly as possible.'[55] As so often happens in the student–teacher relationship, the protégé had grown into a critic of his old tutor. Seventy years on from his enthusiastic Charterhouse days, Vaughan Williams had left Lucy Broadwood far behind.

'The Cherry Tree Carol'

'The Cherry Tree Carol', 1871

At seventy, Vaughan Williams recalled a vivid memory of a childhood Christmas, when his family stayed with an aunt 'much bitten' by the William Morris movement, the walls of her house painted with sunflowers, and the windows filled with 'bottle' glass.[1] His aunt was a 'first-rate' musician, and she loved to celebrate Christmas, gathering her musical children around the piano in the evenings to sing from 'Stainer and Bramley', a well-known volume of carols. One Christmas, when he was about ten, they sang 'The Cherry Tree Carol' and it remained 'a fragrant possession' for the rest of his life.[2] At seventy-eight, he described his reaction to the carol as more than simple admiration for a fine tune, although as a boy he had not understood what invoked that 'sense of intimacy' – the feeling that he had always known it.[3] This remembered occasion was Vaughan Williams's first step on the path towards folk-song collecting – and yet the woman who set the scene for this significant experience is not named. Who was this 'Arts and Crafts' aunt?

Vaughan Williams's extended family of Wedgwoods and Darwins included several members who married cousins. In his immediate family, his mother, Margaret, was the daughter of cousins Caroline Darwin and Josiah Wedgwood, and Caroline's brother Charles Darwin married his Wedgwood cousin Emma. Within this complex tangle of family relationships, any older woman with a family connection could be an 'aunt' and, correspondingly, her children cousins. This unnamed Christmas-time 'aunt' was not necessarily a sister of Vaughan Williams's mother or father but could have been a female relation further along the branches of his family tree. The necessary identifying features are her love of William Morris, her 'first-rate' musicianship, and the musical ability of her children.

The aunts most prominent in Vaughan Williams's early life were Sophy and Lucy, his mother's sisters. Sophy gave him his first music lessons, and some of his childhood compositions were dedicated to her – but she lived with the family at Leith Hill Place and never married so cannot be a candidate.

Lucy was 'the officially musical one' and her 'flair for composition was encouraged'.[4] She married Matthew James Harrison, a naval officer who was away from home for long periods. At these times Lucy would often stay at Leith Hill Place with her five children, all younger than Vaughan Williams. In 1882, when he was ten, the oldest surviving Harrison cousin was only five, and the fifth child had not yet been born.[5] They were not old enough to contribute to the carol singing.

On the Vaughan Williams side of the family the aunts are more shadowy. Arthur Vaughan Williams, the composer's father, had several siblings but only three brothers survived into older age. Walter receives a passing mention in Ursula's biography but there appears to be scant information about him elsewhere. The other two uncles, Roland and 'Edwardie', continued to be involved in the life of the family at Leith Hill Place after Arthur's death, but their wives, Aunt Emily and Aunt Laura, do not step into the foreground of Vaughan Williams's memoirs.[6]

In an account of the Wedgwood family circle, Ralph Vaughan Williams is described as 'the first Wedgwood, apart from his cousin Effie and his great-aunt Emma, to show the slightest gift for music . . .'[7] The Vaughan Williams family regularly visited Great-Aunt Emma, wife of Charles Darwin, at Down House in Kent. She was an accomplished pianist, but she was not a fan of William Morris: in fact, she was as 'indifferent to houses and fashionable furniture as she was to clothes'.[8]

The other musical Wedgwood – 'Effie' – was Katherine

Euphemia, Margaret's cousin.[9] In 1873 she married Sir Thomas Farrer and the couple lived at Abinger Hall, near Leith Hill Place. Effie trained seriously as a singer and was interested in unconventional lifestyles – she was a vegetarian, an early cyclist and a member of the Theosophical Society; she also dabbled in the occult. The Arts and Crafts movement may have appealed to her, but she had no children of her own, and her four stepchildren were all considerably older than Vaughan Williams. When he was ten the oldest was twenty-eight, and the youngest sixteen. This does not fit well with the composer's description of musical children gathered around the piano.[10]

Reading through Ursula's biography one particular Christmas memory stands out. While getting ready for a party, young Ralph sees that his cousin Stephen is dressed in velvet, while his own suit is made of mere velveteen. His mother, Margaret, tells him it is because she is not as rich as Stephen's mother. The richer mother was Emily Massingberd, wife of Margaret's cousin Edward Langton.[11] She was a direct relative, and close in age to Margaret. Her children – Charlotte Mildred, Stephen, Mary and Diana – were Vaughan Williams's contemporaries. He calls them cousins, and they were all able musicians.

The two families regularly spent time together. In later years Diana remembered 'summer days at L.H.P. [Leith Hill Place] – . . . raisin bread in the dining room – at 11 o'c . . . Sarah at the tea table, the summer Quarendon apples at the further side of the K[itchen] garden – a little boy making what I thought were lovely sounds out of his head on the pf. [pianoforte] in the drawing room . . .'[12] The Vaughan Williams family made return visits to the Massingberds' Lincolnshire estate where, at twenty,

Ralph wrote a piece called 'Happy Days at Gunby' which the two families performed together.[13] Their mother was also a musician – in a portrait from 1878 Emily Massingberd stands proudly holding a viola in the foreground. She meets the William Morris criterion, too – after her husband's death in the early 1870s, she commissioned for herself a striking Arts and Crafts-style home, the Red House, in Bournemouth.[14]

Massingberd was a feminist, and an active campaigner for women's suffrage. In 1892 she founded the Pioneer Club in London to provide 'a meeting-ground for women workers of all kinds'.[15] She said about the club: 'Here we have no social distinctions, we all meet together on the common ground of sisterhood . . . We are of all creeds and politics, of different professions and of no professions, although most of us "do" something, but united together in the desire to promote the advancement of women's interests.'[16]

It appears that it was the campaigner 'Aunt' Emily who introduced Vaughan Williams to 'The Cherry Tree Carol' and it was at the Red House, Derby Road, Bournemouth that his journey towards folk-song collecting began.

⌒

'The Cherry Tree Carol' was one of forty-two published as *Christmas Carols New and Old* in the 1860s, edited and arranged by the Revd Henry Ramsden Bramley and Sir John Stainer.[17] Their intention was to '. . . obtain traditional Carol Tunes and Words which have escaped the researches of previous collectors'. The book contains a number of previously unpublished old songs, as well as original compositions by 'eminent Musicians'.[18]

The book was beautifully produced, its oxide-red cover dec-orated with marginal panels of embossed gold. In a central panel the Virgin Mary holds the baby Jesus against a black sky spark-ling with gold stars. Inside, each page is illustrated with engravings by a collection of contemporary artists. Those commissioned from 'the brothers Dalziel' present a Victorian Christmas world of starlit nights, snow-blanketed hills and wassailing choirs of quaintly dressed children. The piano arrangements are simple, and Vaughan Williams could have leafed through the book on a win-ter's afternoon and played the carols himself.

What was it about 'The Cherry Tree Carol' that made it stand out from the others? On first hearing, it is a simple melody that would suit a nursery rhyme. Most of the tunes in the book are ascribed to composers but fourteen are described as 'Traditional'. The major-ity of these – such as the still familiar 'The First Nowell', 'A Child This Day is Born' and 'The Wassail Song' – are set in conventional major scales and harmonies. A small number, including 'God Rest You, Merry, Gentlemen', are in minor scales. 'The Cherry Tree Carol' is noted in a standard major scale but there is something about the arrangement which gives the song a distinctive flavour.

Although the key signature indicates that it is in G major, there is an emphasis all through the piece on the note D – akin to the continuous note of a hurdy-gurdy or bagpipe under the melody. [19] Because of its insistence, the listener unconsciously registers D as the tonic – or first note – of the scale. This emphasis gives the song a Mixolydian flavour.[20] The young Vaughan Wil-liams did not understand what attracted him to this particular carol, but it is the only one in the book with the trace of a modal scale. The unexpected arrangement of notes caught 'Ralphy's' attention – a break in the standard intervals and harmonies – which he cherished.

The words might also have intrigued him. In 1907 when commenting on Cecil Sharp's manuscript of *English Folk Song: Some Conclusions* he suggests that carols should be included in the chapter on folk poetry: 'To my mind hardly any ballad poetry is more beautiful than "the 1st Noel" "The Lord at 1st did Adam make" or "The angel Gabriel" or "God rest you merry gentlemen"'.[21] The words of 'The Cherry Tree Carol' have the character of a fairy tale, in which the highest sprig of the cherry tree bends down to Mary so that she can reach the fruit. Even the title, with its promise of summer fruit in the midst of winter, may have attracted him. When he co-edited *The Oxford Book of Carols* in 1928, 'The Cherry Tree Carol' was included with the Stainer and Bramley tune.

⌒

A portrait of Emily Massingberd, dated 1871, shows a soft blue-and-lilac image of femininity, her face gazing out at us passively, hands clasped restfully in her lap. In the 1878 portrait completed three years after her husband's death there has been a transformation.[22] She is caught in motion, her viola and bow in hand, eyes amused, mouth slightly open, perhaps asking, 'What shall I play?' Her hair scraped back, and dressed in black, at first glance she could be mistaken for a fresh-faced young man. In a later photograph she appears with her grown-up children, the long hair of her daughters tied and pinned in complicated braids, her own hair cut short and uncompromising. The Pioneer Club motto – *They say. What say they? Let them say* – speaks of her defiance in the face of potential disapproval.

Her obituary, written by Pioneer Club member Mary Mack Wall, records a strong will. After Massingberd had directed an entertainment at the club one evening, Mack Wall said to her, 'You must be very tired.' She replied, 'No, I am never tired'.[23]

Emily Massingberd by J. C. Moore, 1878

Her first public speech was given at an entertainment she laid on for the workmen who built the Red House. After this success, she campaigned for temperance and anti-vivisection as well as female suffrage. Mack Wall describes a woman of vivid energy:

> Generous and unselfish to an extreme degree, 'a perfect housemate' willing to sacrifice everything but principle, to peace, [*sic*] clear-headed, with a quick eye for domestic details and a kind manner of supervising, endowed, too, with musical, artistic and dramatic talents, she laid herself out lavishly . . . for the good of all with whom she came into contact.

This generosity of spirit can be seen in the design of the Red House – visitors stepping into the hallway would read *'and yours my friends'* inscribed over the internal archway. The main room was big enough for open meetings, music performances and amateur dramatics. It was a house designed for entertaining, where children staying over for Christmas parties could hide in the minstrel's gallery, dress up, and make music.

Stephen Massingberd – who wore the velvet trousers – was three years older than Ralph and was a contemporary at Charterhouse school, where they performed together.[24] It was he who pointed out to Vaughan Williams that 'This man Parry declares that a composer must write music as his musical conscience demands.'[25] His adoption of this creed helps to explain Vaughan Williams's dogged perseverance when faced with a lack of enthusiasm for his youthful composition. Stanford, his teacher at the RCM, would say about his early work, 'Damnably ugly, my boy. Why do you write such things?'[26] His family on the Wedgwood/Darwin side were equally doubtful about his ability. Although he thought he could have made a 'quite decent fiddler' they persuaded him to take up the safer option of the organ.[27] Gwen Raverat, granddaughter of Charles and Emma Darwin, recalled as a child hearing family discussions about ' "that foolish young man" . . . who would go on working at music "when he was so hopelessly bad at it" ', and her aunt Henrietta wrote, 'He has been playing all his life, and for six months hard, and yet he can't play the simplest thing decently.'[28]

In contrast the Massingberd cousins supported his aspirations as a musician and composer. After his mother's death Stephen inherited Gunby Hall where he and his wife, Margaret (*née*

Lushington), started the Lincolnshire Musical Festival at Spilsby. This provided opportunities for Vaughan Williams to try out his material – Margaret commissioned him to set Christina Rossetti's poem 'Sound Sleep' for the 1903 event.[29] Diana, an accomplished musician, sang in the Magpie Madrigal Society, an amateur choir based in London whose upper-class members (Lucy Broadwood was one) mostly sang English madrigals of the sixteenth and seventeenth centuries but occasionally performed music written by RCM professors and students, including Parry, Stanford, Holst – and Vaughan Williams.[30] In a letter to Holst in 1901 Vaughan Williams suggests that his cousin had some influence on what pieces the choir performed.[31] Cousin Diana was one of the last friends Vaughan Williams and Ursula visited before his death in 1958: 'Ralph said, "Do you remember *Happy Days at Gunby?*" '[32] This creative family, with their musical abilities and liberal politics, were congenial and encouraging company for the young Ralph as he began to take himself seriously as a composer.

⌒

Emily Massingberd died young, in 1897 – not quite fifty. The Bournemouth house later became a hotel and the myth grew up that it had been built for Lillie Langtry by the Prince of Wales (later Edward VII) during their affair – based solely on the initials 'E.L.L.' carved into the foundation stone. Langtry's full married name was Emilie Charlotte Langtry but in this narrative it is argued that the initials stand for Emilie LeBreton Langtry.[33]

There are no concrete facts to connect the nineteenth-century celebrity with the house. On the other hand, there is much to connect Massingberd. Her name in 1877, when the house was built, was Emily Langton-Langton – E.L.L. – the double Langton a result of marrying her cousin, Edmund Langton. The motto set out underneath the minstrel's gallery – *They say. What say they? Let them say* – was also inscribed in stained glass at the Pioneer Club.[34] Conclusively, Mack Wall's obituary for Massingberd states that she built the house.[35]

Despite proof of Massingberd's ownership of and residence at the house, the Lillie Langtry myth lives on, perpetuated in the official National Heritage description where the association with Langtry is cited as one of the reasons for its Grade II status.[36] A Borough of Bournemouth plaque on the front of the house reiterates the story. A woman idolised for her looks and amorous adventures has eclipsed the memory of the contemporary feminist campaigner. When I tell my brother this story, he remembers that a friend interested in all things paranormal had stayed at the hotel because it was rumoured to be haunted by Lillie Langtry's ghost.

⌒

I travel to Bournemouth on a grey September day to seek out Massingberd's house, arriving on a ring road that winds round endless roundabouts. When Vaughan Williams visited the town as a boy, the seaside resort was less than eighty years old, built on open heath as a speculative venture by a local landowner. Arriving on the A338 there is no hint of the young town's genteel core.

Eventually I turn off the urban highway and find myself abruptly in a planned Victorian suburb of wide, leafy roads.

The Red House sits prominently on a corner. These days it looks fussy and conventional – a lavish example of mock-Tudor. In the 1870s it was startingly modern with its tall chimneys, hipped roofs, balconies and pavilions built from timber and plaster, with vertically hung tiles. Its design reflects the ideals of the Arts and Crafts movement – one of those Victorian responses to industrialisation – which championed traditional skills and individual craftsmanship in the face of mass-production.

Walking up to the door, I notice the 'bottle' glass in the gable of the front porch. Beneath this a man is tidying up the flower border. I ask him if non-residents can eat lunch here. He is friendly, smiles, but says no, they only do bed and breakfast these days. Even though many Americans come to stay because of the Lillie Langtry story, once here they prefer to eat out. I ask whether it would be possible to have a quick look inside, and he kindly assents. Feeling guilty, because I have not divulged my true interest in the house, I walk quickly through the entrance hall – *and yours my friends* is still written over the archway – looking for sunflowers (I see none – the walls are hung with numerous pictures of Lillie Langtry and Prince Bertie) and up the stairs to a door labelled 'Minstrel's Gallery'. From this dark, dusty balcony, next to a music system and an abandoned pile of CDs, I look down briefly into a large room.

The bones of the space Vaughan Williams knew remain: the double-height ceiling, the panelled dado, a Jacobean-style man-telpiece of dark wood, and the striking full-height window forming the end of the room – its top half decorated with stained-glass panels, including a portrait of Shakespeare, and at its foot a low dais for performers. This is the room in which he heard 'The Cherry Tree Carol'. Here he first experienced that sense of recognition about a piece of music – 'something entirely new yet absolutely familiar' – which indicated a great work. It became one of those childhood memories that are crystallised in the mind and conjured up at will, focused and in full colour. I try to imagine what he experienced – the smell of woodsmoke, the voices of his young cousins, the rub of unfamiliar velveteen on his skin – but I feel I am here on false pretences, unable to linger, and only manage to snap a photograph before leaving in a hurry.

Afterwards, when sifting through images online I find a photograph of the room taken from the dais looking towards the minstrel's gallery – a view I did not manage to obtain. It occurs to me that as a young man, when family and teachers doubted his abilities, he took courage from the defiant Massingberd motto that he saw many times as a child, proclaimed in script along the base of the balcony: *They say. What say they? Let them say.*

⌢

It is not known whether Emily Massingberd, Lucy Broadwood and Adeline were ever together in one place, but it is possible.[37] On a summer's day in the mid-1880s the paths of all three could have crossed at Leith Hill Place while attending one of the regular dances to which cousins and friends were invited in the school holidays.[38] At such gatherings the young Vaughan Williams arranged chamber music for whichever instruments were available in the house. Emily, Lucy and Adeline, all accomplished musicians, were welcome guests.

On this summer's day, the older women sit on the airy terrace looking out towards the distant line of the south downs, while the young people, including a flaxen-haired Adeline, play in the meadow below. Through the open drawing-room windows, they hear Ralphy playing the piano. Aunt Emily murmurs that the boy shows promise on the keyboard, and his mother replies that they hope he will earn his living as a church organist.[39] Adeline's mother makes a note to herself that although Ralphy is a nice boy he would not be an advantageous match for any of her daughters. It occurs to Lucy that his musical ability would be useful for noting down folk songs from the Leith Hill Place staff. The tranquil afternoon continues, the children run off to the kitchen garden to pick summer apples, the women sip tea in the shade, and later, after everyone has rested in the cool bedrooms of the old house, the dance begins.

CODA

Fen and Flood

[Phone rings] Hello. Yes, yes, speaking. Alert! Sound the alarm! Action stations! Hey ho, away, look alive boys, do our duty, men![1]

On the night of 31 January 1953 the North Sea coast was overwhelmed by a terrible flood. Hurricane-force winds whipped up a predicted high tide into a massive surge. The tidal wave hit King's Lynn at 6.30 p.m. and then sped around the coast towards the Thames estuary and the City of London. One hundred people were killed in Norfolk as the water coursed down streets, burst through doors and poured down chimneys. Britain's worst natural disaster of the twentieth century left over three hundred people dead and forty thousand homeless.[2] In the Netherlands nearly two thousand people perished.

Six months earlier Ursula and Ralph Vaughan Williams had spent an idyllic evening at Heacham by the sea, north of King's Lynn. They were staying at the home of their friend Paddy

Hadley, a pupil of Vaughan Williams in the 1920s, and now a professor of music at Cambridge University. Ursula remembered that they bathed in the sea before dinner and then sat in Hadley's garden where 'hundreds of stars fell out of the sky, and the air was gentle and summery and smelt of lavender fields, now almost ready to be cut'.[3]

Vaughan Williams, who at the age of eighty was the pre-eminent composer of his generation, was booked to deliver a talk at the King's Lynn Festival. His subject was East Anglian folk song, and he took the opportunity to look back at his collecting days in the town nearly half a century before and to recall the thrill of discovering the songs of the fishing community in the North End. If he had hoped to revisit the yards and cottages where he heard 'The Captain's Apprentice', he was too late. During the 1930s the borough council's programme of slum clearance had demolished much of the North End, with the tenants rehoused in newly built estates. But if he had walked past the Tilden Smith pub on that summer evening he might have heard that folk singing was still alive. John Seymour, on his sailing trip through England three years later, noted that '*The Tilden* is still a fisherman's pub. You hear some good songs there.'[4]

⌒

During the 1953 floods the village of Heacham felt the full force of the tidal surge: nine people were drowned.[5] The devastation of his village and the surrounding area moved Paddy Hadley to compose a cantata with libretto by Charles Cudworth, called *Fen and Flood*. This set of songs was designed both as a tribute and an act of defiance, to show 'how man's wit and resource stood against the powers of water on the low lying, fertile but dangerous East Anglian coast', and it was dedicated to Vaughan Williams.[6]

Hadley wrote the piece for the male choir of Caius College, Cambridge, accompanied by two pianos. After Vaughan Williams heard the first performance in May 1955 he felt that an arrangement for mixed choir and soloists would have 'wider possibilities for performance', and he proposed to undertake the task himself. This was unusual: Vaughan Williams had arranged other people's music only a few times and none had been by contemporary composers. Something in the piece touched him. After some initial doubts Hadley became enthusiastic about the idea, saying that his former teacher 'superimposed a magic that wasn't there before'.[7]

With the sound of a wind machine in the background a telephone rings on stage and we hear the words of Superintendent Fred Calvert. He was contacted on the night by the harbour master who could see the water already lapping over the tops of the banks and knew disaster was imminent. Calvert sent out police cars into the threatened areas to broadcast the alert and the words became the libretto: *Alert! . . . Hurry along there! . . . Rescue and relief are coming! . . . They must get through!* In an extraordinary twist, at the 1956 King's Lynn premier of Vaughan Williams's arrangement, this part was performed by Fred Calvert himself. The piece concludes with a heart-stirring rendition of a hymn, 'St Nicholas', the patron saint of sailors.

☙

In 1939 A. L. Lloyd and Francis Dillon recorded a Saturday-night singing session at the Eel's Foot pub in Eastbridge, Suffolk.[8] In the same year, despite doubts about mixing art with politics,

South Lynn, 1953 floods

Vaughan Williams agreed to provide a guarantee of £100 for the Workers Music Association (WMA) in the hope that it would 'help people realize what is in the long run worth while [*sic*]'.[9] The WMA founded Topic Records that year, their first release being 'The Man that Waters Down the Workers' Beer' by Paddy Ryan.[10] After the war Lloyd and other researchers, including Ewan MacColl, went out into the field to record singers such as Norfolk's Sam Larner, Harry Cox and Walter Pardon; Fred Jordan in Shropshire; and the Copper family near Brighton. The availability of this music on vinyl was the seed for a renewed interest in folk music during the 1950s and '60s.[11] It turned out that the art of the folk singer was not dead, as Vaughan Williams had supposed – the singers had carried on after the collectors left. One of his last projects was a collaboration with Lloyd: the jointly edited *The Penguin Book of English Folk Songs* – aimed at 'the partisans of the new folk song revival' – was published in 1959, the year after his death.[12]

A few years earlier, in 1955, Topic brought out *The Singing*

Sailor, a collection of folk songs about life under sail performed by Lloyd, MacColl and Harry H. Corbett. One of the tracks – 'The Cruel Ship's Captain' – is a version of 'The Captain's Apprentice', sung by Lloyd. He uses Carter's tune with a variant of the words which locates the events off the frozen Greenland shore. This appears to be an adaptation by Lloyd, as none of the historical lyrics name Greenland. It reflects his knowledge that King's Lynn was once a whaling port, combined with Vaughan Williams's claim that the song was local to the town.[13] This change in the lyrics was the latest of many over the years, to fit each singer's purpose. Lloyd's version, unaccompanied, individual and raw, provides a glimpse into the world of Duggie Carter.

⌒

The first performance of Vaughan Williams's arrangement of *Fen and Flood* for mixed choir and orchestra took place in St Nicholas' Chapel, North End, where Robert Eastick's parents were married in May 1827; where Duggie Carter married Alice in 1865; and where he and Joe Anderson later sang in Revd Huddle's congregation. In a series of very short songs the cantata tells the story of the surrounding countryside's transformation from its wild state into a domesticated landscape. The opening song describes the primordial fen with its infinite skies, slow-flowing rivers and myriad fish, fowl and eels before moving on to the arrival of the monks, the rise of Ely Cathedral, the drain-age by Dutch engineers, and the rebellion of the fen dwellers. Part Two starts with a cheerful arrangement of the folk song, 'The Painful Plough', to represent the taming of the land and the plentiful bounty it produces to support all other trades, including shipping, before the mood abruptly turns darker, with an introduction: 'Here is a tale of Lynn'.

And it might be this that made Vaughan Williams keen to work on the cantata: there follows a rendition of 'The Captain's Apprentice' – called here the 'The Lynn Apprentice' – which contrasts dramatically with his previous treatments of Carter's tune. The edited lyrics of the 1908 piano arrangement are used, but with an additional opening verse adapted from one of the Dorset versions:

> You captains bold that sail the ocean,
> That have got servants one, two, three;
> I pray you never to ill-use them,
> For you plainly see 'twas the death of me.[14]

This warning, sung by the unaccompanied soprano, is followed by the women of the chorus who repeat the last two lines. The baritone takes up the next three verses, with the male chorus on the refrain. Underlying this, the relentless two-note phrase introduced by the piano and repeated in each bar, takes on a malevolent persistence, building in volume and orchestral layering until, as the boy dies under the captain's 'barbarous cruel entreatment', the tension peaks as the sopranos ululate their anguish over the men's words. The full ensemble performs the final warning verse, the strings swirling up and down the scale in wild grief while the outraged solo soprano screams, 'Take special care of your apprentice'. Vaughan Williams is no longer ruled by the Edwardian constraints of simple arrangements and folk-like harmonies: at last the horror of the cabin boy's tale is given voice.

Last Words

(18 August 1856, 3.45 p.m.)[1]

They said they saw Robert Eastick, bucket in hand at the forecastle, but no one saw him fall. And yet someone sang out, 'Boy overboard!'

The mystery was why the boy was up there at all. It was no place to draw water, high up at the bow, and so far from the captain's quarters at the rear. The contents of the bucket would have slopped out over the deck long before it could be used to scrub the cabin floor.

Only four inches of upstanding timber planking stood as a barrier between the deck of the John Sugars and the drop to the glassy surface of the Indian Ocean below, but sailors were used to such hazards. The day was clear – a 'nice, beautiful day' as the Austrian crew member, George Murdock, recalled when Robert Eastick's case was heard at the Old Bailey. There was no need to fear a sudden heave of the ship as the boy went about his task.

Food was not abundant on board – the ship's carpenter described *in his court testimony how the crew were 'only middlingly off for provision' during the voyage. Other crew members reported that the captain had starved the boy as punishment. After several weeks at sea it was a thin-limbed lad of fifteen who stood on the deck, passing the rope through his hands until the bucket hit the surface. He saw the splash of white foam rise up at its base and watched how it glided silently below the clear water, its stained timber pearled with bubbles. Hauling the bucket made his arm throb painfully. It was red-raw, where the skin had been rubbed against the hatch down to the cabin. Captain Doyle had done that. It began with the simple matter of a knife left in the wrong place.*

'What is this knife on the table?' the captain had demanded.

'That is the knife you cut some cheese with for breakfast.'

'I did not.'

'Yes, sir, you did.'

The crew's court testimonies show that Robert persisted in answering back. His firm words suggest he was a boy who stood up for himself, or perhaps there was a simplicity about him that could not ignore a false statement. Doyle lost his temper. Nobody witnessed the attack but several of the crew reported that they heard the boy shout, 'Murder!' None went to his rescue. Did Doyle pick up the knife in the heat of the moment and thrust it towards the boy?

'Murder!'

Robert made a dash for the steps up to the deck – called the companion – but before he could reach the top the captain was upon him, his arm crooked around the boy's neck, pulling him back.

'Go and do your duty!' he roared in Robert's ear.

'No, I shall not if you use me like that!'

The Jamaican cook, Prince Montague, emerged on deck, curious to see what the noise was about. Doyle somehow managed to get in front of the boy, who was clinging to the 'companion', and caught hold of his hands to force him down the stairs. In the struggle the boy's arm was rubbed against the brass fittings, scraping away his skin, blood rushing to the surface.

'Ah, you rascal!' he cried. 'Surely somebody will take my part. George! George! Look what he is trying to do, he is trying to break my arm and neck!'

The boy lost his grip and, as he fell back down the stairs, Captain Doyle helped him on the way with a jab of his boot to the boy's head. It was a drop of six feet.

George Murdock remained at the wheel and said nothing. As a common seaman it was not his place to stand between a captain and his apprentice. Later he found Robert in the kitchen, working with Montague. This was the boy's main job, to help the cook prepare dinner and wait at table for the captain and the first and second mates. His cheeks were stained with tears. As he worked on the dough for a pudding he complained of his treatment – 'Look here, how that fellow has hit me' – showing Murdock and Montague his injured arm – 'I can endure it no longer.'

The seaman and the cook were both aware of rough treatment given out to the boy during the voyage. Murdock had heard with his own ears the captain vow that the lad would rue the day he came on board the John Sugars. *He'd flogged him with a rope end that time, an inch and a half thick. Enough to do damage. Montague had seen how the captain rationed the boy's food and punished him with no dinner. It was never clear what the lad had done to deserve such persecution. The other apprentice was not so ill-used. Both boys had been forced to march up and down the deck like soldiers for hours without stopping, holding a great big handspike like a musket, but that was a more common punishment. It did not result in black-and-blue bruises, and bloodied skin.*

After Robert had served the captain his dinner, he was required to clean the cabin floor. He took a bucket and made his way to the forecastle. By 18 August Robert had been at sea for over three months – long enough for a young boy to feel entirely cut off from his previous life, and to slip into deep hopelessness. The ship might as well have been a prison, with constant hard labour, bad food and little of it, and the ever-present threat of violence from Doyle. After this particularly vicious attack he was utterly forlorn. He had appealed to the other members of the crew for sympathy, but none were prepared to defend him.

Looking out over the bow of the ship as he went to collect water, he saw nothing but endless sea and sky. And then he fell. The captain's attack, the kick to the head, the fall down the stairs, might have caused some injury that made him faint away as he balanced precariously on the deck. Or perhaps at that moment the glittering sea below seemed a beautiful alternative to his daily torment. There might have been a feeling of joy, his limbs free of gravity, his mind free from anxiety. Once his feet left the deck there was little doubt he would drown. No boat was lowered, nor any rope thrown.

Notes

A note on names

Throughout the text I have used surnames as standard to identify people. However, I refer to Vaughan Williams's two wives as Adeline and Ursula to avoid confusion over the shared surname; and I use Virginia to describe Virginia Woolf, for a similar reason – the letters and journal entries used in the book date from when she was still Virginia Stephen.

Abbreviations used in the notes

Archives and Collections

VWML   Vaughan Williams Memorial Library Online Catalogue, https://www.vwml.org/. Abbreviation is followed by the catalogue reference

VWL   Hugh Cobbe, Katherine Hogg and Colin Coleman (eds), *Letters of Vaughan Williams*. Website database of annotated transcriptions of correspondence of the British composer Ralph Vaughan Williams (1872–1958), http://vaughanwilliams.uk/. Abbreviation is followed by the individual online correspondence reference

People frequently cited

RVW   Ralph Vaughan Williams
UVW   Ursula Vaughan Williams

Works frequently cited

BIOG   Ursula Vaughan Williams, *RVW: A Biography of Ralph Vaughan Williams* (Oxford: OUP, 1964)
CAM   Alain Frogley and Aidan Thomson (eds), *The Cambridge Companion to Vaughan Williams* (Cambridge: CUP, 2013)
JFSS   *Journal of the Folk-Song Society* followed by date
MA   'Musical Autobiography' by RVW in Hubert Foss, *Ralph Vaughan Williams* (London: George G. Harrap & Co. Ltd.,1950) pp. 18–38
MANN   David Manning (ed.), *Vaughan Williams on Music* (Oxford: OUP, 2008)
NM   Ralph Vaughan Williams, *National Music* (London: OUP, 1963)
WORKS   Michael Kennedy, *The Works of Ralph Vaughan Williams* (London: OUP, 1964)

Full details of all works cited in the notes are given in the Bibliography.

1 The original words of the plaque read, '*Ralph Vaughan Williams (1876–1958):* Searching for English folk songs the young composer visited King's Lynn and district in January

1905 and collected 61 in a week. The fisherfolk of the North End impressed Ralph Vaughan Williams, particularly James "Duggie" Carter (aged 61). Their songs influenced several of his orchestral works including three "Norfolk Rhapsodies" and "A Sea Symphony". Ralph Vaughan Williams met the fisherfolk in January 1905 in this public house then called "The Tilden Smith".' The plaque has since been updated and reads, 'This building was the Tilden Smith public house where the North End Fisherfolk came to enjoy their songs and tunes. In 1905 the composer Ralph Vaughan Williams collected more than 70 of these melodies which became the basis of the beautiful Norfolk Rhapsodies.'

2 UVW, *Paradise Remembered* pp. 195–7. Ursula's autobiography was largely written during the 1970s but not published until 2002.

3 Ibid. p. 199.

4 Ibid. p. 199.

5 UVW, *The Complete Poems* p. 223, 'Remembering Paradise'. Her autobiography is titled *Paradise Remembered* in an allusion to the poem.

6 James, ' "The Captain's Apprentice" and the Death of Young Robert Eastick of King's Lynn'.

PART I

Approaching King's Lynn

1 VWL189 15 January 1905.

2 BIOG p. 70.

3 de Val, *In Search of Song* p. 73.

4 Karpeles, *Cecil Sharp* p. 46.

5 This letter appears in BIOG pp. 69–70 and is described as a letter to the *Morning Post*. It was not printed in that newspaper and it appears that RVW's letter is actually directed towards another paper which has referred to the *Morning*

Post correspondence in its own pages. It is not certain that the letter was published in any paper – it currently remains untraced – but it is likely that the Tilney vicar was alerted to the content of the letter in some sort of publication.

6 Meteorological Committee, *Meteorological Observations* 1909; *Lynn Advertiser* Friday 13 January 1905 p. 5.

7 Samual, 'Vaughan Williams and Kings Lynn' p. 22.

8 VWL189 15 January 1905. The hotel is now converted into private apartments.

9 *Eastern Daily Press* Saturday 17 September 1910 p. 8. Report on lecture given by RVW on 'English Folk Song' to National Convention of Choirmasters, School Teachers and Music Teachers held in Norwich.

10 Samual, 'Vaughan Williams and Kings Lynn' p. 22; *Eastern Daily Press* Saturday 17 September 1910 p. 8.

11 *Lynn Advertiser* Friday 13 January 1905 p. 5.

12 It was at the festival in the following year that Vaughan Williams lectured on East Anglian Folk Song and spoke enthusiastically about the importance of his 1905 visit.

13 Jones, *Alfred Wallis, Artist and Mariner*.

14 Kettle's Yard Resources. 'Alfred Wallis' cites letter from Alfred Wallis to H. S. Ede 6 April 1936 p. 4.

15 RVW et al, 'Preface' JFSS 1906 p. 142.

16 Johann Gottfried Herder (1744–1803) is seen as the 'father of national culturalism' because of his highly influential ideas expressed in a number of late eighteenth-century publications.

17 RVW et al, 'Songs Collected from Norfolk' JFSS 1906 p. 162.

18 Date based on dated sketches by Baines held at King's Lynn Museum.

19 *Norwich Mercury* 22 September 1880 p. 3.

20 Seymour, *Sailing through England* pp. 33–4. John Seymour recorded his conversation with Charlie Fysh in the Tilden Smith pub in the mid-1950s.

21 Ibid.

22 *Boston Guardian* 20 October 1883.

Meeting Duggie Carter

1 See, for example, a report in the *Eastern Daily Press* 2014 https://www.edp24.co.uk/lifestyle/heritage/king-s-lynn-pub-where-fishermen-sang-to-ralph-vaughan-635938.

2 RVW et al, 'Preface' JFSS 1906 p. 141.

3 The plaque was updated in 2015. It no longer claims that Vaughan Williams visited the pub, but points out that the North End fisherfolk enjoyed their songs and tunes there; and that the composer collected more than seventy 'which became the basis of the beautiful Norfolk Rhapsodies'.

4 Seymour, *Sailing through England* p. 32. The recordings featured in a series called *Voyages of 'Jenny III'* on the Light Programme (later Radio 4) in 1956.

5 UVW, 'Ralph Vaughan Williams and Folk Music' p. 15.

6 Howson, 'The self sufficient singers of the Tilden Smith'. Howson's research into old singers recorded in the 1950s and '60s has established that there was a group of younger singers, all fishermen in the North End, at least some of whom frequented the pubs at the same time that Vaughan Williams was collecting in 1905, although they were more likely to frequent pubs in the summer when fishing produced more surplus cash: see *Lynn Advertiser* 12 February 1909 p. 3: 'In the summer fishermen would spend a shilling or two, but now they could not do so as the money was required to buy bread for their wives and families.'

7 Helsdon, *Vaughan Williams in Norfolk*: *Singers*; *Eastern Daily Press* Saturday 17 September 1910 p. 8. RVW is reported as saying he collected from the fishermen 'when they could get away from their work'. I have drawn on the itinerary researched by Alan Helsdon throughout this section.

8 VWL1412 27 March 1940.

9 BIOG pp. 72–3.

10 BIOG p. 69.

11 James, 'James Carter, Fisherman of King's Lynn' p. 24.

12 Birth certificate, marriage certificate and 1881 and 1911 census confirm he was born in 1844.

13 The provenance of the image has not yet been traced. Katie Howson notes that a copy was given to the VWML by Bob Thomson, folklorist, who told her that it may have been passed to him by Mike Herring, a fellow song collector (personal communication). It is unlikely to have been produced for a newspaper in 1905 because RVW was not famous at that point. It is possible that the photo was taken for a reason unconnected with RVW, such as the occasion of the men's confirmation – as noted in Midgley, *The Northenders* p. 69.

14 RVW et al, 'Preface' JFSS 1906 pp. 141–2.

15 Helsdon, *Vaughan Williams in Norfolk*.

16 *Eastern Daily Press* Saturday 17 September 1910 p. 8.

17 True's Yard Fisherfolk Museum website.

18 Lee, 'Enquiry into the Sewerage'.

19 VWML RVW2/3/63.

20 VWML RVW2/3/77.

21 The instructions for collection provided by the Folk-Song Society in 1904 included the suggestion that 'in view of the special difficulty of the work in taking down songs, the collector should make no attempt to write down words or music until after the first verse has been gone through. He will probably find that he is then able to grasp the rhythmic structure of the tune, the mode in which it is cast, and to settle upon a key-signature and time-signature.' Quoted in Onderdonk, 'Vaughan Williams and the Modes' pp. 609–26; in BIOG p. 73 UVW wrote about this trip that 'with each foray after songs he was getting more experienced and more able to capture both tune and words without asking for repetitions'.

22 UVW, 'Ralph Vaughan Williams and Folk Music' p. 16.

23 RVW et al 'Songs collected from Norfolk', p. 162.

24 James, ' "The Captain's Apprentice" ' p. 581.

25 James, 'James Carter, Fisherman of King's Lynn' p. 24.

26 RVW speaking in '*O Thou Transcendent': The Life of Vaughan Williams*. Tony Palmer Films 2007.

27 These figures are based on Helsdon's data in *Vaughan Williams in Norfolk*. They exclude songs collected in Tilney and Sheringham and the repeats/variants of songs sung by more than one person.

St James' Workhouse (King's Lynn, 13 August 1854)

1 This story of the workhouse collapse, including the detail of the key in Andrews's hand, is adapted from contemporary reports in *The Norfolk News, Eastern Counties Journal, and Norwich Yarmouth and Lynn Commercial Gazette* Saturday 20 August 1854 p. 6; and *The Illustrated London News* 2 September 1854 p. 209.

2 There's no evidence that Robert was in the workhouse – in 1851 his address was Town Clerks Office Yard, St James' Street. In 1861 his mother, Elizabeth, was still there – it was called County Court Office Yard by then, which is to the rear of the old St James' workhouse. The yard is listed in the same position in the census, after the grammar school, and has some of the same people listed.

PART II

The Hebrides Connection: South Uist

1 Carmichael, *Carmina Gadelica* p. 23.
2 Stiubhart, *The Life and Legacy of Alexander Carmichael* p. 6.
3 Ibid.
4 Carmichael, *Carmina Gadelica* p. 23.

In Search of a Good Tune

1 Sharp, *Folk Songs from Somerset* pp. 16–17.
2 Ibid. p. 61.
3 VWML CJS2/9/90.
4 Sharp, *Folk Songs from Somerset* p. 61.
5 VWML GG/1/20/1251.
6 VWL3386 in a letter to Simona Pakenham in 1958.
7 This assumes the photo was taken in 1909 when Sharp first met Shadrach. Ages etc. from 1901 and 1911 census.
8 1911 census.
9 Sutcliffe, 'Cecil Sharp's People'.
10 VWML CJS2/9/590.
11 Sharp, *English Folk Song* pp. 128–9.
12 RVW spells it 'Bennefer' but the accepted spelling is with one 'n'.
13 Howson, 'The Other Mrs Benefer'; *Ipswich Journal* Saturday 12 August 1882; *Bury and Norwich Post* Tuesday 15 August 1882.
14 Sharp, *English Folk Song*, p. 128.
15 RVW and A. L. Lloyd chose Harper's version of 'Oxford City' for publication in *The Penguin Book of English Songs* (1959).
16 Broadwood et al, 'Songs from Various Counties' JFSS 1913 pp. 335–6.
17 MANN, 'English Folk-Songs' p. 195. The application of evolutionary theory to folk song has been widely criticised since the late twentieth century on the grounds that it assumes continual progress, denies individual agency, and leads to reductionism. For a useful summary of recent views see P. E. Savage, 'Cultural Evolution of Music'.
18 Moeran et al, 'Songs Collected in Norfolk' JFSS 1922 pp. 4–5.
19 MANN, 'English Folk Songs' p. 195.
20 VWML RVW2/2/12

21 Whitman, *Leaves of Grass* 'Song of the Exposition', lines 15–21 cited in MANN, 'Who Wants the Composer?' p. 39.
22 Stanford, *The National School Book* p. iii.
23 Dowland, *Andreas Ornithoparcus his Micrologus* p. 36.
24 Sharp, *English Folk Song* pp. 47–8.
25 Onderdonk, 'Vaughan Williams and the Modes' p. 613.
26 For an analysis of this criticism and an alternative view see Onderdonk, 'Vaughan Williams and the Modes' pp. 609–26.
27 Sharp, *English Folk Song* p. 48.

A Kind of Folk-Song Symphony

1 WORKS Appendix 2 pp. 647–81. Essex, Surrey, Sussex, London, Berkshire, Buckinghamshire, Yorkshire, Wiltshire, Dorset and Kent.
2 WORKS Appendix 1 pp. 416–22. During 1904 he was still focusing on Tudor-period French folk-song arrangements, settings of Rossetti, Arnold, Whitman, Stevenson. *In the Fen Country* is folk-like, as was 'Harnham Down'. Also 'Ballade and Scherzo' (unpublished) for string quintet. Scherzo is based on a folk song he'd collected: 'As I Walked Out'.
3 Evans, 'Modern British Composers' IX p. 232.
4 Evans 'Modern British Composers' X p. 305.
5 *The Globe* Saturday 25 August 1906.
6 *Norfolk Chronicle and Norwich Gazette* 1 September 1906 p. 8.
7 WORKS p. 428–9.
8 *Daily Telegraph* 12 March 1908 p. 13.
9 *Western Mail* 5 August 1913.
10 *Guardian* [Bournemouth] 23 May 1914.
11 Meaning the performer can stretch, slow, or hurry the tempo as she/he sees fit, thus imparting flexibility and

emotion to the performance. https://www.freemusicdic-tionary.com/definition/rubato/

12 WORKS p. 428.

13 Ibid. p. 429.

14 Hogger, *'Preface', R. Vaughan Williams*.

15 UVW, 'Ralph Vaughan Williams and Folk Music' p. 16.

16 Faber Music, 'David Matthews's "Norfolk March"'.

17 Evans, 'Modern British Composers' X p. 305.

18 CAM Alain Frogley, 'History and Geography: the early orchestral works and the first three symphonies' p. 89.

19 VWL151 notes by Ralph Vaughan Williams to Cecil Sharp relating to Sharp's draft *English Folk Song*.

20 Ibid.

21 RVW et al, 'Preface' JFSS 1906 p. 141.

22 RVW et al, 'Songs Collected from Norfolk' JFSS 1906 p. 162.

23 Payne, 'Vaughan Williams and folk-song' p. 3.

24 Harvey, 'English Folk Songs' pp. 3–9.

25 UVW, 'Ralph Vaughan Williams and Folk Music' p. 16.

26 MANN, 'The Justification of Folk Song' p. 249.

27 Ibid. p. 247.

28 MANN, 'Traditional Arts in the Twentieth Century' p. 243.

29 RVW, 'Preface' JFSS 1906 p. 141. As RVW notes these were largely modal in character. This bias towards the modal scales has been criticised in more recent times for producing an unbalanced view of wider folk song. For an analysis see Onderdonk, 'Vaughan Williams and the Modes'.

30 Sharp, *Folk-Songs of England Book II: Folk Songs from the Eastern Counties* General Preface, no page number.

31 Ibid.

32 Moeran, 'Folk-songs and some Traditional Singers in East Anglia' p. 31.

33 RVW et al, *The Penguin Book of English Folk Songs* p. 9.

The Unromantic Truth

1 RVW et al, 'Songs Collected from Norfolk' JFSS 1906 p. 162. James Catnach was a major publisher of chapbooks in London in the early nineteenth century.

2 The air frequently collected for the words of 'Oxford City' bears a similarity in melodic pattern – listen for example to George Maynard's version of 1959, https://www.vwml.org/record/VWMLSongIndex/SN29300.

3 Kidson's review of Lucy Broadwood's *English Traditional Songs and Carols* in *Musical Times* 1 November 1908 p. 716 cited in Roud, *Folk Song in England* pp. 100–101.

4 Graham et al, 'The Late Mr. Frank Kidson' *Journal of the English Folk Dance Society* 1927 p. 51.

5 Sharp, *English Folk Song* p. 9.

6 Palmer, *Bushes and Briars* p. 84.

7 Ibid.; discussed in detail in James, ' "The Captain's Apprentice" '; and Waltz et al, *The Ballad Index*.

8 Nash, 'The Abandoning of the "Long s" in Britain in 1800' pp. 3–19. The broadside has no imprint (i.e. no information about the printer) which became illegal in 1799. The broadside also uses the long 's' – that looks like an 'f' in old texts – and is therefore likely to pre-date 1801 when they suddenly went out of fashion. The execution of a person with the surname Mills is not listed in the Bristol executions of the eighteenth century (although it is possible he was not hanged) and has not been found in the Old Bailey online trial transcripts. Thomas (or John) Mills captained a ship called *Fly* from Bristol to St Kitts in 1763–4 and again in 1765–6, but he died on board with seven of the crew (Richardson, 'Bristol Africa and the Eighteenth-Century Slave Trade').

9 Halpert cited in Ashton, 'Truth in Folksong'.

10 Sharp, *English Folk Song* p. 114.

11 Jellicoe, *Shorelines* p. 96 from the reminiscence of Mr Rogers, Southwold fisherman.

12 Green, 'McCaffery: A Study in the Variation and Function of a Ballad' p. 10.

13 Dunn, *The Fellowship of Song* p. 220. Chris Messenger interviewed in Blaxhall, Suffolk in October 1975.

14 The tune was sung twice with the 'Captain's Apprentice' words, once with the words of 'Oxford City'.

15 Southwell, 'Notes on the Arctic Whale-Fishery from Yarmouth and Lynn' p. 208. Nine ships in total between 1774 and 1821.

16 Rudmose Brown, 'Whaling: Greenland and Davis Strait Fishery'.

17 Southwell, 'Notes on the Arctic Whale-Fishery from Yarmouth and Lynn': White's Directory (Norfolk) 1840 entry for King's Lynn states, '. . . but since the demand for oil has been greatly decreased by the introduction of gas, this hazardous, but often lucrative, trade has been here discontinued . . .'

18 Melville, *Moby-Dick* pp. 187–93.

19 Email from Tim Radford 06.01.2021; Waltz et al, *The Ballad Index* R078 – earliest version collected in Newfoundland 1920, song collected by Maud Karpeles in the 1930s; VWML HAM/5/37/11 Letter from collector Hammond to Lucy Broadwood October 1905. The songs he collected from Elliot 'nearly all have to do with the sea, Elliot having been a fisherman off Newfoundland. He went out with about 60 other men chiefly from Dorset, I gather, starting from Dartmouth about 55 years ago [i.e. circa 1850]. He is now some 70 odd years old. He knows nothing of the original source of most of his songs having learnt them all or nearly all while fishing.'

20 Huntington, *Songs the Whalemen Sang* pp. 57–9.

21 Email from A. Bowdoin Van Riper, Research Librarian, Martha's Vineyard Museum 22.12.2020.

22 Ibid.

23 'Captain James, who was hung & gibbeted in England for starving to death his cabin-boy', published in Newburyport, north of Boston (copy supplied by Steve Gardham);

American Antiquarian Society, 'Captain James, who was hung and gibbeted in England, for starving to death his cabbin-boy [*sic*]' printed by Nathaniel Coverly, Milk Street, Boston and dated 1810–1814; the Madden Collection, 'A Copy of Verses Made on Capt. ELDEB's Cruelty to his Boy' described as British by the American Antiquarian Society. Broadsides that are not dated, have no imprint, and use the long 's', as with the Captain Mills and Eldeb broadsides, can be dated as prior to 1800 or 1801, if British.

24 Presumably the Newburyport version was the source for the *Two Brothers* text (but this does not rule out the Eldeb version being earlier). The *Two Brothers* text is shorter than the ballad sheets and does not include the details on purple gore and faeces. Neither of the other two journal versions include the full details of these tortures – perhaps they were too explicit for the sailors and/or too long for their taste.

25 For example, Marsh, *Forget-me-not Songster* pp. 89–91; see also VWML rn835.

26 Waltz et al, *The Ballad Index*. At the time of writing a reference to the Captain Eldeb broadside is not included.

27 VWML rn835.

28 Palmer, *The Oxford Book of Sea Songs* pp. 119–22.

29 Nichols, 'Historical Chronicle' April 1766.

30 *Public Advertiser* Saturday 26 April 1766.

31 Palmer, *The Oxford Book of Sea Songs* p. 122.

32 Sharp, *English Folk Song* p. 12.

Cruelty at Sea

1 Nichols, 'Historical Chronicle June 1764' p. 301.

2 Miller, *The Adventures of Benjamin Miller* p. 8.

3 Dyson, *Business in Great Waters* p. 114. Merchant Shipping Act 1854.

4 Ibid. p. 114. The year was 1877.

5 Ibid. p. 113.

6 Ibid.

7 Waltz et al, *The Ballad Index*.

8 Hughes, *Trial of Henry Rogers*.

9 Palmer, *The Oxford Book of Sea Songs*, text from Boston broadside, printed by Coverley 'between 1810 and 1814' p. 122.

10 *East London Observer* Saturday 19 September 1857 p. 4.

11 *East London Observer* Saturday 26 December 1857 p. 4.

12 *Globe* Tuesday 27 October 1857. *Act for Improving the Condition of Masters, Mates, and Seamen, and Maintaining Discipline in the Merchant Service*. The Mercantile Marine Act 1850 required masters to record events on board in a ship's official log which was inspected on their return from foreign trips – this is how Robert Eastick's case was picked up.

13 Old Bailey Proceedings Online, 'Trial of Johnson William Doyle'.

14 *Morning Chronicle* 14 September 1857 p. 3.

15 *Globe* 27 October 1857.

16 *The Times* 25 April 1878.

17 Dyson, *Business in Great Waters* p. 116.

18 Crabbe, 'Peter Grimes' pp. 252–63.

19 Lloyd, *Leviathan!* album sleeve notes: 'Early in the 19th century a whale skipper was charged in King's Lynn with the murder of an apprentice. A broadside ballad, in the form of a wordy gallows confession and good night, appeared, and in course of circulating round the East Anglian countryside it got pared down to the bone. The poet George Crabbe was interested in the case and took it as a model for his verse-narrating of Peter Grimes, which subsequently formed the base of Britten's opera.' Lloyd appears to have made assumptions in his summary re the date of the murder, the location on a whaling boat and the connection with Crabbe's poem.

20 Spiegelman, 'Peter Grimes: The Development of a Hero' pp. 541–60 cites M. Schafer, *British Composers in Interview* (London: Faber, 1963) p. 116.

21 Brett, 'Britten and Grimes' cites *Radio Times* 8 March 1946 p. 3.

A New Ballad of Captain Doyle or
'The Unrepentant Master'

1   These verses have been written by the author, based on the story of Doyle's life and illegal activities taken from public archives and contemporary newspapers including the *Shipping and Mercantile Gazette* 10 April 1851; the *Morning Post* 16 July 1853; the *Norwich Mercury* 26 April 1856; Lloyds List 1 December 1856; the *Morning Chronicle* 2 September 1857; the *Morning Chronicle* 7 September 1857 p. 3; the *Morning Chronicle* 14 September 1857; the *Globe* 27 October 1857; the *Morning Chronicle* 12 November 1857; the *Norfolk Chronicle and Norwich Gazette* 5 December 1857. Further material on Lascars from Our Migration Story, 'The Lascars: Britain's colonial sailors'.

2   Our Migration, 'The Lascars: Britain's colonial sailors'.

PART III

Magic Casements

1   VWL3275. RVW's message to the schoolchildren of Swaffham Primary School contained in a letter to the head teacher E. A. Barber, 10.07.58. He used the same phrase in his lecture 'What is music' given in 1954, published in NM p. 206 '. . . these great patterns in sound . . . open the magic casements and enable us to understand what is beyond the appearances of life'; and in a defence of the Third Programme in *Music and Musicians* 6/2 1957 p. 15; MANN pp. 119–21.

2   His grandfather Joe Wedgwood was already eighty when the family moved into Leith Hill Place and died when Ralph was seven.

3   BIOG p. 258.

4 National Trust, 'Leith Hill Tower'.

5 Interpretation panel at Leith Hill Tower 13.09.19.

6 Hall, *Fenland Survey* p. 2.

7 Ibid.

8 Barrett, *Tales from the Fens*; Barrett, *More Tales from the Fens*.

9 Barrett, *Tales from the Fens* p. ix.

10 Bloom, *The Skaters of the Fens* p. 61.

11 Barrett, *Tales from the Fens* p. 5.

12 Barrett, *More Tales from the Fens* p. 45–9.

Beauty of the Plain Alone

1 Wedgwood, *Fenland Rivers* pp. ix–xi.

2 *Unofficial Countryside* is the title of Richard Mabey's book originally published in 1973 in which he looked for nature burgeoning in docks, city canals and car parks. The description of the 'official wilderness' is from Farley et al, *Edgelands* p. 8.

3 Lowenthal, *Finding Valued Landscapes* p. 18 cites Nicolson, *Mountain Gloom and Mountain Glory* 1959 p. 16.

4 VWL263 June 1899.

5 Pike, 'Rivalry on Ice'; *Penrith Observer* 19 March 1895 and 26 March 1895.

6 Alldritt, *Vaughan Williams* p. 59; BIOG p. 41.

7 The sketch by Amos was made in 1930 in anticipation of a hoped-for reunion – see Northrop Moore, *Vaughan Williams: A Life in Photographs* p. 25.

8 Wordsworth, *A Guide through the District of the Lakes* p. 94.

9 Whittaker, 'In the Footsteps of Ralph Vaughan Williams' p. 6. The poem is quoted in full in this article. Original held at British Library MS Mus. 163. Supplementary Vaughan Williams Manuscripts. Vol. XI. 'The Log Book – Seatoller'; Easter 1895.

10 BIOG p. 41.

11 Probably George Moore who was studying philosophy and writes about how he found RVW 'querulous' on a later trip, cited in Levy, *Moore: G. E. Moore and the Cambridge Apostles* p. 187.

12 BIOG p. 41.

13 VWL263 June 1899.

14 Kant, *Critique of Judgment* p. 124.

15 VWL227 [1894?]

16 VWL257 [December 1897?].

17 VWL133 [?Early 1902]

18 BIOG p. 37.

19 In order of quotes: Burke, *Musical Landscapes* p. 85; WORKS p. 84; Foss, *Ralph Vaughan Williams* p. 111; CAM, Frogley, 'The Early Orchestral Works and the First Three Symphonies' p. 88; France, 'The Reception of Ralph Vaughan Williams's *In the Fen Country*' p. 3, cites Simona Pakenham; Marshall, *Music in the Landscape* p. 76.

20 Huisman, 'Misreading the Marshes' pp. 105–16 cites Felix, *The Life of St. Guthlac*, XXIV, translated by B. Colgrave, *Felix's Life of Saint Guthlac. Introduction, Text Translation and notes* (Cambridge: Cambridge University Press 1985) p. 87.

21 Kingsley, *Hereward, the Last of the English*, p. 9.

22 Pullman, *The Book of Dust Vol. 2* p. 249.

23 Pike, 'Rivalry on Ice'.

24 Pearce, *Tom's Midnight Garden* p. 189.

25 Bloom, *The Skaters of the Fens* p. 58.

26 Bartholomew, 'Sheet 19 – Cambridge, Huntingdon'.

27 Leaska, *Virginia Woolf* p. 143.

28 Ibid. pp. 135–6.

29 Ibid.

30 Ibid. p. 140.

31 Ibid. pp. 143 and 140.

32 Ibid. p. 143.

33 Ibid. p. 161.

34 Nicolson, *The Flight of the Mind* p. 27.

35 Cowper Powys, *John Cowper Powys: Autobiography* p. 168.
36 Ibid. p. 183.
37 Ibid. p. 189.
38 BIOG p. 65.
39 VWL4449 [1895?].
40 VWL261 May 1899.
41 VWL177 30 December 1903.
42 VWL126 [December 1900?].
43 The première was in 1909, but the first version and dedication date from April 1904.

Folk-Like

1   MANN, 'English Folk Songs' p. 188.
2   VWL201 February 1898.
3   Ibid.
4   MA p. 31.
5   Holyoake, 'Towards a Folk Song Awakening' p. 14 cites contemporary reports on Vaughan Williams lectures which appeared in the *Bournemouth Guardian*, *Bournemouth Observer and Chronicle*.
6   MA p. 33.
7   WORKS p. 408.
8   WORKS p. 53.
9   MANN, 'English Folk-Songs' p. 188.
10 WORKS p. 417.
11 Evans, 'Modern British Composers' X p. 305.
12 WORKS cites *The Times* p. 91.
13 *The Referee* 28 February 1909 p. 5.
14 *Staffordshire Sentinel* 23 February 1909 p. 6.
15 VWL2412 22 May 1952.
16 The work was salvaged, revised and performed over twenty-five years later but was not published in RVW's lifetime – see WORKS p. 417.
17 WORKS p. 87, *Times* critic on *Rhapsodies*.

18 CAM, Aidan J. Thomson, 'Becoming a national composer' p. 61 cites Sydney Grew, 'English and Modern Ideas of Music' *Musical Opinion and Music Trade Review* 33/386 (1 November 1909) pp. 89–90.

19 Ibid. p. 62.

20 MA p. 34. As Kennedy points out (WORKS p. 91) the only orchestral work written before the visit to Paris which Vaughan Williams allowed to be published was *Norfolk Rhapsody No. 1.*

21 *Harnham Down* and *Boldre Wood* were performed in 1907 but were withdrawn.

22 Ross, ' "There, in the Fastness of Rural England" ' p. 44.

23 WORKS p. 137.

Monday 26 October 1857 (London, sunrise *c.*7.30)

1 This section is based on census material and Old Bailey Proceedings Online, 'Trial of Johnson William Doyle'.

2 Matilda was born before Eastick's mother, Elizabeth (*née* Rogers), married Robert Eastick Snr. It may be that the illegitimate pregnancy was the reason Elizabeth left Ireland. There is a five-year gap between Matilda and the next child, Mary Ann, who was born in the year after marriage to Robert Snr. If true, Matilda was Robert's half-sister – but she calls herself his sister at the court trial.

3 Hitchcock et al, 'St Clement Danes'.

4 Strype, *A Survey of the Cities of London and Westminster.*

5 London School of Economics and Political Science, *Charles Booth's London.*

6 Old Bailey Proceedings Online, 'Trial of Johnson William Doyle'.

7 Ibid. These are Matilda's words as set out in the transcript.

PART IV

The Hebrides Connection: Barra

1 Campbell, *Hebridean Folksongs I* pp. 151–3.
2 Lorne-Gillies, 'A Life of Song'.
3 VWML LEB/6/73/2 and VWML LEB/6/73/4 article about 'Songs of the Hebrides' in the *Glasgow Herald* by Ernest Newman (14 January 1926) and letter by 'C.M.P.' to the editor in response, regarding the application of scientific principles to the study of Hebridean song.
4 Mary Morrison was recorded singing 'Latha Dhomh's Mi am Beinn a' Cheathaich' in 1950 – see Kist o Riches website www.tobarandualchais.co.uk/en/fullrecord/22602. The composition is attributed in Barra oral tradition to a seventeenth-century poetess from Mingulay, who was known as Nic Iain Fhinn.
5 Campbell, *Hebridean Folksongs I* pp. 7–10 cites Goodrich Freer, *Outer Isles* 1902 p. 254.
6 Kennedy-Fraser, *Hebridean Song and the Laws of Interpretation* pp. 5–6.
7 Roud, *Folk Song in England* pp. 24–5.

One of Life's Free Pleasures

1 MANN, 'English Folk-Songs' p. 188.
2 Ibid.
3 VWML RVW1/1/122 Letter from Georgiana Heatley to Ralph Vaughan Williams 1.04.1903 and List of Essex singers (n.d.) VWML RVW1/1/146.
4 BIOG p. 66.
5 Dineen, *Ralph's People* p. 17.
6 BIOG p. 66.
7 Ibid.
8 VWML RVW2/4/3.

9 RVW, 'Various Songs' JFSS 1905 p. 98.

10 MANN, 'English Folk-Songs' p. 186.

11 VWL2967 14 January 1955. Vaughan Williams considered Henry Burstow to be more of a collector than a singer – an uncommon example of a collector from the same social circle as the singers. The Copper family of Rottingdean are another well-known example.

12 Burstow, *Reminiscences of Horsham* p. 110. No author given but it is known to have been William Albery – see also WORKS pp. 647–9.

13 BIOG p. 66.

14 VWML RVW2/4/19. The composer noted that the Revd John Broadwood (Lucy Broadwood's uncle) used to give Mr Garman half a crown to hear the 'The Ploughboy's Dream'.

15 RVW 'Preface' JFSS 1906 pp. 141–2. RVW thanks the Heatley sisters, Revd Huddle and Mr Ansfield the game-keeper for finding out singers and helping with notation. He also refers to Revd Geoffry Hill for introducing him to Mr Smith in St Nicholas Hospital, Salisbury in the section on Wiltshire songs: RVW et al, 'Songs Collected from Wiltshire' p. 211.

16 It is possible that RVW visited Ingrave with Lucy Broadwood on 4 April with a phonograph when they recorded 'Bushes and Briars' and 'Tarry Trousers', sung by a woman who might have been Mrs Humphreys or Broadwood – but I think it was Georgiana Heatley. She is known to have learnt some of the songs sung to her by local people. The voice does not sound like an old, working-class woman from Essex but it is not trained enough to be Broadwood (VWML SN30592).

17 BIOG p. 67, WORKS pp. 648–59. Repeat visits included four sessions with Mr Broomfield, and three with Mr Punt, most of them in local pubs.

18 BIOG p. 69.

19 Ansfield is listed as gamekeeper at Leith Hill Place Cottages in the 1901 census – though as a visitor so perhaps he only lodged there when necessary.

20 Two tunes collected on that first day were later used by RVW in *The English Hymnal* – one, which he called 'Monk's Gate', is better known as the tune to 'He who would valiant be'.

21 Ivor Gatty is thanked for his help in collecting by RVW, 'Songs from Norfolk' JFSS 1910 p. 90.

22 Wilkinson, *Tours to the British Mountains* p. 12. Although the book came out in 1824 the actual tour took place in 1787 and his manuscript was circulated amongst friends before publication. This is when Wordsworth saw it – see British Library Online, 'Manuscript of "The Solitary Reaper"'.

23 NM, 'Making your Own Music' p. 238.

24 Dunn, *The Fellowship of Song* p. 217. James Knights 11 September 1974.

25 Peter Kennedy collection, 'Two Norfolk Singers: Harry Cox & Sam Larner'.

26 Stewart, *Lifting the Latch: A Life on the Land* p. 37.

27 Stradling et al, 'Put a Bit of Powder on it, Father' cites transcriptions of Pardon's conversations with Peter Bellamy (published in *Folk Review*, August 1974, pp.10–15) and Karl Dallas (published in *Folk News*, August 1977 pp. 14–15).

28 Dunn, *The Fellowship of Song* p. 179.

29 James, 'James Carter, Fisherman of King's Lynn' p. 24.

30 Sharp, *English Folk Song* p. 134.

31 MANN, 'The Justification of Folk Song' p. 248.

32 MANN, 'How to Sing a Folk-Song' p. 220.

33 Ibid. p. 219.

34 Dunn, *The Fellowship of Song* p. 210. The first speaker is Frank Reeve in June 1975, then in his mid-sixties; the second is James Knights in September 1974, aged ninety-four; and the third is Bob Hart in July 1974, aged eighty-two – Topic Songs released a record by him, 'Song from Suffolk', in 1973.

35 Folktrax, *Here's a Health to the Barley Mow*.

36 Thompson, *Lark Rise to Candleford* pp. 69–72.

37 VWML RVW1/1/122 Letter from Georgiana Heatley to Ralph Vaughan Williams 1.04.1903.

38 James, 'James Carter, Fisherman of King's Lynn' p. 24.

Exchange Was No Robbery

1 MANN, 'The First Fifty Years' p. 115.

2 Ibid. p. 116.

3 BIOG p. 72.

4 WORKS p. 74 citing RVW's lectures in 1902/1903.

5 Ibid. p. 71.

6 MANN, 'The First Fifty Years' p. 117; NM, 'When Do We Make Music?' p. 227.

7 MANN, 'Preface to *The English Hymnal*' p. 32.

8 Christian Research, 'UK Church Overview'. Church of England statistics for twentieth-century church attendance shows around 280,000 Anglicans and 120,000 Catholics attending in 1901 compared to roughly 120,000 and 90,000 respectively in 2007; Wright in 'Vaughan Williams and *The English Hymnal*' states that hundreds of thousands of copies were sold and it was widely and rapidly adopted.

9 MA p. 34.

10 Parry, 'Inaugural Address' JFSS 1899 pp. 1–3; Mackenzie, 'Speech by Sir A. C. Mackenzie' pp. 12–13.

11 Sharp et al, *Folk Songs from Somerset* p. xiii.

12 Fox Strangways et al, *Cecil Sharp* p. 45.

13 Sharp, *Ballad Hunting in the Appalachians*. Diary entry 27 August 1916.

14 Fox Strangways et al, *Cecil Sharp* p. 36.

15 VWL3622 March 1936. Memo from RVW to EFDS Committee on copyright.

16 For a critique of this approach as cultural appropriation see Harker, *Fakesong*.

17 Grainger, *Thirteen Folk Songs* notes for 'Bold William Taylor'.
18 NM, 'The Evolution of the Folk-Song' p. 38.

A Great Fancy for the Old-Fashioned Songs

1 RVW wrote this extract at the head of his score for 'Harnham Down', 'begun July 1904, finished 1907'. WORKS p. 418.
2 Dunn, *The Fellowship of Song*. Bob Hart, who was born in 1892 at Sotherton and lived near Southwold, Suffolk, was interviewed on 25 June 1974 p. 187.
3 Stewart, *Lifting the Latch* p. 38.
4 Bearman, 'Percy Grainger, the Phonograph, and the Folk-Song Society' p. 441; and Parry JFSS 1899 'Inaugural Address' pp. 1–3.
5 RVW, 'Songs Collected from Essex' JFSS 1906 p. 144. *Portamento* means a slide from one note to another, especially in singing or playing the violin.
6 Grainger, 'The Impress of Personality in Traditional Singing' JFSS 1908 p. 164.
7 Freeman, "'It Wants All the Creases Ironing Out"' p. 427 cites Michael Yates, 'Percy Grainger and the Impact of the Phonograph', *Folk Music Journal*, 6/3 (1992), p. 266.
8 Sharp, *English Folk Song* p. 173.
9 Ibid. pp. 174–5.
10 Bearman, 'Percy Grainger, the Phonograph, and the Folk-Song Society' p. 441.
11 Leather, *The Folklore of Herefordshire*.
12 This section is adapted and developed from the story told in BIOG pp. 98–9.
13 Lunn et al, *Ralph Vaughan Williams: A pictorial biography* p. 34.
14 Fox Strangways et al, *Cecil Sharp* pp. 34–5.
15 Ibid. p. 35.
16 Karpeles, *Cecil Sharp: His life and work* p. 39.

17   Ibid. p. 38 – information from a letter written by Louisa Hooper after his death.

18   See note 13 under 'Meeting Duggie Carter' re provenance of the image.

19   Francis, 'Ralph Vaughan Williams: The Folk Song Arrangements' p. 32, citing an unpublished letter held in the British Library from Barry Barker to Ursula Vaughan Williams which contains the anecdote.

20   WORKS p. 648.

21   Graebe, 'Gustav Holst, "Songs of the West"' p. 28 cites Michael Kennedy from a talk 'Vaughan Williams in Spring', presented at St Mary de Lode church, Gloucester, 2 May 2008.

22   King, 'Resources in the Vaughan Williams Memorial Library' p. 758.

23   Leather et al, 'Carols from Herefordshire'. Leather remarks that RVW 'has given much time and trouble to noting the music from singers and from records' p. 6.

24   Birt, '"Wise and Fair and Good as She"' p. 2.

25   RVW, 'Ella Mary Leather' JFSS 1928 p. 102.

26   Ibid.

27   BIOG pp. 83–4. The story is adapted from UVW's telling which included the tramps' conversation.

28   Broadwood et al, 'Songs Collected by Percy Grainger' JFSS 1908 p. 231.

29   VWL151 [?May 1907].

30   Sharp, *English Folk Song* p. 118.

31   VWL151 [? May 1907]

32   VWL4925 [Summer 1910].

33   Graham, *The Gentle Art of Tramping* p. 21.

34   NM, 'National Music' p. 15.

35   Hugh Cobbe, 'Vaughan Williams, Germany and the German Tradition' Frogley, *Vaughan Williams Studies* p. 86.

36   It might also have been in 1922 – in a letter from Leather [VWML EML/1/79] dated 15 September 1922 she writes, 'I suppose it is owing to lack of employment elsewhere that the

Ledbury Country is swarming with gypsy hop-pickers,' as if in response to a remark he has made about the number of hop-pickers in the area. She also mentions the financial success of the Three Choirs Festival at Gloucester (see also note 35 in following chapter).

A Wind on the Heath

1 Stevenson, *Songs of Travel and Other Verses* published 1896.
2 Only eight songs were performed during his lifetime. The ninth song, 'I Have trod the Upward and Downward Slope', was not discovered until after Vaughan William's death – see WORKS p. 420.
3 WORKS p. 51.
4 British Library Catalogue, 'Ralph Vaughan Williams and Gustav Holst walking in the Malvern Hills'. The image was taken by their walking companion, William Gillies Whittaker, a fellow composer and friend of Holst. The pieces they conducted were Holst's *The Hymn of Jesus*; and Vaughan Williams's *Fantasia on a Theme by Thomas Tallis*.
5 BIOG p 111.
6 UVW, 'Ralph Vaughan Williams and Folk Music' p. 15.
7 VWL4448 n.d. but 1895.
8 VWL126 [?December 1900].
9 VWL347 10 August 1913.
10 WORKS p. 63 note 3.
11 NM, 'The Letters and the Spirit' p. 125.
12 WORKS p. 592. Vaughan Williams's sense of an exploration of life's purpose, rather than a religious pilgrimage, is emphasised by his explanatory production note of 1954 which points out that the name 'Pilgrim' is used throughout the libretto, as being of more universal significance than Bunyan's title which was 'Christian'.
13 Ibid. p. 605.

14 Stephen, *Studies of a Biographer* 'In Praise of Walking' pp. 254–5.

15 Ibid. p. 259. Adeline and her mother kept in touch with Leslie Stephen after Stella's death and helped to nurse him during his final illness in 1904.

16 Ibid. p. 285.

17 The poetry of Wordsworth is embedded in RVW's vocabulary – in a letter to Percy Scholes [VWL1475] in 1940 he remarks that he is reminded too much 'of old far off unhappy things' taken from *The Solitary Reaper*: 'Will no-one tell me what she sings? / Perhaps the plaintive numbers flow / for old, unhappy, far-off things, / and battles long ago'. He mentions the poem again in NM, 'Making your own music' p. 238.

18 WORKS p. 100.

19 Whitman, *Leaves of Grass*, 'Darest Thou Now O Soul', the basis for RVW's choral work 'Toward the Unknown Region'. Kennedy thought there was a reference to the first ideas for this in a letter to Holst in 1904. WORKS p. 64.

20 WORKS p. 420. *Songs of Travel*, 'Whither Must I Wander' was first performed in 1902, full cycle in 1904; p. 75. *The Pilgrim's Progress*: in December 1904 he collects 'Our Captain Calls' from Mrs Verrall which he adapted for 'He Who Would Valiant Be' – one of the small factors which set him thinking of *The Pilgrim's Progress*; pp. 64 and 92. *Toward an Unknown Region*: mention of a cantata in a letter to Holst suggests first thoughts of this in 1904; and he had begun to sketch a large-scale work in 1903 which would become *A Sea Symphony*.

21 Whitman, *Leaves of Grass* Book XXVI 'Passage to India'. Verse 8 set by RVW in *A Sea Symphony*.

22 VWL2245 Monday [?21 May 1951], RVW to Rutland Boughton: 'I, on purpose, did not call the Pilgrim "Christian" because I want the work to be universal and apply to any body who aims at the spiritual life whether he is Xtian, Jew, Buddhist, Shintoist or 5th day [sic] Adventist.'

23 BIOG pp. 167–8. He walked with Dorothy and Bobby Longman and sometimes Fanny Farrer pp. 167–8.

24 Ibid. p. 393.

25 Borrow went to school in Norwich and witnessed boxing matches on Mousehold Heath on the north-east edge of Norwich. He is commemorated in Norwich with road names – Lavengro Road and George Borrow Road, and a pub called the Romany Rye.

26 Borrow, *Lavengro* p. 479.

27 WORKS p. 309. For a full exploration of the themes and connection between these works of literature and RVW's work, see Roger Savage, 'Vaughan Williams, the Romany Ryes, and the Cambridge Ritualists' pp. 383–418.

28 Borrow, *Lavengro* p. 202.

29 WORKS p. 305. Kennedy claimed that 'all [RVW's] life he had been haunted by *The Scholar Gipsy*' by Matthew Arnold (1853) although he only wrote one song based on the poet's lyrics at this early point in his career: 'Dover Beach', complete by 1899. After the Second World War he wrote a more major work, 'An Oxford Elegy', based on extracts from 'The Scholar Gipsy' and 'Thyrsis', first performed in 1952.

30 Arthur Symons quoted in Taylor, 'Britain's Gypsy Travellers'.

31 WORKS p. 101; BIOG p. 401.

32 VWL501 13 July 1922 to Percy Scholes; VWL4925 [Summer 1910] to Harold Child.

33 RVW collected versions of these three songs in 1904 and also collected from ballad sellers in London during that year – see WORKS Appendix 2.

34 Whitman, *Leaves of Grass* Book XXVI 'Passage to India' verse 5.

35 There is no record that Leather used a phonograph to record Jones in 1922 so it is probable that RVW was with her on the occasion – but also possible that Leather sent

him an uncatalogued phonograph recording for transcription. However, RVW manuscripts of two songs from Elli Smith sung on 8/9 September near Gloucester (VWML RVW2/11/3/2; VWML RVW2/11/3/1) appear to be 'in the field' notations and place RVW in the right place to visit Leather; the dates fit with the Three Choirs Festival, which he regularly attended, and which was in Gloucester that year, 3–8 September.

36 BIOG p. 167.
37 VWL501 July 13 [1922]
38 BIOG p. 362.
39 Aarons, 'Juanita Casey: Writer, Artist and Horse Breeder'.
40 Whitman, *Leaves of Grass* 'Passage to India' p. 8; British Library Collection, 'Walt Whitman's Passage to India'; Borrow, *Lavengro* p. 202. Stevenson, *Songs of Travel and Other Verses* 'VI. The infinite shining heavens' p. 9.
41 NM, 'The Letter and the Spirit' pp. 122 and 125.

The Dream of John Sugars (Hastings, 1885)

1 The events described in this chapter about the shipowner John Sugars are drawn from testimony given in the Thames Police Court and Central Criminal Court in 1857 as reported in newspapers between 2 September and 1 November 1857; and Greenwich Police Court and Central Criminal Court as reported in newspapers between 4 February 4 and 20 May 1860; and Old Bailey Proceedings Online, 'Trial of Johnson William Doyle Monday, October 26th, 1857'. Biographical details are from census returns and records of births, marriages and deaths; also from reports in newspapers, including the cancelled trip in the hot-air balloon.

PART V

'The effect of music upon the minds of children . . .'

1 Cited in Baring-Gould et al, *English Folk-Songs for Schools* p. iii.
2 Sharp, *English Folk Song* p. 172.
3 VWL151 [? May 1907]
4 Sharp, *English Folk Song* p. 177.
5 MANN, 'Who wants the English composer?' p. 41.
6 Sharp, *English Folk Song* p. 174; VWL151 [? May 1907].
7 VWL5051 February 20 [1950].
8 VWL151 [? May 1907].
9 Ibid. Notes on Chapter 7, p. 17; Introduction, p. 3.
10 NM, 'National Music' p. 71.
11 NM, 'Nationalism and Internationalism' p. 155.
12 MANN, 'Let Us Remember' p. 252.
13 NM, 'The Making of Music' p. 236. These essays were originally given as lectures in 1954.

Separate Atoms

1 BIOG, p. 309.
2 Ibid. p. 180.
3 Neighbour 'Ralph, Adeline, and Ursula Vaughan Williams' p. 338.
4 UVW, *Paradise Remembered* p. 199.
5 Ross, '"There, in the Fastness of Rural England"' p. 44. Letter cited by Ross from UVW to Lionel Pike (1989) in which she reported that Vaughan Williams said that his London Symphony should be called 'Symphony by a Londoner'. Original source: Lionel Pike, *Vaughan Williams and the Symphony* (London, 2003) p. 7.
6 UVW, *Paradise Remembered* p. 121.

7 BIOG p. 310.
8 Neighbour 'Ralph, Adeline, and Ursula Vaughan Williams' p. 338.
9 BIOG p. 91.
10 BIOG p. 47. This is taken from a short story by Adeline's brother Hervey in which, according to Ursula, the character Marjorie is Adeline: 'An Afternoon' from *A Romantic Man and Other Tales* (Martin Secker, 1920).
11 BIOG p. 91.
12 BIOG p. 62.
13 BIOG pp. 122 and 133.
14 Alldritt, *Vaughan Williams: Composer, Radical, Patriot* p. 177.
15 BIOG pp. 60 and 90. My italics.
16 BIOG p. 85.
17 BIOG p. 47. This is again taken from Hervey's short story (note 10 above) in which Adeline is thinly disguised as Marjorie.
18 As an illustration of the small world RVW operated in, Maitland had completed his degree at Trinity (the same college as RVW), was taught moral science by Henry Sidgwick, and was an Apostle. After his death, his wife, Adeline's sister, married Sir Francis Darwin, son of Charles Darwin, and Vaughan Williams's first cousin once removed.
19 BIOG p. 46.
20 Adeline's mother, Mary, was the sister of Julia Stephen, Leslie Stephen's second wife. Julia had three children from a previous marriage – George, Stella and Gerald – and four with Stephen – Vanessa, Thoby, Virginia (later Woolf) and Adrian.
21 In 1897 Adeline was twenty-seven, Virginia fifteen.
22 Leaska, *Virginia Woolf* p. 55.
23 Ibid. pp. 30, 54, 75, 74.
24 Ibid. p.74. 'Dyke' refers to the Devil's Dyke on the South Downs, a deep valley five miles north of Brighton which was a major tourist attraction during this period with a dedicated branch line.
25 Ibid. p. 70.

26 Ibid. p. 98.
27 Ibid. p. 99.
28 Ibid. p. 98.
29 Ibid. p. 101.
30 Ibid. p. 111.
31 Ibid. p. 111.
32 Ibid. pp. 111–12.
33 Nicolson, *The Flight of the Mind* p. 30. Letter to Emma Vaughan April 1900.
34 Leaska, *Virginia Woolf* p. 123; Nicolson, *The Flight of the Mind* p. 17. Letter to Thoby Stephen June 1898.
35 Nicolson, *The Flight of the Mind* p. 39. Letter to Emma Vaughan 23 October 1900.
36 BIOG p. 49.
37 Neighbour 'Ralph, Adeline, and Ursula Vaughan Williams' pp. 339 and 341 footnote 17. Ursula did not discuss this idea with Vaughan Williams. She said, 'There are things one cannot and does not ask.'
38 VWL206 *circa* 1 August 1906.
39 VWL207; 6 August 1906. 'A real picture of seduction.'
40 VWL142; 20 August 1906.
41 Nicolson, *The Flight of the Mind* p. 92. Letter to Emma Vaughan 30 August 1903.
42 Ibid. p. 102. Letter to Violet Dickinson October/November 1903.
43 Ibid. p. 149. Letter to Emma Vaughan 1 November 1904.
44 VWL283 10 June 1897.
45 VWL253 September 1897.
46 Boyes, ' "An Individual Flowering" ' p. 7 notes that he collected songs from Berkshire, Buckinghamshire, Cambridgeshire, Cumberland, Derbyshire, Dorset, Durham, Essex, Gloucestershire, Hampshire, Herefordshire, Hertfordshire, Kent, Norfolk, Northumberland, Suffolk, Surrey, Sussex, Wiltshire and Yorkshire.
47 BIOG p. 68.

48 BIOG pp. 80–1.

49 BIOG p. 55.

50 BIOG p. 39.

51 VWL4455 9 April 1900; VWL131 4 October 1900. He began these lectures in October 1902; VWL107 27 December 1901. These were probably the two Barnes settings: 'Linden Lea' and 'Blackmwore by the Stour'.

52 VWL181 16 June 1903 and VWL297 4 July 1898.

53 VWL132 1 December 1900.

54 VWL127 9 April 1900.

55 VWL4454 21 April 1898; VWL118 [1899?].

56 VWL293 9 April 1898.

57 VWL132 1 December 1900.

58 VWL175 28 October 1901.

59 VWL4455 9 April 1900.

60 VWL131 4 October 1900.

61 VWL190 1 February 1905.

62 BIOG p. 48.

63 VWL297 4 July 1898; VWL4457 13 October [1899?].

64 BIOG p. 55.

65 BIOG pp. 49–50.

66 VWL298 31 December 1899.

67 VWL280 15 December 1899.

68 VWL107 27 December 1901.

69 BIOG p. 91.

70 Alldritt, *Vaughan Williams* pp. 147–8.

71 BIOG p. 48. Adeline had 'an ability to be cruelly critical'.

72 UVW, *Paradise Remembered* p. 162.

A Firm and Generous Friend

1 VWL514 3 April 1923. St George's Square was the Broadwood family's London home up until the death of Lucy's mother in 1898.

2 MA p. 23.

3 MA p. 20. He writes that he was first introduced to Bach's music at Rottingdean school, which he attended in 1883–7 but he might have meant in his letter to Broadwood that she helped him to understand and interpret Bach's work.

4 MANN, 'Let Us Remember' p. 252.

5 Broadwood et al, *English County Songs*. In MANN, 'Let Us Remember', published in 1942, he says it was in 1898 that he heard 'Lazarus' for the first time (p. 252), but in MA (p. 32), published in 1950, he says it was 1893 which is more likely as this is when *English County Songs* was published. The 1950 version is probably a correction of the earlier typo.

6 Broadwood et al, *English County Songs* p. 103. 'The Thresher' and 'Cold Blows the Wind' are included in the book; the other three songs were 'We are Frozen-Out Gardeners', 'Gilderoy' and 'By Chance It Was I Met My Love'. The words of 'Dives and Lazarus' date from at least the early seventeenth century as the song is mentioned in Fletcher, *Monsieur Thomas: A Comedy* – in Act 3 Scene 3 'Dives and Lazarus' is one of the songs proposed to be sung although it is not known what tune was used. The play was published in 1639 but written earlier (the author John Fletcher died in 1625).

7 Harvey, 'English Folk Songs' p. 5.

8 MANN, 'Let Us Remember' p. 252.

9 BIOG p. 62.

10 VWML CJS1/12/2/10/3 Letter from Lucy Etheldred Broadwood to Cecil Sharp (3 March 1909) re Ralph Vaughan Williams and various songs.

11 de Val, *In search of Song* p. 42. Broadwood's diary entry 20 September 1887.

12 Ibid.

13 The young Vaughan Williams's enthusiasm might have been influenced by an attraction to the older woman, but

there is no hint of this in their known correspondence – he always addressed her respectfully as Miss Broadwood, never Lucy, while she addressed him as Ralph, a reflection of her seniority. It is likely that he saw her as an aunt or teacher-like figure – he had known her from birth and, when a teenager, the fourteen-year age difference (she was born in August 1858, he not until October 1872) would have seemed substantial.

14 BIOG p. 62, and more explicitly in UVW, 'Ralph Vaughan Williams and Folk' p. 15. '. . . Ralph knew of folk songs both from the earlier book [John Broadwood] and from the publication of *Sussex Songs* in 1889 when he was seventeen . . . Lucy had interested Ralph in the subject . . .'

15 Graebe, *As I Walked Out* p. 162. John Broadwood's book is usually known as *Old English Songs* as the printed title is very long: 'OLD ENGLISH SONGS as now sung by the Peasantry of the WEALD OF SURREY AND SUSSEX and collected by one who has learnt them by hearing them sung every Christmas from Early Childhood by The Country People who go about to the Neighbouring Houses, Singing. "WASSAILING"AS IT IS CALLED AT THAT SEASON.' The date of collection was 1843 but it was published privately in 1847; de Val, *In Search of Song* p. 9.

16 Graebe, *As I Walked Out* p. 162.

17 de Val, *In Search of Song* p. 37. Letter from Alfred Hipkins to Broadwood 1884. He was an authority on musical history and keyboards.

18 Graebe, *As I Walked Out* p. 163. Publication date was January 1890 although in BIOG it is given as 1889 p. 62.

19 de Val, *In Search of Song* p. 46.

20 Ibid. pp. 51–3.

21 Broadwood, 'Introduction' p. 139.

22 WORKS p. 13. Kennedy cites *R.C.M [Royal College of Music] Magazine*, Easter Term 1959, Vol LV, No.1. The employee was J. Ellis Cook.

23 Northrop Moore, *Vaughan Williams* pp. 15 and 34.

24 This man has been identified as Joseph Berry in the past, but according to the 1891 census, Joseph, son of Edmund Berry, was then only twenty so would have been a teenager at the time of this photo. His father is listed as the groom and coachman and was forty-nine in 1891 which seems to be a better fit for the man in the photo. Living in Leith Hill Place Lodge in 1891 was William Longhurst, Stableman, age thirty – possibly Anne's brother. Isaac Longhurst, a labourer, lived in Forest Green with his wife Emily, but may have performed at another family member's house in Broadmoor when Vaughan Williams heard him sing in December 1903. Longhurst was by then in his early seventies.

25 MANN, 'Let Us Remember' pp. 251–2. The concert was in 1888.

26 BIOG p. 36; MA p. 25.

27 BIOG pp. 51–2.

28 de Val, *In Search of Song* pp. 60–2.

29 WORKS p. 45. He argues that an undated letter to Holst, which mentions this work, must date from either 1900 or 1901 based on other material in the letter. The two volumes edited by Vaughan Williams were not published until 1905 and 1910.

30 *Grove's Dictionary of Music and Musicians* was first compiled and edited by George Grove (1879–89); Fuller Maitland edited the second edition (1904–10).

31 de Val, *In Search of Song* pp. 84–5. Broadwood diary entry March 1901. These were 'Linden Lea' and 'Blackmwore by the Stour', published in 1902.

32 Belloc, Broadwood and Beyond Project website. Venables is cited from an unpublished manuscript, 'Lucy Etheldred Broadwood', by Mary Venables, February 1930, Surrey History Centre Accession no. 2297/6. Another well-documented protégé was James Campbell McInnes, a baritone, sixteen years her junior and from a Northern

working-class background – see de Val, *In Search of Song* p. 81.

33 VWL129 14 July 1902.

34 VWL180 2 October 1902; BIOG p. 64.

35 MANN, 'Let us remember . . .' p. 253.

36 Ibid. pp. 252–3. The 'flattened seventh' describes the practice of taking down (or lowering) the seventh note of an eight-note scale by a semitone – for example, in the C-major scale (C-D-E-F-G-A-B-C) the seventh note would normally be B natural but would become B flat. This is a characteristic of folk-song 'modal' scales which use different intervals between notes to the conventional classical scales of major and minor. In the C-major example, the flattened B would create a scale in the Mixolydian mode. If the E was also flattened, the mode would be Dorian, and if in addition the A was flattened it would become Aeolian.

37 Ibid. 'Let Us Remember' p. 253.

38 VWL179 24 July 1902.

39 Broadwood et al, 'Songs from the Collection of Lucy E. Broadwood' pp. 142–225.

40 VWL180 2 October 1902.

41 Holyoake, 'Towards a Folk Song Awakening' pp. 11–12.

42 MANN, 'English Folk Songs' p. 188. The surname of the singer is spelt in a variety of ways in various publications, but this is the spelling on his marriage certificate – see Dineen *Ralph's People* Fig. 2.

43 de Val, *In Search of Song* p. 90.

44 CAM, David Manning, 'The Public Figure: Vaughan Williams as writer and activist' p. 232.

45 de Val, *In Search of Song* pp. 94–5.

46 RVW, 'Lucy Broadwood: An Appreciation' JFSS 1927 p. 45.

47 VWL637 30 October 1928; VWL638 1 November 1928. Vaughan Williams edited the music, Percy Dearmer co-edited the words with Martin Shaw.

48 VWL640 7 November 1928: letter from Adeline to Broad-wood explaining why the letter was written in her hand.

49 VWL637 30 October 1928.

50 Ibid.

51 VWL638 1 November 1928.

52 RVW, 'Lucy Broadwood, 1858–1929' JFSS 1948 p. 138.

53 de Val, *In Search of Song* p. 160.

54 Ibid. p. 159. Letter from Broadwood to her sister Bertha 22 July 1924.

55 VWL4405 19 July 1958.

'The Cherry Tree Carol'

1 By 'bottle' glass I think Vaughan Williams meant to describe the practice of using thick, uneven, circular glass – similar to the bottom of bottles – in modern windows to imply great age, sometimes called 'bullseye' glass.

2 MANN, 'Let Us Remember' p. 251.

3 MA p. 32. The moment is mentioned again in BIOG p. 62.

4 BIOG pp. 13 and 5.

5 Arbuthnott, 'Commander Matthew James Harrison: An Overview'.

6 BIOG p. 17. The Lord Justice Sir Roland Bowdler Vaughan Williams had four children who were close contemporaries of Ralph; and the Leith Hill children visited their other uncle, the Revd Edward Vaughan Williams and their two cousins at North Tidworth, Wiltshire. Uncle 'Edwardie' once took Ralph to the bell-ringers' practice there.

7 Wedgwood, *The Wedgwood Circle* pp. 344–5.

8 Ibid. pp. 345 and 233. Emma had taken piano lessons with Chopin.

9 Their fathers were brothers.

10 Vaughan Williams kept in touch with the stepchildren throughout his life. Evangeline Knox, who married Effie's

oldest stepson, was a student at the RCM with Vaughan Williams and later co-founded with him the Leith Hill Choir festival. It is possible (I have no evidence) that Vaughan Williams introduced Evangeline to the Farrer household.

11 When married to Edward, and until she inherited Gunby Hall (1867 to 1887), Emily was known as Mrs Langton-Langton – a combination of her husband's and her own surname (they were cousins), but she changed to the ancestral name of Massingberd when she inherited the Gunby Estate, Lincolnshire, in 1887 – see National Trust, *Women and Power*.

12 BIOG p. 251.

13 Ibid. p. 395. Composed 1892.

14 Mack Wall, 'Obituary: Mrs Massingberd', no page number.

15 Ibid.

16 National Trust, *Women and Power*.

17 Bramley et al, *Christmas Carols New and Old* (London, 1871) pp. 60–1.

18 Ibid. 'Preface', no page number.

19 The key signature at the beginning of a piece indicates which notes should be sharpened (♯) or flattened (♭) throughout. The key signature for 'The Cherry Tree Carol' is F♯. In classical scales this could indicate the key of G major or E minor – in this case it is G major.

20 The notes in a Mixolydian scale starting on D would be D-E-F♯-G-A-B-C-D compared to the notes in a G-major scale G-A-B-C-D-E-F♯-G i.e. they are the same notes but starting at different points in the sequence.

21 VWL151 [?May 1907].

22 Portrait dated 1878; her husband died 1875.

23 Mack Wall, 'Obituary: Mrs Massingberd'.

24 Alldritt, *Vaughan Williams: Composer, Radical, Patriot* p. 32.

25 MA p. 22. The book Stephen was reading was *Studies of Great Composers* by Hubert Parry, published in 1887.

26 Ibid. p. 28.

27 Ibid. p. 20.

28 Raverat, *Period Piece* p. 273.

29 CAM, Sophie Fuller, 'The Songs and Shorter Secular Choral Works' p. 116; BIOG pp. 64–5.

30 Ibid. p. 116.

31 VWL111 [1901?]. In the letter Vaughan Williams says he has been playing one of Holst's pieces to Diana and has 'persuaded her to take an interest in it'. Broadwood also had influence.

32 BIOG p. 395.

33 Unknown author, *Lillie Langtry*.

34 Zimmern, 'Ladies' Clubs in London' p. 686.

35 Mack Wall, 'Obituary: Mrs Massingberd', no page number.

36 Historic England, 'Langtry Manor Hotel'.

37 Massingberd inherited Gunby in 1887 after which she was less often in Bournemouth. Broadwood only moved permanently to London in 1893 and so was often at the family home nearby. The Fishers could have been staying at Leith Hill Place itself – guests were invited to stay for the dances.

38 BIOG p. 25.

39 Ibid. p. 30. This was seen by the family as 'a safe and respectable career'.

CODA

Fen and Flood

1 Words from 'The Floods' in *Fen and Flood – A Cantata Part II* by Patrick Hadley, arranged by RVW

2 Tregaskis, 'Devastation on England's East Coast after 1953's "Big Flood"'.

3 BIOG p. 323.

4 Seymour, *Sailing through England* p. 32.

5 Dixon, 'The Floods of 1953'.

6 BIOG p. 361.

7 Oxford University Press Online, 'Fen and Flood'.

8 Young, *Electric Eden* p. 124.

9 VWL1574 13 July [1939]. Letter from Ralph Vaughan Williams to Alan Bush.

10 Irwin, 'Topic Records celebrated its 80th Anniversary'.

11 Ibid. The Topic Record Club's first release included the Topic Singers and Band performing 'The Internationale'.

12 RVW et al, *The Penguin Book of English Folk Songs* p. 7.

13 Lloyd, *Leviathan!* sleeve notes: see note 19 under 'Cruelty at Sea' above for full text.

14 VWML LEB/5/206.

Last Words

1 The dialogue and events in this section are adapted and expanded from Old Bailey Proceedings Online, 'Trial of Johnson William Doyle October 26 1857'.

Bibliography

All historic newspapers accessed online at *British Newspaper Archive Online* at www.britishnewspaperarchive.co.uk in partnership with The British Library Board unless otherwise stated.

All information on birth, marriage, death and census material accessed online at www.ancestry.co.uk unless otherwise stated.

Aarons, Sonia, 'Juanita Casey: Writer, Artist and Horse Breeder Who Lived Archetypal Bohemian Life', *Independent* 05.12.2012 https://www.independent.co.uk/news/obituaries/juanita-casey-writer-artist-and-horse-breeder-who-lived-archetypal-bohemian-life-8382233.html

Adams, Williams A., 'A brief history of the Songs of Travel', *Ralph Vaughan Williams Society Journal,* No. 25 October 2002

Alldritt, Keith, *Vaughan Williams: Composer, Radical, Patriot – a Biography,* London, Robert Hale, 2015

American Antiquarian Society, 'Captain James, who was hung and gibbeted in England, for starving to death his cabbin-boy [*sic*]', Isaiah Thomas Broadside Ballad Collection 2021 https://www.americanantiquarian.org/thomasballads/items/show/59

Arbuthnott, Robina, 'Commander Matthew James Harrison: An Overview', *Historical Biographies: Ancestors, relatives & people of interest to JJ Heath-Caldwell*, webpage article https://www.jjhc.info/harrisonmatthew1926 accessed 11.08.2019

Ashton, John, 'Truth in Folksong: Some developments and applications', *Canadian Journal for Traditional Music*, 1977

Baring-Gould, Sabine, and Cecil Sharp, *English Folk-Songs for Schools*, London: J. Curwen & Sons, 1906

Barnouw, Jeffrey, 'The Morality of the Sublime: Kant and Schiller', *Studies in Romanticism*, Vol. 19, No. 4, German Romanticism (Winter, 1980), pp. 497–514, 1980 https://www.jstor.org/stable/25600265 accessed 20.02.20

Barrett, W. H., Enid Porter (ed.), *Tales from the Fens*, London: Routledge & Kegan Paul, 1963

Barrett, W. H., Enid Porter (ed.), *More Tales from the Fens*, London: Routledge & Kegan Paul, 1964

Bartholomew Sheet 19 – Cambridge, Huntingdon, Bartholomew's 'Half Inch Maps' of England and Wales, 1902–1906, *National Library of Scotland* https://maps.nls.uk/view/97131068 accessed 18.03.2020

Bearman, C. J., 'Kate Lee and the Foundation of the Folk-Song Society' *Folk Music Journal* Vol. 7, No. 5 (1999), pp. 627–43 1999 http://www.jstor.org/stable/4522632 accessed: 17.09.2016

Bearman, C. J., 'Cecil Sharp in Somerset: Some Reflections on the Work of David Harker', *Folklore*, April. Vol. 113, No. 1 pp. 11–34, 2002 https://www.jstor.org/stable/1261004

Bearman, C. J., 'Percy Grainger, the Phonograph, and the Folk Song Society', *Music & Letters* Vol. 84, No. 3 (August) Oxford University Press pp. 434–55, 2003 https://www.jstor.org/stable/3526314 19-02-2019

Belloc, Broadwood and Beyond Project Online, 'Belloc, Broadwood and Beyond: The Folk Song in Sussex', 2021 https://belloc-broadwood.org.uk/lucy-broadwood-biography/

Birt, Richard, ' "Wise and Fair and Good as She": An appraisal of Ella Mary Leather – the forgotten gatherer of folk lore', *Ralph Vaughan Williams Society Journal*, No. 13 October pp. 2 and 24, 1998

Bloom, Alan, *The Skaters of the Fens*, Cambridge: W Heffer & Sons Ltd, 1958

Borrow, George, *Lavengro*, London: Collins' Clear-Type Press [1st edn 1851] n.d.

Boston Guardian, 20 October 1883

Boyes, Georgina, ' "An Individual Flowering": Ralph Vaughan Williams's work in Folklore', *Ralph Vaughan Williams Society Journal*, Issue No. 46 October pp. 7–8, 2009

Bramley, Revd Henry Ramsden, and John Stainer (eds), *Christmas Carols New and Old*, London: Novello 1871 https://www.ccel.org/b/bramley/carols/home.html

Brett, Philip, 'Britten and Grimes', *The Musical Times* December 1977, Vol. 118, No. 1618 pp. 995–7 and 999–1000, 1977 https://www.jstor.org/stable/959289

British Library Catalogue Online, 'Manuscript of "The Solitary Reaper" by William Wordsworth', webpage article 2021 https://www.bl.uk/collection-items/manuscript-of-the-solitary-reaper-by-william-wordsworth

British Library Catalogue Online, 'Ralph Vaughan Williams: Correspondence', MS Mus. 1714/1/4: 1910–1913

British Library Catalogue Online, 'Walt Whitman's Passage to India', webpage article 2021 https://www.bl.uk/collection-items/walt-whitmans-passage-to-india

British Library Catalogue Online, 'Ralph Vaughan Williams and Gustav Holst walking in the Malvern Hills' MS Mus. 1714/10/6 1919–1937 2021

British Newspaper Archive Online, 2021 https://www.britishnewspaperarchive.co.uk/

Broadwood, Lucy E. and J. A. Fuller Maitland (eds), *English County Songs*, London: J. B. Cramer and Co. 1893 Facsimile https://imslp.org/wiki/English_County_Songs_(Broadwood,_Lucy_Etheldred) accessed 07-08-19

Broadwood, Lucy E., 'Introduction', *Journal of the Folk-Song Society*, Vol. 1, No. 4 pp.139–141, 1902

Broadwood, Lucy E. and Frank Kidson, 'Songs from the Collection of Lucy E. Broadwood', *Journal of the Folk-Song Society*, 1902, Vol. 1, No. 4 pp. 142–225, 1902 http://www.jstor.com/stable/4433862 accessed 12.08.20

Broadwood, Lucy E., Percy Grainger, Cecil J. Sharp, Ralph Vaughan Williams, Frank Kidson, J. A. Fuller-Maitland and A. G. Gilchrist, 'Songs Collected by Percy Grainger', *Journal of the Folk-Song Society*, May 1908, Vol. 3 No. 12 pp. 170–242, 1908

Broadwood, Lucy E., Ralph Vaughan Williams and A. G. Gilchrist, 'Songs from Norfolk', *Journal of the Folk-Song Society*, Vol. 4 No. 15 December pp. 161–83, 1910

Broadwood, Lucy E., Cecil J. Sharp, G. S. K. Butterworth, Ralph Vaughan Williams, Frank Kidson and A. G. Gilchrist, 'Songs from Various Counties', *Journal of the Folk-Song Society* Vol. 4 No. 17 January pp. 325–47, 1913

Burke, J., *Musical Landscapes*, Exeter: Webb & Bower 1983

Burstow, Henry, *Reminiscences of Horsham being recollections of Henry Burstow, The celebrated Bellringer and Songsinger*, Horsham: Free Christian Church Book Society, 1911

Bury and Norwich Post, Tuesday 15 August 1882

Campbell, J. L. (ed.), *Hebridean Folksongs I: A Collection of Waulking Songs Made by Donald MacCormick in Kilphedir in South Uist in the year 1893*. Edinburgh: John Donald [1st edn 1969], 2018

Carmichael, Alexander, *Carmina Gadelica*, Edinburgh: Floris Books [1st edn 1900], 2006

Christian Research website, 'UK Church Overview', webpage article 13.07.2018 https://www.christian-research.org/reports/archives-and-statistics/uk-church-overview

Clark, Richard, 'Capital Punishment UK website' 2021 http://www.capitalpunishmentuk.org/bristol.html

Cobbe, Hugh, Katherine Hogg, and Colin Coleman (eds), 'Letters of Ralph Vaughan Williams', website 2021 http://vaughanwilliams.uk/

Connock, Stephen, *Toward the Sun Rising*, Albion Music Ltd, 2018

Cowper Powys, John, *John Cowper Powys: Autobiography*, London: Macdonald, 1967

Crabbe, George, 'Peter Grimes', Letter XXII, part of the long verse narrative, *The Borough: A Poem in twenty-four letters*, London [6th edn 1816]

Cubbin, Sue, *'That Precious Legacy': Ralph Vaughan Williams and Essex Folksong*, Essex Record Office, 2006

Daily Telegraph, 12 March 1908

de Val, Dorothy, *In Search of Song: The Life and Times of Lucy Broadwood*, London and New York: Routledge [1st edn 2011] 2016

Dineen, Frank, *Ralph's People: The Ingrave Secret*, Albion Music Ltd, 2001

Dixon, Emily, 'The Floods of 1953: Bravery on a night of death and destruction', *Eastern Daily Press*, 30.01.2013 https://www.edp24.co.uk/lifestyle/the-floods-of-1953-bravery-on-a-night-of-death-552584

Dowland, John (translator), *Andreas Ornithoparcus HIS Micrologus OR Introduction: Containing the Art of Singing*, London: Thomas Adams, 1609 https://imslp.org/wiki/Musicae_activae_micrologus_(Ornithoparchus%2C_Andreas)

Dunn, Ginette, *The Fellowship of Song: Popular Singing Traditions in East Suffolk*, London: Croom Helm, 1980

Dyson, John, *Business in Great Waters: The Story of British Fishermen*, London: Angus & Robertson, 1977

East London Observer, Saturday 19 September 1857 and 26 December 1857

Eastern Daily Press, Saturday 17 September 1910

Editor, The 'Ralph Vaughan Williams', *Music & Letters* Vol. 1 No. 2 (April) pp. 78–86, Oxford University Press, 1920 http://www.jstor.org/stable/726801 accessed: 09-04-2016 14:27 UTC

Eisentraut, Jochen, 'Case Study 2: Vaughan Williams', *National Music* in context' in *The Accessibility of Music: Participation, Reception and Contact*, Cambridge: CUP pp. 147–76, 2012

Evans, Edwin, 'Modern British Composers. IX. Ralph Vaughan Williams', *Musical Times* 1 April Vol. 61 No. 926 pp. 232–4, 1920

Evans, Edwin, 'Modern British Composers. X. Ralph Vaughan Williams (Contd.)', *Musical Times*, 1 May Vol. 61, No. 927 pp. 302–5, 1920

Faber Music website, 'David Matthews's "Norfolk March"', 17.3.2016 webpage article https://www.fabermusic.com/news/david-matthewss-norfolk-march17032016

Farley, P., and M. Symmons Roberts, *Edgelands: Journeys into England's True Wilderness*, London: Jonathan Cape, 2011

Fletcher, John, *Monsieur Thomas: A Comedy*, London: John Waterson 1639 Facsimile https://archive.org/details/monsieurthomasco00flet/page/n59

Folktrax [archived website at https://folktrax-archive.org/index.htm], *Here's a Health to the Barley Mow 1955 The Ship at Blaxhall*, Suffolk 1955. Film permanently available at East Anglian Film Archive Online http://www.eafa.org.uk/catalogue/5 © 2011

Foreman, Lewis (ed.), *Ralph Vaughan Williams in Perspective*, Albion Press, 1998

Foss, Hubert, *Ralph Vaughan Williams*, London: George G. Harrap & Co. Ltd, 1950

Fox Strangways, A. H., and Maud Karpeles, *Cecil Sharp*, Oxford: OUP [1st edn 1933], 1955

France, J., 'The Reception of Ralph Vaughan Williams's "In the Fen Country"', *Ralph Vaughan Williams Society Journal*, No. 65 February pp. 3–6, 2016

Francis, John, 'Ralph Vaughan Williams: The Folk Song Arrangements', *Ralph Vaughan Williams Society Journal*, No. 80 February pp. 29–35, 2021

Francmanis, John, 'National Music to National Redeemer: The Consolidation of a "Folk-Song" Construct', *Popular Music*, Vol. 21 No. 1 January pp. 1–25, Cambridge: CUP, 2002 https://www.jstor.org/stable/853584 accessed: 20-05-2019 16:51 UTC

Free Music Dictionary 2019 https://www.freemusicdictionary. com/definition/rubato/

Freeman, Graham '"It Wants All the Creases Ironing Out": Percy Grainger, the Folk Song Society and the ideology of the archive', *Music & Letters*, Vol. 92 No. 3 pp. 410–36, 2011 www.ml.oxfordjournals.org

Frith, Simon, '*The Imagined Village: Culture, Ideology and the English Folk Revival* by Georgina Boyes; *The British Folk Scene: Musical Performance and Social Identity* by Niall MacKinnon; *Transforming Tradition: Folk Music Revivals Examined* by Neil V. Rosenberg' [Review] *Popular Music*, Vol. 13 No. 3, Australia / New Zealand Issue October pp. 345–53 Cambridge: Cambridge University Press, 1994 https://www. jstor.org/stable/924636 accessed: 20.05.2019

Frogley, Alain (ed.), *Vaughan Williams Studies*, Cambridge: CUP, 1996

Frogley, Alain, and Aidan Thomson J. (eds), *The Cambridge Companion to Vaughan Williams*, Cambridge: CUP, 2013

Gammon, Vic, 'Folk Song Collecting in Sussex and Surrey, 1843–1914', *History Workshop* No. 10 Autumn 1980, Oxford: OUP pp. 61–89, 1980 https://www.jstor.org/stable/4288312 accessed: 29.09.2019

Gardham, Steve [copy provided by], 'Captain James who was hung and gibbeted in England for starving to death his cabin boy', Newburyport, Boston USA. Broadside n.d.

Globe, Saturday 25 August 1906 and Tuesday 27 October 1857

Guardian [Bournemouth], 23 May 1914

Graebe, Martin, 'Gustav Holst, "Songs of the West", and the English Folk Song Movement', *Folk Music Journal*, Vol. 10 No. 1 pp. 5–41, 2011

Graebe, Martin, *As I Walked Out: Sabine Baring-Gould and the Search for the Folk Songs of Devon and Cornwall*, Oxford: Signal Books, 2017

Graham, John, and R. Vaughan Williams, 'The Late Mr. Frank Kidson', *Journal of the English Folk Dance Society*, No. 1 pp. 48–51, 1927 https://www.jstor.org/stable/4520964

Graham, Stephen, *The Gentle Art of Tramping*, London: Bloomsbury [1st edn 1927], 2019

Grainger, Percy, 'Collecting with the Phonograph', *Journal of the Folk-Song Society* Vol. 3 No. 12 May pp. 147–62, 1908 https://www.jstor.org/stable/4433924 accessed 19.02.2019

Grainger, Percy, 'The Impress of Personality in Traditional Singing', *Journal of the Folk-Song Society*, Vol. 3 No. 12 May pp. 163–6, 1908 www.jstor.org/stable/4433925 accessed 19.02.2019

Grainger, Percy, *Thirteen Folksongs*, Thames Publishing. Notes transcribed by Thomas P. Lewis, 'A Source Guide to the Music of Percy Grainger' 1982 http://www.minervaclassics.com/grainger/prognot1.htm

Green, A.E., '"McCaffery": A Study in the Variation and Function of a Ballad', *Lore and Language*, pp. 5–11, 1971 https://collections.mun.ca/digital/collection/lorelang/id/76/rec/5

Gregory, David, 'Fakesong in an Imagined Village? A Critique of the Harker-Boyes Thesis', *Canadian Folk Music*, Vol. 43 No. 3 pp. 18–26, 2010

Hall, David, and John Coles, *Fenland Survey: An essay in landscape and persistence*, English Heritage, 1994

Harker, David, *Fakesong: The Manufacture of British 'Folksong' 1700 to Present Day*, Milton Keynes: Open University Press, 1985

Harvey, Adam, 'English Folk Songs and Other Traditional Tunes in the Works of Ralph Vaughan Williams: A Checklist', *Ralph Vaughan Williams Society Journal*, No. 54 June pp. 3–9, 2012

Heffer, Simon, *Vaughan Williams*, London: Faber and Faber, 2000

Helsdon, Alan, *Vaughan Williams in Norfolk: The 1905–6 Collections from King's Lynn*, CD-ROM. Musical Traditions MTCD253, 2015

Historic England, 'Langtry Manor Hotel' List Entry Number 1324733 2021 https://historicengland.org.uk/listing/the-list/list-entry/1324733 accessed 05.05.2021

Hitchcock, Tim, and Robert Shoemaker, *Tales from the Hanging Court*, London: Hodder Education, 2007

Hitchcock, Tim, Sharon Howard and Robert Shoemaker, 'St Clement Danes' *London Lives, 1690–1800* www.londonlives.org, version 2.0, 17 June 2018 http://www.londonlives.org/static/StClementDane.jsp#fn1_1

Hogger, Stephen (ed.), 'Preface', *R. Vaughan Williams Norfolk Rhapsody Study Score* Oxford: OUP, 2014

Holyoake, Michael, 'Towards a Folk Song Awakening: Vaughan Williams in Bournemouth,1902', *Ralph Vaughan Williams Society Journal*, No. 46 October, pp. 9–15, 2009

Howson, Katie, 'The Other Mrs Benefer', *Unsung Histories* webpage article 8.03.2021 https://unsunghistories.info/the-other-mrs-benefer

Howson, Katie, 'The Fishermen that Got Away', *Unsung Histories* webpage article 16.04.2021 https://unsunghistories.info/the-fishermen-that-got-away

Howson, Katie, 'The Self-sufficient Singers of the Tilden Smith', *Unsung Histories* webpage article 16.04.2021 https://unsunghistories.info/the-self-sufficient-singers-of-the-tilden-smith

Hughes Esq, Bond, *Trial of Henry Rogers, The Captain, William Miles, First Mate, and Charles E. Seymour, Second Mate of the Ship 'Martha and Jane' of Sunderland for the wilful murder on the high seas of Andrew Rose, a Seaman, tried at the Liverpool Summer Assizes, before Mr Baron Easton on the 19th August 1857 with the particulars of the execution of the captain, the fate of the two mates being yet undecided.* London: Lewis & Son, 1857 http://lawcollections.library.cornell.edu/trial/catalog/sat:2102

Huisman, F, 'Misreading the Marshes: Past and present perceptions of the East Anglian Fens, UK', *Archaeological approaches to breaking boundaries: interaction, integration and division*: proceedings of the Graduate Archaeology at Oxford Conferences 2015–16. Oxford, British Archaeological Reports (BAR)

Huntington, Gale, *Songs the Whalemen Sang*, Dover Publications [1st edn 1964], 1970

Illustrated London News, 2 September 1854

Ipswich Journal, Saturday 12 August 1882

Ireland, John, Alun Hoddinott, Norman Demuth, Michael Kennedy, Adrian Boult, John Barbirolli, Herbert Howells, Arthur Bliss, Steuart Wilson, George Dyson and Frank Howes, 'Tributes to Vaughan Williams', *Musical Times* October Vol. 99, No. 1388 pp. 535–9, 1958

Irwin, Colin, 'Topic Records celebrated its 80th anniversary in 2019 as the oldest independent record label in the world', *Topic Records* webpage article 2019 https://www.topicrecords.co.uk/topic-records-full-length-biography/

James, Elizabeth, 'James Carter, Fisherman of King's Lynn', *Ralph Vaughan Williams Society Journal*, No. 14 February pp. 23–4, 1999

James, Elizabeth, ' "The Captain's Apprentice" and the Death of Young Robert Eastick of King's Lynn: A Study in the Development of a Folk Song', *Folk Music Journal* Vol. 7 No. 5 pp. 579–94, 1999

Jellicoe, Robert J., *Shorelines: Voices of Southwold Fishermen*, Norwich: Black Dog Books, 2021

Jones, Robert, *Alfred Wallis, Artist and Mariner*, Tiverton: Halsgrove Press, 2001

Kant, Immanuel, *Critique of Judgment*, translated with an introduction by Werner S. Pluhar, Indianapolis: Gregor Hackett

Publishing Company (original work by Kant published 1790), 1987

Karpeles, Maud, *Cecil Sharp: His life and work*, London: Routledge & Kegan Paul Ltd, 1967

Kemp, Peter, *The British Sailor: A social history of the lower deck*, London: J.M. Dent & Sons, 1970

Kennedy, Michael, *The Works of Ralph Vaughan Williams*, London: OUP, 1964

Kennedy, Michael, Rosamund Strode, Elizabeth Poston, Imogen Holst and Frank Howes, 'Ralph Vaughan Williams: The Centenary of His Birth Folk', *Music Journal* Vol. 2 No. 3 pp. 167–73, 1972 http://www.jstor.org/stable/4521896 accessed 25.02,2017

Kennedy, Michael, 'The Unknown Vaughan Williams', *Proceedings of the Royal Musical Association* Vol. 99 pp. 31–41, 1972–73 https://www.jstor.org/stable/766153

Kennedy-Fraser, Marjory, *Hebridean Song and the Laws of Interpretation*, Glasgow & Edinburgh: Patterson Sons & Co., 1922 https://archive.org/stream/hebrideansonglaw00kennuoft/ hebrideansonglaw00kennuoft _djvu.txt accessed online at Internet Archive 10 January 2019

Kettle's Yard Resources, 'Alfred Wallis' *Kettle's Yard University of Cambridge Artists and Exhibitions teachers' packs*, 2021 https:// www.kettlesyard.co.uk/wp-content/uploads/2014/10/ Alfred-Wallis-Teaching-Resource.pdf

Kidson, Frank, 'The Ballad Sheet and Garland', *Journal of the Folk-Song Society* Vol. 2 No. 7 pp. 70–104, 1905

Kimmel, William, 'Vaughan Williams's Melodic Style', *Musical Quarterly* Vol. 27 No. 4 October pp. 491–99 1941 http:// www.jstor.org/stable/739496 accessed 09.04.2016

King, Andrew, 'Resources in the Vaughan Williams Memorial Library: The Ella Mary Leather Manuscript Collection' *Folk Music Journal* Vol. 9 No. 5 pp. 749–812, 2010 https://www. jstor.org/stable/25654210

Kingsley, Charles, *Hereward, the Last of the English*, Boston: Ticknor & Fields, 1866

Kist O Riches/Tobar an Dualchais website, *National Trust for Scotland's Canna Collection of recordings by John Lorne Campbell* CW0034C www.tobaranddualchais.co.uk accessed 10.01.2019

Knevett, Arthur, and Vic Gammon, 'English folk song collectors and the idea of the peasant', *Folk Music Journal*, Vol. 11 No. 1 pp. 44–66, 2016

Knevett, Arthur, 'Folk Songs for Schools: Cecil Sharp, Patriotism, and The National Song Book', *Folk Music Journal*, Vol. 11 No. 3 pp. 47–71, 2018

Leaska, Mitchell A. (ed), *Virginia Woolf: A Passionate Apprentice: The Early Journals*, London: Hogarth Press, 1990

Leather, Ella M., Lucy E. Broadwood, A. G. Gilchrist, Ralph Vaughan Williams, Frances Tolmie and Cecil J. Sharp, 'Carols from Herefordshire', *Journal of the Folk-Song Society* June Vol. 4 No. 14 pp. 3–51, 1910 http://www.jstor.com/stable/4433939

Leather, Ella Mary, *The Folklore of Herefordshire*, Logaston Press [1st edn 1912], 2018

Lee, Kate, 'Some Experiences of a Folk-Song Collector', *Journal of the Folk-Song Society* Vol. 1 No. 1 pp. 7–12 and 16–25, 1899 http://www.jstor.org/stable/4433850 accessed: 25.02.2017

Lee, William, *Enquiry into the Sewerage, Drainage and Supply of Water, and the Sanitary Condition of the Inhabitants of the Borough of King's Lynn*, 1853 http://www.thornburypump.co.uk/FiddamansLynn/leerept.html

Leistra-Jones, Karen, ' "When Once You Have Fallen into an Equable Stride": The Peripatetic in Vaughan Williams's Songs of Travel', *Journal of Musicological Research* 36:4 pp. 259–91, 2017 https://doi.org/10.1080/01411896.2017.1380494

Levy, Paul, *Moore: G. E. Moore and the Cambridge Apostles*, Oxford: OUP, 1981

Lloyd, A. L., *Leviathan! Ballads and songs of the Whaling Trade*, Sleeve notes 1967 https://mainlynorfolk.info/lloyd/songs/thecruelshipscaptain.html

London School of Economics and Political Science, *Charles Booth's London: Poverty maps and police notebooks*, website 2016 https://booth.lse.ac.uk

Lorne-Gillies, Anne, 'A Life of Song: The Autobiography of Marjory Kennedy-Fraser (1857–1930)', Islands Book Trust Review n.d. https://electricscotland.com/history/women/MKF05LifeOfSongReviewByAnneLorneGillies.pdf accessed 12.01.2019

Lowenthal, D., *Finding Valued Landscapes Working Paper No. 4*, London, University College 1978 http://www.ilankelman.org/miscellany/EPR4.pdf accessed 24.02.2020

Lunn, John E., and Ursula Vaughan Williams, *Ralph Vaughan Williams: A pictorial biography*, London: OUP, 1971

Lynn Advertiser, 13 January 1905 and 12 February 1909

Mack Wall, Mary, 'Obituary: Mrs Massingberd', *The Englishwoman's Review of Social and Industrial Questions (New Series)* No. CCXXXIL April 1897 https://books.google.co.uk/books?id=63–_DQAAQBAJ&printsec=frontcover&source=gbs_ge_summary_r&cad=0#v=onepage&q&f=false. accessed 25.09.2019

Mackenzie, Sir A. C., 'Speech by Sir A.C. Mackenzie', *Journal of the Folk-Song Society*, Vol. 1 No. 1 pp. 12–13, 1899

Madden Collection, 'A Copy of Verses Made on Capt. ELDEB's Cruelty to his Boy', *The Madden Collection* Volume 4, item 378, Rare Books Department Cambridge University Library n.d.

Manning, David (ed.), *Vaughan Williams on Music*, Oxford: OUP, 2008

Marsh, Richard (publisher), *Forget-me-not Songster: containing a choice collection of old ballad songs as sung by our grandmothers*, New York: Richard Marsh 372 Pearl Street 1847 https://www.google.co.uk/books/edition/The_Forget_me_not_Songster_Containing_a/uo4mi3pj6AMC?hl=en&gbpv=1&

dq=Come+all+ye+noble+and+bold+commanders&pg=PA89
&printsec=frontcover

Marshall, Em, *Music in the Landscape*, London: Robert Hale, 2011

Melville, Herman, *Moby-Dick or The Whale*, London: Penguin Classics [1st edn 1851], 2003

Meteorological Committee, *Meteorological Observations at Stations of the Second Order for the Year 1905*, Meteorological Committee: Edinburgh, 1909 https://digital.nmla.metoffice.gov.uk/deliverableUnit_39b7c2e2-ca25-4b04-b96c-add099ef5de6/

Midgley, Patricia, *The Northenders: A disappeared community*, Fakenham: Lanceni Press Ltd, 1987

Miller, Benjamin, *The Adventures of Benjamin Miller whilst serving in the 14th Battalion of the Royal Regiment of Artillery 1796 to 1815*, Naval & Military Press, n.d.

Miller, Stephen, ' "You will be interested to hear of a project to form a Folk Song Society": W. H. Gill and the Founding of the Folk-Song Society', *Folk Music Journal* Vol. 11 No. 1 pp. 73–88, 2016

Moeran, E. J., A. G. Gilchrist, Frank Kidson, Ralph Vaughan Williams and Lucy E. Broadwood, 'Songs Collected in Norfolk', *Journal of the Folk-Song Society* Vol. 7 No. 26 December pp. 1–24, 1922

Moeran E. J., 'Folk-songs and some Traditional Singers in East Anglia', *Countrygoer,* Autumn 1946 pp. 31–5

Morning Chronicle, 14 September 1857

Nash, Paul, 'The abandoning of the "long s" in Britain in 1800', *Journal of the Printing Historical Society New Series*, 3 Summer pp. 3–19, 2001

National Archive www.ancestry.co.uk

National Trust, The, *Women and Power: Emily Massingberd*, webpage article 2018 https://www.nationaltrust.org.uk/gunby-estate-hall-and-gardens/features/women-and-power-emily-massingberd

National Trust, The, 'Leith Hill Tower', webpage article https://www.nationaltrust.org.uk/leith-hill/features/leith-hill-tower 2021

Neighbour, Oliver, 'Ralph, Adeline, and Ursula Vaughan Williams: Some Facts and Speculation (With a Note about Tippett)', *Music and Letters* Vol. 89 No. 3, August pp. 337–45, 2008 https://www.jstor.org/stable/30162996 accessed 06.05.2020

Newton, Anthony, 'Vaughan Williams and the Idea of Folk Song in the Norfolk Rhapsodies', *Ralph Vaughan Williams Society Journal*, No. 46 October pp. 3–6, 2009

Nichols, John, 'Historical Chronicle June 1764', *Gentleman's Magazine*, London: E. Cave, June 1764 https://babel.hathitrust.org/cgi/pt?id=inu.30000080773892&view=1up&seq=311&q1=june

Nichols, John, 'Historical Chronicle April 1766', *Gentleman's Magazine*, London: E. Cave, April 1766 https://babel.hathitrust.org/cgi/pt?id=inu.30000080773876&view=1up&seq=221&q1=april

Nicolson, Nigel and Joanne Trautmann (eds), *The Flight of the Mind: The Letters of Virginia Woolf 1888–1912*, London, Hogarth Press, Vol. I, 1975

Norfolk Chronicle and Norwich Gazette, 12 March 1881 and 1 September 1906

Norfolk News, Eastern Counties Journal, and Norwich, Yarmouth, and Lynn Commercial Gazette 20 August 1854

Norfolk Pubs website, 'Tilden Smith', 2021 http://www.norfolkpubs.co.uk/kingslynn/tkingslynn/kltis.htm accessed 26.05.20

Northrop Moore, Jerrold, *Vaughan Williams: A Life in Photographs*, Oxford: OUP, 1992

Norwich Mercury, 22 September 1880

Old Bailey Proceedings Online, 'Trial of Johnson William Doyle October 26th 1857' (www.oldbaileyonline.org, version 8.0, 02 September 2019), (t18571026-998).

Olson, Ian A., ' "Fakesong": The Manufacture of British "Folk-song" 1700 to the Present Day by Dave Harker' [Review], *Folk Music Journal* Vol. 5 No. 2 pp. 223–4, 1986 https://www.jstor.org/stable/4522210 accessed 20.05.2019

Onderdonk, Julian, 'Vaughan Williams and the Modes', *Folk Music Journal* Vol. 7 No. 5 1999

Our Migration Story, 'The Lascars: Britain's colonial sailors', webpage article 2021 https://www.ourmigrationstory.org.uk/oms/the-lascars-britains-colonial-era-sailors 26.01.21

Oxford Reference Online OUP 2021 https://www.oxfordreference.com/view/10.1093/oi/authority.20110803100418377

Oxford University Press website, *'Fen and Flood' Conductor's score and parts on hire.* Publisher listing online 2021 https://global.oup.com/academic/product/fen-and-flood-9780193366060?cc=gb&lang=en&#

Palmer, Christopher, 'Patrick Hadley: The Man and His Music', *Music and Letters* Vol. 55, No. 2 April, pp. 151–66, 1974 Oxford University Press: https://www.jstor.org/stable/733850 accessed: 08-04-2021

Palmer, Roy (ed.), *Oxford Book of Sea Songs*, Oxford: OUP, 1986

Palmer, Roy (ed.), *The Sound of History: Songs and Social Comment*, London: Pimlico, 1988

Palmer, Roy (ed.), *Bushes and Briars: Folk Songs collected by Ralph Vaughan Williams*, Burnham-on-Sea, Somerset: Llanerch Publishers, 1999

Parry, Hubert, 'Inaugural Address', *Journal of the Folk-Song Society*, Vol. 1 No.1 pp. 1–3, 1899

Payne, Elsie, 'Vaughan Williams and folk-song; Part 1', *Ralph Vaughan Williams Society Journal,* No. 13 Oct pp. 3–10, 1998

Pearce, Philippa, *Tom's Midnight Garden*, Oxford: OUP, 1958

Penrith Observer, 19 March 1895

Peter Kennedy Collection, 'Two Norfolk Singers: Harry Cox and Sam Larner', interview by Charles Parker at their homes in 1962. From the Peter Kennedy collection 1962 https://www.youtube.com/watch?v=dyqsqnKpwEo&t=533s.

See also https://sounds.bl.uk/World-and-traditional-music/ Peter-Kennedy-Collection and archived website https:// folktrax-archive.org/menus/cassprogs/2217norfolk.htm

Pike, W. S., 'Rivalry on ice: Skating and the memorable 1894/95 winter', *Weather*, February pp. 48–54 1995, https://rmets. onlinelibrary.wiley.com/doi/10.1002/j.1477-8696.1995. tb06076.x accessed 02.08.2017

Public Advertiser, Saturday 26 April 1766, Burney Newspapers Collection https://www.bl.uk/collection-guides/burney-collection

Pullman, Philip, *The Book of Dust Vol. 2: The Secret Commonwealth*, Oxford: David Fickling Books, 2019

Raverat, Gwen, *Period Piece: A Cambridge Childhood*, London: Faber & Faber [1st edn 1952], 2002

Referee, 28 February 1909

Richardson, David (ed.), *Bristol, Africa and the Eighteenth-Century Slave Trade to America Vol. 3 The Years of Decline 1746–1769*, Bristol Record Society's Publications: Stroud, 1991 http://www.bris.ac.uk/Depts/History/bristolrecordsociety/publications/brs42.pdf

Ross, Ryan, ' "There, in the fastness of Rural England": Vaughan Williams, folk song and George Borrow's Lavengro', *Musical Times*, Winter pp. 43–56, 2015

Rosselli, John, 'An Indian Governor in the Norfolk Marshland: Lord William Bentinck as Improver, 1809–27', *Agricultural History Review*, Vol. 19, No. 1 pp. 42–64, 1971 https://www. jstor.org/stable/40273414 accessed: 21-01-2020

Roud, Steve, Eddie Upton and Malcolm Taylor (eds), *Still Growing: English Traditional Songs and Singers from the Cecil Sharp Collection*, London: EFDSS 2003

Roud, Steve, *Folk Song in England*, London: Faber & Faber, 2017

Rudmose Brown, R. N., 'Whaling: Greenland and Davis Strait Fishery', *Encyclopaedia Arctica 14: Greenland, Svalbard, Etc. Geography and General Encyclopaedia Arctica* unpublished reference work (1947–51) Trustees of Dartmouth College USA

2020 https://collections.dartmouth.edu/arctica-beta/html/EA14-05.html

Rushton, Julian (ed.), *Let Beauty Awake: Elgar, Vaughan Williams and Literature*, London: Elgar Editions, 2010

Samual, Edgar, 'Vaughan Williams and King's Lynn', *Ralph Vaughan Williams Society Journal*, No. 14 February pp. 22–3, 1999

Savage, P. E., 'Cultural Evolution of Music', *Palgrave Communications* Vol. 5 Issue 1 pp. 1–12, 2019 https://doi.org/10.1057/s41599-019-0221-1

Savage, Roger, 'Vaughan Williams, the Romany Ryes, and the Cambridge Ritualists', *Music and Letters* Vol. 83 No. 3 August 2002 pp. 383–418, Oxford: OUP, 2002 http://www.jstor.org/stable/3525988 accessed: 09-04-2016 14:25 UTC

Schofield, Derek, 'Sowing the Seeds: Cecil Sharp and Charles Marson in Somerset in 1903', *Folk Music Journal* Vol. 8 No. 4 pp. 484–512, 2004

Seymour, John, *Sailing through England*, London: Eyre & Spottiswoode, 1956

Sharp, Cecil, and Charles Marson, *Folk Songs from Somerset*, London: Simpkin Marshall, Schott & Co, Barnicott & Pearce, 1905 https://archive.org/details/FolkSongsFromSomerset/page/n95

Sharp, Cecil (ed.), *Folk-Songs of England Book II: Folk Songs from the Eastern Counties* collected by R. Vaughan Williams, London: Novello & Co. Ltd, 1908

Sharp, Cecil, *English Folk Song: Some Conclusions*, London: Mercury Books [1st edn 1907], 1965

Sharp, Cecil, *Ballad Hunting in the Appalachians* [self-published booklet 1916] transcribed by Michael Yates http://mustrad.org.uk/articles/shar_txt.htm 2021

Southwell, Thomas, 'Notes on the Arctic Whale-fishery from Yarmouth and Lynn', *Transactions of the Norfolk and Norwich Naturalist's Society*, Vol. VIII, 1908 https://greenland-fishery.org.uk/notes-on-the-arctic-whale-fishery-from-yarmouth-and-lynn/

Spiegelman, Willard, 'Peter Grimes: The Development of a Hero', *Studies in Romanticism* Winter, Vol. 25 No. 4 pp. 541– 60, 1986 https://www.jstor.org/stable/25600621

Staffordshire Sentinel, 23 February 1909

Stammers, M. K., *Ships' Figureheads*, Princes Risborough, Buckinghamshire: Shire Publications, 1983

Stanford, Charles Villiers (ed.), *The National School Book*, London: Boosey & Co., 1905

Stephen, Leslie, *Studies of a Biographer Volume 3*, London: Duckworth & Co., September 1902

Stevenson, Robert Louis, *Songs of Travel and Other Verses*, London: Chatto & Windus, 1896

Stewart, Sheila, *Lifting the Latch: A Life on the Land*, Crawborough: Day Books [1st edn 2003], 2011

Stiubhart, Domhnall Uilleam (ed.), *The Life and Legacy of Alexander Carmichael*, Port of Ness: The Islands Book Trust, 2008

Stradling, Rod, and Mike Yates, 'Put a Bit of Powder on it, Father', Sleeve notes for Walter Pardon CD Musical Traditions 2000 http://www.mustrad.org.uk/articles/pardon2.htm

Strype, John, *A Survey of the Cities of London and Westminster, IV.vii.118* [online] (hriOnline, Sheffield) accessed 17.07.2018 https://www.dhi.ac.uk/strype/TransformServlet?page=book 4_118

Sutcliffe, David, *Cecil Sharp's People* website 2019 https:// cecilsharpspeople.org.uk/ 12.03.21

Taylor, Becky, 'Britain's Gypsy Travellers: A People on the Outside', *History Today* Vol. 61 Issue 6 June (no page numbers), 2011 https://www.historytoday.com/archive/britains-gypsy-travellers-people-outside

Taylor, Irene C., *Sophy Under Sail*, London: Hodder & Stoughton, 1969

Thompson, Flora, *Lark Rise to Candleford*, London: Penguin [1st edn 1939], 1976

Times, The, 25 April 1878 https://www.fusilier.co.uk/boats_ planes/amble_barque_maggie_meggie_dixon.htm

Tregaskis, Shiona, 'Devastation on England's east coast after 1953's "Big Flood" – in pictures', *Guardian* Online Thursday 31.01.2013 https://www.theguardian.com/environment/gallery/2013/jan/31/devastation-east-anglia-1953-flood-in-pictures

True's Yard Fisherfolk Museum website 2021 https://truesyard.co.uk

Unknown author, Interpretation panel at Leith Hill Tower, Surrey 13.09.19

Unknown author, *Lillie Langtry* website http://www.lillielangtry.com/red-house.htm accessed 24.09.19

Vaughan Williams, Ralph, 'Preface', *Journal of the Folk-Song Society*, Vol. 2 No. 8 pp. 141–2, 1906

Vaughan Williams, Ralph, Lucy E. Broadwood, Cecil J. Sharp, Frank Kidson, J. A. Fuller-Maitland, 'Songs Collected from Essex', *Journal of the Folk-Song Society* Vol. 2 No. 8 pp. 143–60, 1906 Stable URL: http://www.jstor.org/stable/4433887 accessed: 24-04-2016

Vaughan Williams, Ralph, Frank Kidson, J. A. Fuller-Maitland, Cecil J. Sharp and Lucy E. Broadwood, 'Songs Collected from Norfolk', *Journal of the Folk-Song Society* Vol. 2 No. 8 pp. 161–83, 1906 http://www.jstor.org/stable/4433888 accessed: 09–04-2016

Vaughan Williams, Ralph, Lucy E. Broadwood, Frank Kidson and Cecil J. Sharp, 'Songs Collected from Wiltshire', *Journal of the Folk-Song Society* Vol. 2 No. 8 pp. 210–13, 1906 https://www.jstor.org/stable/4433890

Vaughan Williams, Ralph & Percy Dearmer (eds), *The English Hymnal With Tunes*, Oxford: OUP, 1906

Vaughan Williams, Ralph, 'Lucy Broadwood: An Appreciation', *Journal of the Folk-Song Society* Vol. 8 No. 31 September pp. 44–5, 1927 http://www.jstor.com/stable/4434180 accessed 14.08.20

Vaughan Williams, Ralph, 'Ella Mary Leather. Born March 26th, 1874. Died June 7th, 1928', *Journal of the Folk-Song*

Society December Vol. 8 No. 32 p. 102, 1928 https://www.jstor.org/stable/4434192

Vaughan Williams, Ralph, 'Lucy Broadwood, 1858–1929', *Journal of the English Folk Dance and Song Society*, December Vol. 5 No. 3, pp. 136–8, 1948 http://www.jstor.com/stable/4521288 accessed 23.08.20

Vaughan Williams, Ralph, Frank Howes, Maud Karpeles and Rose Ethel Bassin, 'Portraits', *Journal of the English Folk Dance and Song Society*, December Vol. 5 No. 3 pp.127–46, 1948

Vaughan Williams, Ralph, *National Music*, London: OUP, 1963

Vaughan Williams, Ralph and A.L. Lloyd (eds) *The Penguin Book of English Folk Songs* London: Penguin Books [1st edn 1959], 1968

Vaughan Williams, Ursula, 'Ralph Vaughan Williams and His Choice of Words for Music', *Proceedings of the Royal Musical Association* Vol. 99 pp. 81–9, 1972–3 https://www.jstor.org/stable/766156

Vaughan Williams, Ursula, 'Ralph Vaughan Williams and Folk Music', *English Dance and Song*, Vol. 45 No. 1 Spring pp. 15–17, 1983

Vaughan Williams, Ursula, *Paradise Remembered*, Basingstoke: Albion Music Ltd, 2002

Vaughan Williams, Ursula, *R.V.W.: A Biography of Ralph Vaughan Williams*, Oxford: OUP [1st edn 1964], 2002

Vaughan Williams, Ursula, *The Complete Poems of Ursula Vaughan Williams and a short story – Fall of Leaf*, Basingstoke: Albion Music Ltd, 2003

Vaughan Williams Memorial Library https://www.vwml.org

Waltz, Robert B., and David G. Engle (eds), *The Ballad Index* online 'Captain's Apprentice (II), The', California State University 2021 http://www.fresnostate.edu/folklore/ballads/BdCapMil.html

Wedgwood, Barbara and Hensleigh, *The Wedgwood Circle*, New Jersey: Eastview Editions Inc., 1980

Wedgwood, Iris, *Fenland Rivers: Impressions of the Fen Countries*, London: Rich & Cowan Ltd, 1936

Western Mail, 5 August 1913

Whitman, Walt, *Leaves of Grass,* Philadelphia: David McKay, 1891–92https://www.gutenberg.org/files/1322/1322-h/1322-h.htm

Whittaker, J., 'In the Footsteps of Ralph Vaughan Williams: Seatoller, Cumbria', *Ralph Vaughan Williams Society Journal,* No. 66 June pp. 6–8, 2016

Wilkinson, Thomas, *Tours to the British Mountains, with the descriptive poems of Lowther and Emont Vale,* London: Taylor and Hessey, 1824 https://www.google.co.uk/books/edition/Tours_to_the_British_Mountains/OGcwAAAAYAAJ?hl=en&gbpv=1; accessed online at Google Books

Wordsworth, William, *A Guide through the District of the Lakes in the North of England with a Description of the Scenery &c. for the use of Tourists and Residents* [5th edn], Kendal: Hudson & Nicholson, 1835

Wright, Simon, 'Vaughan Williams and The English Hymnal', *British Library online* n.d. https://www.bl.uk/20th-century-music/articles/vaughan-williams-and-the-english-hymnal

Young, Rob, *Electric Eden: Unearthing Britain's Visionary Music,* London: Faber & Faber, 2010

Zimmern, Alice, 'Ladies' Clubs in London', *Forum,* Vol. 22: September 1896 – February 1897, no page number, 1897 https://books.google.co.uk/books?redir_esc=y&id=XGoXAQAAIAAJ&pg=PA686&sig=ACfU3U0igdyJ94VzyXKzZ6u3EOS_TdG5EQ&focus=searchwithinvolume&q=let+them+say accessed 24.09.19

Acknowledgements

My thanks go to early readers of the draft manuscript, for the gift of their time and their invaluable comments and suggestions: Pip Cartwright, Sally Davison, Simon Davison, John Francis, Katie Howson, Joanna Swainson and Pete Tolhurst; and to my fellow students on the University of East Anglia's MA in Biography and Creative Non-fiction for their constructive feedback on work in progress, especially fellow part-timers in 2019–20: Helen Baczkowska, Winifred Bolton, Hannah Dee and Frances Lord. Thanks, too, to my UEA tutors for their encouragement: Kathryn Hughes, Helen Smith and Ian Thomson.

I'm grateful to the following who responded to my enquiries during the COVID lockdowns and restrictions of 2020–1 when my ability to travel in person to libraries and other institutions was severely limited: members of the Traditional Song Forum, including Julia Bishop, Steve Gardham, Martin Graebe, John Moulden, Brian Peters, Tim Radford, Steve Roud and, in particular, Katie Howson for her generosity in sharing unpublished research with me on Lol Benefer and other aspects of Vaughan Williams's visit to King's Lynn; staff at universities and other institutions including Professor David Cooper, Emeritus Professor of Music, University of Leeds; Bow Van Riper, Research Librarian, Martha's Vineyard Museum; Robert Waltz, Traditional Ballad Index, University of California, Fresno; Liam Sims, Rare Books Department, Cambridge University Library; Anna McKinney, National Trust, Leith Hill Place; Elaine Moll, Librarian Archivist, Hull History Centre; Sarah Taylor, Archives Assistant, Bristol Archives; Brad Beaven, Professor of Social and Cultural History, University of Portsmouth; John D. Bolt, University of Portsmouth; Lee-Jane Giles, University of Plymouth; Alex Bartholomew, East Anglian Music Trust; Malcolm Barr-Hamilton, Vaughan Williams Memorial Library; Lorraine Jones, Proper Music Distribution; and staff at the National Archives and Hampshire Record Office. Thanks also to Alan Helsdon, Andrew King and Elizabeth James for providing information on their research; Robert Jellicoe for giving me access to his *Shorelines* manuscript before publication and useful references on apprenticeships; and my brother, Simon Davison, for sharing and discussing his own research on Vaughan Williams.

At the Ralph Vaughan Williams Society I would like to thank John Francis, Tadeusz Kasa and Stephen Connock for sourcing images, and Graham Muncy and William Hedley for helping with my enquiries, and I am grateful to the Vaughan Williams Charitable Trust – especially Hugh Cobbe and Rosie Johnson – for granting permission to reproduce written material and images.

Heartfelt thanks go to my agent, Joanna Swainson, for her

enthusiasm and support for my original book proposal; and to the team at Chatto & Windus for believing in it, especially Becky Hardie, for her patient editorial guidance, and Mary Chamberlain for her meticulous copy-editing.

This book is dedicated to Pip, Pete and Siân for their enduring friendship, and for listening to me talk about Vaughan Williams for many years – thank you.

Illustration Credits and Text Permissions

Illustration Credits and Text Permissions

Illustration Credits and Text Permissions

Index

Page references in *italics* indicate images.
RVW indicates Ralph Vaughan Williams.